PUBLICATIONS OF
THE MANCHESTER CENTRE FOR ANGLO-SAXON STUDIES

Volume 2

# Apocryphal Texts and Traditions in Anglo-Saxon England

Apocrypha and apocryphal traditions in Anglo-Saxon England have been often referred to but little studied. This collection, by a leading group of scholars in the field, therefore fills a gap in the study of pre-Conquest England, considering the boundaries between apocryphal and orthodox in the period and the uses the Anglo-Saxons made of apocryphal materials. The essays, placed into their context in apocryphal studies by the introduction, cover a broad range of topics: both vernacular and Latin texts, those available in Anglo-Saxon England and those actually written there, and the uses of apocrypha in art as well as literature. The book also includes a number of editions of apocryphal texts which were previously unpublished or inaccessible. By presenting these new texts along with the accompanying range of essays, the collection aims to retrieve these apocryphal traditions from the margins of scholarship and restore to them some of the importance they held for the Anglo-Saxons.

Dr KATHRYN POWELL is Research Fellow at the Centre for Anglo-Saxon Studies, University of Manchester, where DONALD SCRAGG is Professor of Anglo-Saxon Studies; he is also Director of the Centre.

PUBLICATIONS OF
THE MANCHESTER CENTRE FOR ANGLO-SAXON STUDIES

ISSN 1478–6710

*Titles published so far*

1. *Textual and Material Culture in Anglo-Saxon England: Thomas Northcote Toller and the Toller Memorial Lectures*, ed. Donald Scragg
2. *Apocryphal Texts and Traditions in Anglo-Saxon England*, ed. Kathryn Powell and Donald Scragg

# Apocryphal Texts and Traditions in Anglo-Saxon England

edited by
KATHRYN POWELL
and
DONALD SCRAGG

D. S. BREWER

First published 2003
D. S. Brewer, Cambridge

ISBN 0 85991 774 6

D. S. Brewer is an imprint of Boydell & Brewer Ltd
PO Box 9, Woodbridge, Suffolk IP12 3DF, UK
and of Boydell & Brewer Inc.
PO Box 41026, Rochester, NY 14604–4126, USA
website: www.boydell.co.uk

A catalogue record for this book is available
from the British Library

Library of Congress Cataloging-in-Publication Data
Apocryphal texts and traditions in Anglo-Saxon England/ edited by
Kathryn Powell and Donald Scragg.
    p. cm.
Includes bibliographical references and index.
  ISBN 0–85991–774–6 (alk. paper)
1. Apocryphal books – Criticism, interpretation,
etc. – England – History – Middle Ages, 600–1500. 2. Christian literature,
Latin (Medieval and modern) – England – History and criticism.
3. Christian literature, English (Old) – History and criticism. I. Powell,
Kathryn, 1970– II. Scragg, D. G.
BS1700.A73 2003
229′.00942′09021 – dc21                                                    2002154692

This publication is printed on acid-free paper

Typeset by Joshua Associates Ltd, Oxford
Printed in Great Britain by
St Edmundsbury Press Ltd, Bury St Edmunds, Suffolk

# Contents

# Illustrations

Illustrations are reproduced by permission of the British Library and the Bodleian Library, University of Oxford.

# Contributors

Daniel Anlezark, Trinity College, Dublin

Frederick M. Biggs, University of Connecticut at Storrs

Elizabeth Coatsworth, Manchester Metropolitan University

Thomas N. Hall, University of Illinois at Chicago

Joyce Hill, University of Leeds

Catherine Karkov, Miami University of Ohio

Patrizia Lendinara, Universitá di Palermo

Aideen O'Leary, University of Notre Dame

Charles D. Wright, University of Illinois at Urbana-Champagne

# Preface

The subject of this book is central to the study of the culture of Anglo-Saxon England, although, as Joyce Hill points out in the final essay, it has not often been seen as such. It is central because we need to know what is apocryphal in Anglo-Saxon terms, not just in our own, before we can properly evaluate the canonical, and it is clear from the essays that follow that our view and theirs are different. However, in the compass of a single volume it is not possible to rehearse all of even the most signal of the texts current in Anglo-Saxon England which our own day judges to be apocryphal, let alone the traditions that relate to them, and that is certainly not the intention here. The first necessity indeed is to define the terminology and to review the major texts, and Biggs' introductory essay does this admirably well. The essays that follow focus on individual texts, both in Latin and in Old English, and on traditions associated with them. They include studies of two of the most influential texts linked to the Old and the New Testaments respectively: the Book of Enoch – considered by Coatsworth for its influence on Anglo-Saxon art and, *inter alia*, on texts considered by Anlezark – and the Apocalypse of Thomas (Wright), an apocryphal text which was not only widely read throughout medieval Europe but one which was well known in England, as the four independent translations into the vernacular prove. Yet other texts exerted a wide influence also, an influence which scholars have perhaps overlooked, as is shown by Lendinara of a classical text and O'Leary of the legends of the apostles. In accordance with the interdisciplinary focus of this series, there are, as well as textual studies, two studies on art history, Coatsworth's and Karkov's. Throughout, there is reference to attitudes toward all of these texts by contemporaries, particularly, in the case of Hall and Lendinara, to the attitude of that most orthodox of writers, Abbot Ælfric. Wright, Hall and Lendinara offer the texts themselves, in Wright's case newly published Latin versions of the Thomas Apocalypse. In sum, these essays by established scholars constitute a significant advance in our understanding of a neglected area, and will substantially add to our knowledge.

This volume originated in a conference held under the auspices of the Manchester Centre for Anglo-Saxon Studies in July 2001, organized by Susan Rosser as part of the HEFCE/HRB Institutional Fellowship project, Sources, Authorship and the Transmission of Texts and Ideas in Anglo-Saxon England. The conference was also supported by a generous grant from the British Academy, and by the University of Manchester Research Support Fund. Since Susan had offered the University her resignation before the conference took place, DGS took over responsibility for commissioning essays for publication in this volume based on some of the papers presented at the conference. The introductory chapter was specially commissioned, and many of the papers were significantly adapted for their new context. We are most grateful to the contributors for their patience and willingness to do what was asked of them. The greatest part of the editing of the volume has fallen to KP, but we are both responsible for the text in its final version.

KP
DGS

# Abbreviations

| | |
|---|---|
| ASC | Anglo-Saxon Charters |
| *ASE* | *Anglo-Saxon England* |
| *ASPR* | *Anglo-Saxon Poetic Records: A Collective Edition*, ed. George P. Krapp and Elliott van Kirk Dobbie, 6 vols. (New York, 1931–53) |
| *BHL* | *Bibliotheca hagiographica latina: antiquae et mediae aetatis*, 2 vols. (Brussels, 1891–1901; *Subsidia hagiographica* 6); with supplements in 1911 (*Subsidia hagiographica* 12) and 1986 (*Subsidia hagiographica* 70) |
| BL | London, British Library |
| BN | Paris, Bibliothèque Nationale |
| *CANT* | *Clavis Apocryphorum Novi Testamenti*, Maurice Geerard (Turnhout, 1992) |
| *CAVT* | *Clavis Apocryphorum Veteris Testamenti*, J.-C. Haelewyck (Turnhout, 1998) |
| *CCCM* | *Corpus Christianorum, Continuatio Mediaevalis* (Turnhout, 1966– ) |
| *CCSA* | *Corpus Christianorum, Series Apocryphorum* (Turnhout, 1983– ) |
| *CCSL* | *Corpus Christianorum, Series Latina* (Turnhout, 1953– ) |
| *CLA* | *Codices Latini Antiquores*, ed. E. A. Lowe, 11 vols. (Oxford, 1934–66); with supplement (1971) |
| *CPPM* | Johannes Machielsen, *Clavis Patristica Pseudepigraphorum Medii Aevi*, IA-B: *Opera Homiletica*, 2 vols. (Turnhout, 1990) |
| CSASE | Cambridge Studies in Anglo-Saxon England |
| *CSEL* | *Corpus Scriptorum Ecclesiasticorum Latinorum* (Vienna, 1886– ) |
| EEMF | Early English Manuscripts in Facsimile (Copenhagen, 1951– ) |
| EETS | Early English Text Society |
| | os = Original Series |
| | ss = Supplementary Series |
| *EHR* | *English Historical Review* |
| HBS | Henry Bradshaw Society (London, 1891– ) |
| *ICL* | *Initia carminum latinorum saeculo undecimo antiquiorum*, ed. D. Schaller and E. Könsgen (Göttingen, 1977) |
| *MÆ* | *Medium Ævum* |
| MGH | Monumenta Germaniae Historica |
| | AA = Auctores antiquissimi |
| MRTS | Medieval and Renaissance Texts and Studies |
| *NM* | *Neuphilologische Mitteilungen* |
| *ODCC* | *Oxford Dictionary of the Christian Church*, ed. F. L. Cross and E. A. Livingstone, 2nd ed. (London, 1974) |
| *PG* | Patrologia Graeca, ed. J. P. Migne, 162 vols. (Paris, 1857–66) |
| *PL* | Patrologia Latina, ed. J. P. Migne, 221 vols. (Paris, 1844–64) |
| *PQ* | *Philological Quarterly* |
| S (Sawyer) | P. H. Sawyer, *Anglo-Saxon Charters: An Annotated List and Bibliography*, Royal Historical Society Guides and Handbooks (London, 1968) |
| SVTP | Studia in Veteris Testamenti Pseudepigrapha |

# 1

# An Introduction and Overview of Recent Work

FREDERICK M. BIGGS

T HE very idea of apocrypha involves making distinctions – distinctions about works of potentially fundamental importance to religious communities. As books excluded from the bible, apocrypha must be similar enough to be considered like the accepted or canonical books, yet different enough to be separated from them. These judgements change over time as the religious communities themselves evolve, further complicating matters. Thus in discussing a particular period – in our case Anglo-Saxon England – one confronts two distinct, if related, questions: what can this historical evidence reveal about the transmission and development of works identified by modern biblical scholars as apocrypha, and what suggests that the Anglo-Saxons considered these or other similar works to be among this group? Both repay attention.

Information from pre-Conquest England, although not as early as, for example, papyri discovered half a century ago near Qumran,[1] is much older than, for example, Armenian materials, which first appear in manuscripts of the sixteenth or seventeenth centuries and whose significance is only now being investigated.[2] While Anglo-Saxon evidence has largely survived in collections that have been catalogued and studied over the last two centuries, new discoveries are still being made, and the task of evaluating what has already been identified continues.[3] In other words, Anglo-Saxonists still have much to tell biblical scholars about these works. The second question, however, reminds us of the distinct religious and literary cultures of Anglo-Saxon England, in which these works would have taken their place. Advances in the larger field of the study of apocrypha sharpen our understanding of the nature of these works and the significance they

---

[1] *ODCC*, ed. F. L. Cross, 3rd ed., ed. E. A. Livingstone (London, 1997), pp. 457–8.

[2] See, in particular, Michael E. Stone, *Selected Studies in Pseudepigrapha & Apocrypha, with Special Reference to the Armenian Tradition*, SVTP 9 (Leiden, 1991); and 'Selections from *On the Creation of the World* by Yovhannes T'lkuranc'i: Translation and Commentary', in *Literature on Adam and Eve*, ed. Gary Anderson, Michael E. Stone and Johannes Tromp, SVTP 15 (Leiden, 2000), pp. 167–213.

[3] In addition to the works cited later in this essay and in those following, see Frederick M. Biggs and Thomas N. Hall, 'Traditions Concerning Jamnes and Mambres in Anglo-Saxon England', *ASE* 25 (1996), 69–89; Mary Swan, 'The *Apocalypse of Thomas* in Old English' *Leeds Studies in English*, ns 29 (1998), 333–46.

may have assumed for the Anglo-Saxons. Both fields have been active over the past twenty years, and it is on recent developments that this overview will focus.

## Apocrypha, Pseudepigrapha and the Canon

Although there are historical reasons to distinguish between 'apocrypha' and 'pseudepigrapha', it makes sense, especially in light of the Anglo-Saxon evidence, to follow contemporary scholars such as J.-C. Haelewyck in his *Clavis Apocryphorum Veteris Testamenti* and Maurice Geerard in his *Clavis Apocryphorum Novi Testamenti*,[4] who use the first term more generally to refer to all of the material under consideration here. In the narrower sense, the term 'apocrypha', literally 'the hidden things', designates biblical books found in the Septuagint, the Greek version of the Old Testament,[5] but excluded by non-Hellenistic Jews from the Hebrew canon;[6] 'pseudepigrapha', 'with false superscription', can then refer to other writings similar to biblical books but excluded from both traditions. The Christian church inherited all of the books in the Septuagint as canonical, and although notably Jerome made distinctions based on his knowledge of the Hebrew canon, the Latin church, influenced by Augustine and others, affirmed the more inclusive tradition. The result is that the Vulgate, while largely the work of Jerome, contains some books about which he had reservations and others that he did not translate.[7] When Protestant reformers of the sixteenth century returned to the Hebrew canon, a threefold distinction again became useful. For the Anglo-Saxons, however, for whom the Vulgate was the bible, a binary system that distinguishes the apocrypha from the canon seems preferable.

Before turning to the apocrypha in its broader sense, it is necessary to qualify the last sentence with a few words about the Anglo-Saxon bible, which for several reasons might have appeared less clearly defined than one may at first assume. The *Codex Amiatinus*,[8] the justly famous pandect produced along with two others at the twin monastery of Monkwearmouth (or Wearmouth) and Jarrow during Bede's time,[9] may provide a convenient

---

[4] *CAVT*, J.-C. Haelewyck (Turnhout, 1998) and *CANT*, Maurice Geerard (Turnhout, 1992). See James H. Charlesworth's comments on the use of the term 'pseudepigrapha' in the 'Introduction for the General Reader', in *The Old Testament Pseudepigrapha*, 2 vols., ed. Charlesworth (London, 1983–85), I.xxi–xxxiv, at xxiv–xxv.

[5] *ODCC*, pp. 1483–4.

[6] For a more thorough comparison, see G. W. Anderson, 'Canonical and non-Canonical', in *The Cambridge History of the Bible, Volume 1: From the Beginnings to Jerome*, ed. P. R. Ackroyd and C. F. Evans (Cambridge, 1970), I.113–59, at 135–42.

[7] See further, H. F. D. Sparks, 'Jerome as Biblical Scholar', in *Cambridge History of the Bible*, I.510–41, at 532–5; E. F. Sutcliffe, 'Jerome', in *Cambridge History of the Bible, Volume 2: The West from the Fathers to the Reformation*, ed. G. W. H. Lampe (Cambridge, 1969), II.80–101, at 92–3; and *ODCC*, pp. 1710–11.

[8] Florence, Biblioteca Medicea Laurenziana, Amiatino 1; see no. 825 in Helmut Gneuss, *Handlist of Anglo-Saxon Manuscripts: A List of Manuscripts and Manuscript Fragments Written or Owned in England up to 1100*, MRTS 241 (Tempe, AZ, 2001).

[9] See Richard Marsden, *The Text of the Bible in Anglo-Saxon England*, CSASE 15 (Cambridge, 1995), pp. 76–139.

point of reference. In his *Historia abbatum* xv, Bede distinguishes its text, a 'new' translation by which he means the Vulgate, from the 'old' translation in a pandect that abbot Ceolfrith had brought back from Rome;[10] this imported bible was Cassiodorus's since lost *Codex Grandior*.[11] Although the monks at Monkwearmouth-Jarrow clearly favoured Jerome's final revisions,[12] the earlier volume calls attention to the presence of the Old Latin Bible – that is, translations prior to the Vulgate[13] – in pre-Conquest England. While few Anglo-Saxons would have had contact with this particular volume or ones like it, Old Latin readings would have survived in other contexts, especially in the liturgy, sermons and biblical commentaries.[14] Moreover, both the *Codex Amiatinus* and the *Codex Grandior* are notable because complete bibles would have been relatively rare throughout the Anglo-Saxon period even following the Carolingian Reform, which produced its Alcuin Bibles.[15] In addition to *Amiatinus*, only three more complete or nearly complete bibles survive: BL, Royal 1.E.VII and 1.E.VIII (s. x/xi, provenance Christ Church, Canterbury),[16] San Marino, California, Huntington Library, HM 62 (s. xi², possibly from Christ Church, Canterbury; provenance Rochester),[17] and Lincoln, Cathedral Library 1 (A.1.2) + Cambridge, Trinity College B.5.2 (148) (s. xi^ex or xi/xii, provenance Lincoln).[18] Instead, the Anglo-Saxons would have read the bible most often as separate books, with the Psalms and the Gospels being the most familiar because of their place in the liturgy.[19]

---

[10] *Venerabilis Baedae opera historica*, ed. Charles Plummer, 2 vols. (Oxford, 1896), I.379–80; and see the discussion in Marsden, *Text*, pp. 85–6.

[11] See Raphael Loewe, 'The Medieval History of the Latin Vulgate', in *Cambridge History of the Bible*, II.116–17; Marsden, *Text*, pp. 129–39.

[12] This preference is suggested, for example, by their use of a corrupt Irish text of the Psalms which they emended conjecturally so that they might include Jerome's third and final translation of this book from Hebrew; see Loewe, 'Medieval History', p. 117, and Marsden, *Text*, pp. 140–2.

[13] See the *ODCC*, pp. 1180–1. Marsden interprets the description of this volume in the *Institutiones* as implying that Cassiodorus considered it to contain 'the text of Jerome's earlier revision based on the Septuagint version found in Origen's *Hexapla*'; *Text*, p. 131. He also notes that Jerome did not complete this translation, and so the manuscript must have contained a mixture of texts. See also Loewe, 'Medieval History', p. 116, n. 3.

[14] For a discussion, see Paul G. Remley, *Old English Biblical Verse: Studies in Genesis, Exodus and Daniel*, CSASE 16 (Cambridge, 1996), pp. 10–11, *et passim*.

[15] See David Ganz, 'Mass Production of Early Medieval Manuscripts: The Carolingian Bibles from Tours', and Rosamond McKitterick, 'Carolingian Bible Production: The Tours Anomaly', in *The Early Medieval Bible: Its Production, Decoration and Use*, ed. Richard Gameson, Cambridge Studies in Palaeography and Codicology (Cambridge, 1994), pp. 53–62 and pp. 63–77, respectively. In his conclusion, Marsden speculates that 'perhaps only a handful of complete Bibles existed in the whole of England before the end of the tenth century', but that then 'they became more numerous'; *Text*, pp. 444–5.

[16] Gneuss, *Handlist*, no. 449; see Marsden, *Text*, pp. 321–78.

[17] Gneuss, *Handlist*, no. 934.

[18] Gneuss, *Handlist*, nos. 270 and 169. Marsden notes these three bibles and comments that 'their texts and the question of continuity with those of the earlier period await study'; *Text*, p. 42. Fragments of another complete bible from the first half of the ninth century survive in BL, Royal 1.E.VI + Canterbury, Cathedral Library, Add. 16 + Oxford, Bodleian Library, Lat. bib. b. 2 (P), Gneuss, *Handlist*, no. 448; see Patrick McGurk, 'An Anglo-Saxon Bible Fragment of the Late Eighth Century: Royal I E. VI', *Journal of the Warburg and Courtauld Institutes* 25 (1962), 18–34; and Marsden, *Text*, p. 42. The second part of a two volume bible from the turn of the twelfth century also survives at Durham: Cathedral Library A.II.4; Gneuss, *Handlist*, no. 217.

[19] Focusing on manuscripts used in church services, Helmut Gneuss lists twenty-nine with Gospels

Finally, an Anglo-Saxon attempting to grasp the structure of the bible as a whole would have encountered a surprising variety in the ordering of the separate books: Richard Marsden provides a table that shows the differing arrangements for the Old Testament of Jerome, Augustine, the Septuagint, *Amiatinus*, the Theodulfian Bibles, the Alcuin Bibles, the Royal Bible (mentioned above), Ælfric and the Clementine Vulgate (1592).[20] Yet another order is offered in the so-called Gelasian Decree.[21] While the seventy-five and a half pound *Codex Amiatinus* makes a firm statement about the proper content and form of the canon,[22] few Anglo-Saxons would have known the bible in this way, making the excluded books of the Apocrypha more difficult to recognize.

It may also be useful here to identify the books accepted in the Vulgate but omitted from the 1611 King James Bible, also known as the Authorized Version. Most complicated, not only because of the confusing nomenclature, are III and IV Ezra (the Hebrew form of the name, the Greek being Esdras; *CAVT* 179 and 180), printed by Robert Weber in the Appendix to the Vulgate,[23] which correspond to I and II Esdras in the Apocrypha of the King James Bible.[24] In his prologue to I Ezra, Jerome identifies these books as apocryphal,[25] and the so-called Gelasian Decree lists two books of Ezra as canonical.[26] Books 3 and 4 do appear in some early Vulgate manuscripts, and Martin McNamara indicates that they were known in Ireland.[27] The monks at Monkwearmouth and Jarrow, however, did not include them – if indeed they knew them – in *Amiatinus*, and the editors of Bede in the *Corpus Christianorum* do not identify any quotations from them in his works. They are included in the Royal Bible, but in additions from the later Middle Ages.[28] In entries in the database of *Fontes Anglo-Saxonici*, R. C. Love lists IV Ezra XV.4 as the antecedent source for a phrase in Bede's *Explanatio*

---

and twenty-seven with Psalms and Canticles: 'Liturgical Books in Anglo-Saxon England and their Old English Terminology', in *Learning and Literature in Anglo-Saxon England: Studies Presented to Peter Clemoes on the Occasion of his Sixty-Fifth Birthday*, ed. Michael Lapidge and Helmut Gneuss (Cambridge, 1985), pp. 91–141, at pp. 108–9 and 115–16. He also notes that readings from the Old Testament would have been used in the Night Office, but that there is no evidence that the surviving bibles were used in this way: p. 122. See also *The Old English Version of the Gospels: Volume Two, Notes and Glossary*, ed. R. M. Liuzza, EETS os 314 (Oxford, 2000), pp. 1–26.

[20] Marsden, *Text*, pp. 450–1.

[21] *Das Decretum Gelasianum de libris recipiendis et non recipiendis*, ed. E. von Dobschütz, Texte und Untersuchungen 38.4 (Leipzig, 1912), pp. 5–6. See also Wilhelm Schneemelcher, 'General Introduction', in *New Testament Apocrypha*, rev. ed., ed. Schneemelcher, trans. R. McL. Wilson, 2 vols. (Cambridge, 1991–92), I.9–75, at 38–40.

[22] R. L. S. Bruce-Mitford, *The Art of the Codex Amiatinus*, Jarrow Lecture 1967 (Jarrow, 1968); repr. *Journal of the British Archaeological Association* 3rd ser. 32 (1969), 1–25, at 2; Marsden, *Text*, p. 108.

[23] *Biblia sacra iuxta Vulgatam versionem*, editio minor (Stuttgart, 1984), pp. 1910–74.

[24] IV Ezra is itself made up of three parts: in chapters 3–14, an original work containing seven visions (*CAVT* 180; some scholars restrict the name IV Esdras to this part; others refer to it as the Apocalypse of Ezra); two introductory chapters (*CAVT* 182; V Ezra); and two concluding ones (*CAVT* 183; VI Ezra).

[25] Weber, *Biblia sacra*, p. 638.

[26] von Dobschütz, *Decretum*, p. 6.

[27] Martin McNamara, *The Apocrypha in the Irish Church* (Dublin, 1975), p. 27.

[28] Marsden, *Text*, pp. 329–30.

*Apocalypsis*,[29] and IV Ezra VIII.44 as the probable source for a phrase in a spurious charter from the end of the Anglo-Saxon period,[30] but neither proves direct knowledge of the book.[31] Although these examples, then, offer little firm evidence for the knowledge of even IV Ezra in Anglo-Saxon England, motifs ultimately derived from it may appear in the Old English poem *Christ III*; yet here the intermediate source is probably Irish biblical materials,[32] to which we shall have reason to return.

There is also little evidence that the Anglo-Saxons knew Baruch, which formed the last section of Hieremias (Jeremiah) in the Septuagint and thus in Old Latin Bibles,[33] but which became a regular part of the Vulgate only after its inclusion in Theodulfian Bibles.[34] It is not included in the *Amiatinus* or the original part of the Royal Bible,[35] and quotations from it have not been identified in Bede's works edited in the *Corpus Christianorum*. In his entries in *Fontes*, A. N. Doane lists one verse, 'ibi fuerunt gigantes nominati illi qui ab initio fuerunt statura magna scientes bellum' (III.26; 'there were the giants, those renowned men that were from the beginning of great stature, expert in war'),[36] as a 'certain direct source' for *Genesis A* 1264b–69, a passage describing the events that lead to the Flood.[37] In his earlier edition, however, he quotes only Genesis VI.4 opposite these lines, and although his note mentions Baruch III.26–28 as the ultimate source for the 'tradition emphasizing the moral deficiencies of these "giants"',[38] there seems to be nothing that specifically connects these two passages, especially in light of Genesis VI.5, which mentions the 'wickedness' of those whom God destroys. Paul G. Remley also cites Baruch in his analysis of the Old English *Daniel* 33–103, but does not argue for any exclusive links between

---

[29] *Fontes Anglo-Saxonici: World Wide Web Register*, http://fontes.english.ox.ac.uk/, accessed April, 2002. Love claims that IV Ezra XV.4, 'omnis incredulus in incredulitate sua morietur' (Weber, *Biblia sacra*, p. 1967; 'every unbeliever shall die in his unbelief', trans. B. M. Metzger, *Old Testament Pseudepigrapha*, ed. Charlesworth, I.555) corresponds to 'in sua incredulitate morientur' (*PL* 93, col. 160; 'they will die in their unbelief').

[30] Love asserts that IV Ezra VIII.44, 'sed homo qui manibus tuis plasmatus est et tuae imagini nominatus' (Weber, *Biblia sacra*, p. 1952; 'but man, who has been formed by your hands and is called your own image', trans. Metzger, *Old Testament Pseudepigrapha*, ed. Charlesworth, I.543) corresponds to 'homo solus qui ad imaginem suam plasmatus est' ('man alone who was made in his image'); W. de G. Birch, *Cartularium Saxonicum: A Collection of Charters Relating to Anglo-Saxon History*, 3 vols. (London, 1885–93), item 511; see also Sawyer, no. 226; Sawyer has been updated and added to by Susan Kelly, and her online version is available at http://www.trin.cam.ac.uk/chartwww/

[31] For the first, see also Romans XI.20. For the second, see Genesis I.27 and II.7; *plasmo* occurs frequently in this context; for examples, see P. Sabatier, *Bibliorum Sacrorum Latinae versiones antiquae, seu Vetus Italica*, 3 vols. (Rheims, 1743–49), I.13.

[32] For example, the poem identifies Sion as the place of judgement; see my 'The Fourfold Division of Souls: The Old English "Christ III" and the Insular Homiletic Tradition', *Traditio* 45 (1989–90), 35–51, at 43.

[33] The canonical book of Threni (Lamentations) follows Jerimiah in *Amiatinus* without a break or new heading as is normal in older manuscripts; see Marsden, *Text*, p. 137.

[34] See B. Fischer, *Lateinische Bibelhandschriften im frühen Mittelalter*, Vetus Latina: Aus der Geschichte der lateinischen Bibel 11 (Freiburg, 1985), p. 11; and Marsden, *Text*, p. 167.

[35] Marsden, *Text*, pp. 329–30.

[36] All translations of the Vulgate follow the Douai-Rheims version.

[37] *Fontes Anglo-Saxonici*, accessed April 2002.

[38] *Genesis A: A New Edition*, ed. A. N. Doane (Madison, 1978), p. 258.

the poem and this book.[39] Three verses from Baruch, III.36–8, do appear in Ælfric's 'De Natale Domini', *Catholic Homilies* II.1, lines 134–7,[40] but here, as Malcolm Godden notes, the immediate source is Quodvultdeus's sermon *Contra Iudaeos* XI.20–25,[41] and so they in themselves provide no direct knowledge of the entire book.[42] Godden further comments that 'Ælfric's *steore* and *þeawfæstnysse* (lines 135–6) perhaps reflects Vulgate *viam disciplinae* rather than *viam scientiae*',[43] raising the possibility that he emended his source because he knew the original. Both *viam disciplinae* and *viam scientiae* occur in other patristic sources,[44] making it not only less certain which Ælfric would have found in the particular manuscript he used, but also possible that he might have chosen this reading without recourse to Baruch itself.[45]

In contrast to III and IV Ezra and Baruch, the other narrowly defined apocrypal books – Tobias (Tobit), Judith, Sapientia Salomonis (Wisdom of Salomon), Sirach (Ecclesiasticus), and Maccabeorum (1 and 2 Maccabees), as well as additions to Hester (Esther, X.4–XVI.24)[46] and Daniel (the Prayer of Azarias and the Song of the Three Children, III.24–90; Susanna, XIII; and Bel and the Dragon, XIV) – were known to the Anglo-Saxons and used by them. All appear in *Amiatinus*, and indeed, Marsden is able to use the versions in the manuscripts to draw some surprising conclusions about their transmission and availability in Anglo-

---

[39] *Old English Biblical Verse*, pp. 262–5. Earlier in this study, he evaluates James W. Bright's suggestion that *Exodus* reflects the liturgical readings for Easter found in the later form of the 'Gelasian' usage, noting that Bright himself finds nothing that reflects the selection from Baruch (III.9–38): p. 171. See also Remley's index under 'Bible, Old Testament' (p. 466) for further references.

[40] 'Eft se witega hieremias cwæð be ðam hælende ðes is ure god. and nis nan oðer geteald to him. he arærde and gesette steore and þeawfæstnysse his folce Israhel; He wæs siððan gesewen ofer eorðan': *Ælfric's Catholic Homilies, The Second Series: Text* [hereafter cited as *CH II*], ed. Malcolm Godden, EETS ss 5 (London, 1979), pp. 6–7. 'Again the prophet Hieremias said about the saviour, "This is our god and there is none other considered [equal] to him. He raised and established correction and good behaviour for his people, Israel. Afterward, he was seen upon earth."'

[41] 'Accedat et alius testes. Dic et tu, Hieremia, testimonium Christo. *Hic est*, inquit, *deus noster, et non aestimabitur: alius absque illo, qui inuenit omnem uiam scientiae, et dedit eam Iacob puero suo, et Israhel dilecto sibi. Post haec in terris uisus est, et cum hominibus conuersatus est*': *CCSL* 60.242. 'Another witness may be added. You also give, Hieremias, testimony concerning Christ. *This is*, he says, *our God, and there shall be no other accounted of in comparison of him. He found out all the way of knowledge, and gave it to Jacob his servant, and to Israel his beloved. Afterwards he was seen upon earth, and conversed with men.*'

[42] Quodvultdeus identifies the source as 'Heremia', following the Septuagint and Old Latin tradition.

[43] *Ælfric's Catholic Homilies: Introduction, Commentary and Glossary* [hereafter cited as *Ælfric's ... Introduction*], EETS ss 18 (Oxford, 2000), p. 350.

[44] In *De ciuitate Dei* XV.xxiii, Augustine quotes Baruch III.27 using 'viam scientiae' (*CCSL* 48.492). The phrase also appears in Hilary's *De trinitate* IV.xlii and V.xxxix (*CCSL* 62.147–8 and 194). The phrase 'viam disciplinae' is more common. For further examples, see the CD-ROM produced by Brepols in conjunction with the *Corpus Christianorum*, CETEDOC Library of Christian Latin Texts, CLCLT-4 (2000).

[45] These verses are included in the selection from Baruch found in the later Gelasian usage of lections for the Easter Vigil; see Remley, *Old English Biblical Verse*, p. 84.

[46] Jerome gathered the six additions to Hester into a section at the end of the book, obscuring their relationship to the original work; see J. A. F. Gregg, 'The Additions to Esther', in *The Apocrypha and Pseudepigrapha of the Old Testament in English*, ed. R. H. Charles, 2 vols. (Oxford, 1913), I.665–84.

Saxon England.[47] Alcuin includes extracts from Daniel (chapter III), Hester (chapters XIII–XIV), Judith, Tobias, Sapientia, Sirach and II Maccabeorum in his *De Laude Dei*.[48] Bede wrote an 'allegorical' commentary on Tobias, the first on this book.[49] A fragmentary Old English poetic translation of Judith (chapters IX–XV) survives in the *Beowulf*-manuscript,[50] and Ælfric produced a prose paraphrase of it as well.[51] His paraphrase of Maccabees is in rhythmical prose.[52] The Old English poem *Daniel*, in the Junius manuscript, corresponds to chapters I–V of the biblical book, and so includes (in lines 283–408) the Prayer of Azarias and the Song of the Three Children.[53] Some scholars, however, consider this part of the poem to be interpolated, referring to it as *Daniel B*, and P. J. Lucas writes that it 'seems to be a version of the Old English poem *Azarias*, found in the Exeter Book'.[54] The exact relationship between the two Old English poems is further complicated by two Latin Canticles, *Oratio Azariae* and *Canticum trium puerorum*, which circulated independently of the rest of the book, and which Remley argues are the sources of these lines of *Daniel*.[55] In the Vulgate, the stories of Susanna and Bel are preceded by a note indicating that Jerome knew them only from the Greek version associated with Theodotion;[56] Aldhelm refers to Susanna in his prose *De virginitate* LXIV,[57] and to Bel in his poetic *De virginitate*, line 351.[58]

Two other texts that the Anglo-Saxons would have found in some of their bibles, Psalm 151 and the Epistle to the Laodiceans, deserve mention here even though they are printed by Weber in his appendix to the Vulgate and are not included in the Apocrypha of the King James Bible. Psalm 151 draws much of its content from I Samuel, purporting to be spoken by David after his fight with Goliath, but obviously stands outside the neat ordering of 150 Psalms. It was probably part of the Roman Psalter brought by Augustine to Canterbury,[59] and it was included in the *Codex Amiatinus*, but

---

[47] Marsden, *Text*, pp. 151–82. See also Gneuss's lists (in the appendix of his *Handlist*, p. 157) of 'Bibles, complete or presumably complete originally' and 'Old Testament, Books in incomplete Bibles or individually copied'.

[48] Marsden, *Text*, pp. 222–35.

[49] *CCSL* 119B.3–19. See the translation, with and introduction and notes, by W. Trent Foley, *Bede: A Biblical Miscellany*, trans. Foley and Arthur G. Holder, Translated Texts for Historians 28 (Liverpool, 1999), pp. 53–79.

[50] *Judith*, ed. Mark Griffith, Exeter Medieval English Texts and Studies (Exeter, 1997).

[51] It is referred to, following its editor, as Assmann IX; *Angelsächsische Homilien und Heiligenleben*, ed. Bruno Assmann, Bibliothek der angelsächsischen Prosa 3 (Kassel, 1889; repr. with an introduction by Peter Clemoes, Darmstadt, 1964), pp. 102–16.

[52] *Ælfric's Lives of Saints*, ed. Walter W. Skeat, EETS os 76, 82, 94 and 114 (Oxford, 1881–1900; repr. in 2 vols., Oxford 1966), II.66–120.

[53] *Daniel and Azarias*, ed. Robert T. Farrell (London, 1974). Farrell argues that the poem is complete as we have it: pp. 32–3.

[54] Peter J. Lucas, 'Daniel', in *Blackwell Encyclopaedia of Anglo-Saxon England*, ed. Michael Lapidge, John Blair, Simon Keynes and Donald Scragg (Oxford, 1999), p. 137.

[55] *Old English Biblical Verse*, pp. 334–434.

[56] Weber, *Biblia sacra*, p. 1368; see also D. M. Kay, 'Susanna', in *Apocrypha*, ed. Charles, I.638–51, at 640.

[57] *Aldhelmi Opera*, ed. Rudolf Ehwald, MGH AA 15 (Berlin, 1919), 298.

[58] Ehwald, *Aldhelmi*, p. 368.

[59] *Le Psautier Romain et les autres anciens psautiers latins*, ed. Robert Weber, Collectanea Biblica Latina 10 (Rome, 1953), p. ix.

with the heading 'psalmus dauid proprie extra numerum' ('a psalm of David himself outside the normal number').[60] While not in two other eighth-century Roman Psalters, one from Northumbria (Berlin, Staatsbibliothek Preussischer Kulturbesitz, Hamilton 553),[61] the other probably from the south of England (New York, Pierpont Morgan Library, M 776),[62] it is in the Vespasian Psalter (BL, Cotton Vespasian A.i),[63] but on a separate folio added in the ninth century,[64] presumably reflecting the growing influence of Gallican Psalters. Indeed, most of the examples of Psalm 151 in ninth-century and later Anglo-Saxon manuscripts are in Gallican Psalters.[65] Unlike the text in the Vespasian Psalter, however, these are not glossed in Old English even when the other psalms have been.[66] Moreover, Psalm 151 is sometimes preceded by a warning, which in the Salisbury Psalter reads,

> Hic psalmus proprie scriptus est a Dauid . et extra numerum cum pugnauit cum Golia hic in Ebreis codicibus non habetur . sed nec a lxx interprecibus editus est et idcirco repudiandu.[67]

Laodiceans, a tissue of quotations from other Pauline epistles, was presumably composed because the letter mentioned in Colossians IV.16 did not survive. Preserved only in Latin, it is found in many bibles, including BL, Royal 1.E.VIII.[68] Ælfric's reference to it in his letter to Sigeweard concerning the Old and New Testament is the subject of Thomas N. Hall's essay later in this volume.[69]

---

[60] Weber, *Biblia sacra*, p. 1975. See also Marsden, *Text*, p. 141.

[61] Gneuss, *Handlist*, no. 790.

[62] Gneuss, *Handlist*, no. 862.

[63] Gneuss, *Handlist*, no. 381.

[64] *The Vespasian Psalter: British Museum, Cotton Vespasian A. I*, ed. David H. Wright, with a contribution on the gloss by Alistair Campbell, EEMF 14 (Copenhagen, 1967), p. 46.

[65] Cambridge, Corpus Christi College 272 (Gneuss no. 77), 391 (Gneuss no. 104), and 411 (Gneuss no. 106); BL, Arundel 60 (Gneuss no. 304), Cotton Galba A.xviii (Gneuss no. 334), Harley 2904 (Gneuss no. 430); Salisbury, Cathedral Library 180 (Gneuss no. 754); Vatican, Biblioteca Apostolica, Reg. lat. 12 (Gneuss no. 912); see also the following note.

[66] BL, Cotton Vitellius E.xviii (see N. R. Ker, *Catalogue of Manuscripts Containing Anglo-Saxon* [Oxford, 1957], no. 224); London, Lambeth Palace 427 (Ker, *Catalogue*, 280); and Salisbury, Cathedral Library 150 (Ker, *Catalogue*, 379). Only some psalms of the Bosworth Psalter (BL, Additional 37517) have been glossed, but 151 is not among them; see Ker, *Catalogue*, 129.

[67] *The Salisbury Psalter*, ed. Celia Sisam and Kenneth Sisam, EETS os 242 (London, 1959), p. 284: 'this psalm was written by David himself, beyond the normal number when he fought with Goliath. This psalm is not found in Hebrew codices, but was drawn from the Septuagint and so is to be repudiated'; see also the Ramsey Psalter (BL, Harley 2904) 188r, and BL, Cotton Vitellius E.xviii, 131r.

[68] The explicit following the Epistle to the Hebrews at the end of Cambridge, Trinity College B.5.2 (Gneuss, *Handlist*, no. 169), 'epistole Pauli numero xv^cim expl', leads M. R. James to the conclusion that this manuscript 'must have contained the Epistle to the Laodiceans': *The Western Manuscripts in the Library of Trinity College, Cambridge*, 4 vols. (Cambridge, 1900–04), I.186.

[69] *The Old English Version of the Heptateuch, Aelfric's Treatise on the Old and New Testament and his Preface to Genesis*, ed. S. J. Crawford, EETS os 160 (London, 1922), p. 57.

*Modern Definitions of Apocrypha*

The concept of the apocrypha becomes much more complicated when its narrow definition as the Old Testament books found in the Greek but not in the Hebrew canon is expanded to include works referred to by some scholars as Old Testament pseudepigrapha and apocryphal books associated with the New Testament. The number of texts to be considered increases dramatically, and the focus of the study broadens from changes in Jewish communities between the fourth century BC and the first century AD to include more centrally the emergence of Christianity. Given the importance of this period in the histories of both religions, it is not at all surprising that some biblical scholars have tried to restrict the term to works produced before the end of the first centuries of the Christian era, and indeed the relationship of the apocrypha to the canon, which became increasingly fixed during this time,[70] adds further justification to this effort. Thus in the introduction to *Old Testament Pseudepigrapha*, James H. Charlesworth defines his subject as,

> Those writings 1) that, with the exception of Ahiqar, are Jewish or Christian; 2) that are often attributed to ideal figures in Israel's past; 3) that customarily claim to contain God's word or message; 4) that frequently build upon ideas and narratives present in the Old Testament; 5) and that almost always were composed either during the period 200 B.C. to A.D. 200 or, though late, apparently preserve, albeit in an edited form, Jewish traditions that date from that period.[71]

Similarly, in the revised edition of *New Testament Apocrypha*, Wilhelm Schneemelcher repeats the definition from the earlier edition:

> The New Testament Apocrypha are writings which have not been received into the canon, but which by title and other statements lay claim to be in the same class with the writings of the canon, and which from the point of view of Form Criticism further develop and mould the kinds of style created and received in the New Testament, whilst foreign elements certainly intrude.[72]

He also recalls his earlier amplification:

> When we speak of 'Apocrypha of the New Testament', we mean by that Gospels which are distinguished by the fact not merely that they did not come into the New Testament, but also that they were intended to take the place of the four Gospels of the canon (this holds good for the older texts) or to stand as enlargement of them side by side with them. . . . It is further a matter of particular

---

[70] Schneemelcher speaks of the 'provisional closure of the canon (about 200)': 'General Introduction', in *New Testament Apocrypha*, I.51; see also *ODCC*, pp. 279–80.

[71] 'Introduction for the General Reader', p. xxv.

[72] 'General Introduction', pp. 58–9.

pseudepigraphical Epistles and of elaborately fabricated Acts of Apostles, the writers of which have worked up in novelistic fashion the stories and legends about the apostles and so aimed at supplementing the deficient information which the New Testament communicates about the destinies of these men. Finally, there also belong here the Apocalypses in so far as they have further evolved the 'revelation' taken over from Judaism.[73]

These definitions, while open to criticism,[74] reflect and participate in the significant scholarly achievement extending over centuries of identifying and understanding a core of texts that are apocrypha. The continued interest in these texts and the problems they present can be seen in some important series devoted to them, notably the *Series Apocryphorum* of the *Corpus Christianorum* as well as the French translations in *Apocryphes*, and other specialized publications such as *Apocrypha, Journal for the Study of Pseudepigrapha (and Related Literature)*, *Pseudepigrapha Veteris Testamenti Graece*, and *Studia in Veteris Testamenti Pseudepigrapha*.

One ground for criticising these definitions that is particularly relevant to Anglo-Saxonists is the difficulty of setting a closing date on the production of new apocrypha.[75] From a purely practical standpoint, any later text might always be significant to a modern scholar since it could incorporate material from a lost earlier one. Moreover, the opportunity to create a new apocryphon, or to produce a work that is then understood in the following generations to be one, remains as long as the bible itself is known and read as a special kind of book within religious communities. The result of this difficulty in closing the apocrypha is that recent scholarship, as exemplified by *CAVT* and *CANT*, tends to be inclusive in its listing of works. This trend is useful for scholars of pre-Conquest England since the Anglo-Saxons themselves, without modern scholarly tools such as textual criticism and comparative materials, would have found it much more difficult to assess the antiquity and authenticity of any particular text. The danger, however, of this inclusivity is that the core meaning of apocrypha will be diluted so any work concerning a biblical figure or story or imitating a biblical genre may be considered in this group.

This challenge suggests a slight shift in the definition of the apocrypha to those books perceived to be composed under similar circumstances as the canonical books and for similar purposes, and yet, for various reasons, not accepted as authoritative. The passive 'perceived' allows for different decisions at different times (or even by different yet contemporary individuals) about which books are meant, while preserving the common idea that makes these works both profoundly interesting and yet often unsettling: they add significant details to biblical narratives and so may reveal more of God's divine plan; however, they may also include ideas that could

---

[73] 'General Introduction', p. 59.

[74] Schneemelcher discusses some criticisms: 'General Introduction', pp. 59–60.

[75] See Eric Junod, 'Apocryphes du Nouveau Testament: une appellation erronée et une collection artificielle. Discussion de la nouvelle définition proposée par W. Schneemelcher', *Apocrypha* 3 (1992), 17–46.

lead the faithful astray. The origin and involvement of these works in Judaism's self-definition, the emergence of Christianty and Christianity's self-definition indicate the stakes involved for religious groups in making the right decision about the status of each contested book.

## Some Patristic and Anglo-Saxon Uses of the Term

The Anglo-Saxons would have inherited both an interest in and a distrust of the apocrypha from the Latin fathers, in particular Jerome and Augustine. As noted earlier, these two differ sharply in their assessment of the Septuagint, with Jerome denying the divine inspiration of this translation and Augustine affirming it.[76] Yet, even though they consider different books as apocryphal, their attitudes toward this material are often similar. In a letter explaining how to raise a daughter, Jerome turns from a discussion of the order in which to read the books of the bible to the apocrypha:

> caueat omnia apocrypha et, si quando ea non ad dogmatum ueritatem, sed ad signorum reuerentiam legere uoluerit, sciat non eorum esse, quorum titulis praenotatur, multaque his admixta uitiosa et grandis esse prudentiae aurum in luto quaerere.[77]

In spite of his warnings, he recognizes that these works can be read profitably – if not for doctrine, then for the miracles (*signum*) they contain – and indeed both he and Augustine often treat apocrypha with respect.[78] Both, however, also draw attention to times when apocryphal writings stem

---

[76] See, for example, Jerome's comment in his prologue to the Pentateuch: 'Et nescio quis primus auctor septuaginta cellulas Alexandriae mendacio suo extruxerit, quibus divisi eadem scriptitarint, cum Aristheus eiusdem Ptolomei υπερασπιστησε et multo post tempore Iosepphus nihil tale rettulerint, sed in una basilica congregatos contulisse scribant, non prophetasse', Weber, *Biblia sacra*, p. 3; 'I do not know whose false imagination led him to invent the story of the seventy cells at Alexandria, in which, though separated from each other, the translators were said to have written the same words. Aristeas, the champion of that same Ptolemy, and Josephus, long after, relate nothing of the kind; their account is that the Seventy assembled in one basilica consulted together and did not prophesy'; trans. W. F. Fremantle, *Theodoret, Jerome, Gennadius, Rufinus: Historical Writings, etc.*, A Select Library of Nicene and Post-Nicene Fathers of the Christian Church, 2nd ser., vol. 3 (1893; repr. Grand Rapids, MI, 1969), 516. In contrast, in *De civitate Dei* XV.xxiii, Augustine declares, 'Merito enim creduntur septuaginta interpretes accepisse propheticum spiritum, ut, si quid eius auctoritate mutarent atque aliter quam erat quod interpretabantur dicerent, neque hoc diuinitus dictum esse dubitaretur', *CCSL*, 48.491; 'We are justified in supposing that the seventy translators received the spirit of prophecy; and so if they altered anything by its authority and used expressions in their translation different from those of the original, we should not doubt that these expressions also were inspired by God', trans. Henry Bettenson, *The City of God* (Middlesex, 1972), p. 640.

[77] *CSEL* 55.303; 'Let her avoid all apocryphal writings, and if she is led to read such not by the truth of the doctrines which they contain but out of respect for the miracles contained in them; let her understand that they are not really written by those to whom they are ascribed, that many faulty elements have been introduced into them, and that it requires infinite discretion to look for gold in the midst of dirt', trans. W. H. Fremantle, *The Principal Works of Jerome*, Nicene and Post Nicene Fathers 6 (1893; repr. Grand Rapids, MI, 1983), 194.

[78] See Jerome's prologue to the books of Salomon (Weber, *Biblia sacra*, p. 957), and his remark about Barnabus's apocryphal epistle, *De viris inlustribus* VI (*PL* 23.619). See Augustine, *De diuersis quaestionibus lxxxiii* LIX (*CCSL* 44.110), and *Tractatus in Euangelium Ioannis* CXXIV.ii (*CCSL* 36.681–2).

from and/or lead to heretical doctrines.[79] At the beginning of his commentary on Matthew, Jerome recalls the opening of Luke's Gospel, which draws attention to other writings about Christ's life, and comments that these records – he lists the Gospel of the Egyptians, Thomas, Mathias, Bartholomew, the Twelve Apostles, Basilides, and Apelles – were the origin of diverse heresies.[80] Isidore of Seville sums up the patristic attitude toward apocrypha, noting the connection of many of them with heretics: 'in iis apocryphis etsi invenitur aliqua veritas, tamen propter multa falsa nulla est in eis canonica auctoritas'.[81]

Similarly, the Anglo-Saxon attitude toward the apocrypha is marked by caution; however, significant differences can be seen especially between Bede, who is interested in learning and evaluating all that he can about these texts, and Ælfric, who fears apocryphal traditions spreading around him. One of the most detailed statements on this subject is Bede's discussion of the reference to Enoch in the Epistle of Jude 14–15:

> prophetavit autem et his septimus ab Adam Enoch dicens
> ecce venit Dominus in sanctis milibus suis
> facere iudicium contra omnes et arguere omnes impios
> de omnibus operibus impietatis eorum quibus impie egerunt
> et de omnibus duris quae locuti sunt contra eum peccatores impii.[82]

Bede considers Jude's source here to be the Book of Enoch (*CAVT* 61), which, he claims, the Church considers among the apocryphal scriptures ('inter apocryphas scripturas'):

> non quia dicta tanti patriarchae abicienda ullatenus possint aut debeant aestimari sed quia liber ille qui sub nomine eius offertur non uere ab illo scriptus sed sub titulo nominis eius ab alio quodam editus uidetur.[83]

Alluding to Genesis VI.2 (the beginning of the Flood story) and the controversy over the meaning of the 'sons of God' who select wives from the 'daughters of men', he cites the discussion of giants being descended from angels rather than from humans as proof that the book contains many unbelievable things ('multa incredibilia'), an example which, as R. E. Kaske

---

[79] See Jerome, *Contra Vigilantium* VI (*PL* 40.344–5), *Apologia aduersus libos Rufini* II.xxv (*CCSL* 79.62), *Dialogi contra Pelagianos libri iii*, I.xxxii (*CCSL* 80.39–40), *Tractatus lix in psalmos*, 'De psalmo cxxxii' (*CCSL* 78.281). See Augustine, *Epistula* 237 (*CSEL* 57.526–7) and *De ciuitate Dei* XV.xxiii (*CCSL* 48.491).

[80] *Commentarii in Euangelium Matthaei*, 'Praefatio', *CCSL* 77.1.

[81] *Etymologiarum siue Originum libri xx*, VI.ii.52, ed. W. M. Lindsay, 2 vols. (Oxford, 1911); 'although some truth is found in these apocrypha, nevertheless, because of much falsehood, there is in them no canonical authority'.

[82] 'Now of these Enoch also, the seventh from Adam, prophesied, saying: Behold, the Lord cometh with thousands of his saints to execute judgement upon all, and to reprove all the ungodly for all the works of their ungodliness, whereby they have done ungodly, and of all the hard things which ungodly sinners have spoken against God.'

[83] *Super epistulas catholicas expositio*, *CCSL* 121.340; 'not because the sayings of such a patriarch can or ought in any way to be considered rejected, but because that book which is presented under his name is considered not truly written by him, but edited by some other one under the title of his name'.

noted,[84] he could have drawn from Augustine's *De ciuitate Dei* XV.xxiii,[85] and which therefore does not necessarily suggest that he had direct knowledge of Enoch itself. What is also surprising, however, is that Bede, unlike Augustine, acknowledges that Jude could have relied on an apocryphal book, and that, for this reason, his own letter was at first excluded by many from the canon:

> Vnde et haec eadem Iudae epistola quia de apocrypho libre testimonium habet primis temporibus a plerisque reiciebatur, tamen auctoriate iam et uetustate et usu meruit ut inter sanctas scripturas computetur maxime quia tale testimonium de apocrypho Iudas assumpsit quod non apocryphum ac dubium sed uera luce et lucida esset ueritate perspicuum.[86]

While he takes the core of this remark from Jerome's discussion of Jude in *De uiris inlustribus* IV,[87] his use of Jerome rather than Augustine shows a more nuanced approach to this material.

While there is little evidence that Bede knew any Old Testament apocrypha (other than the books from the Septuagint discussed earlier)[88] first-hand, a comment in his *Retractio in Actus Apostolorum* suggests that he was familiar with 'passiones apostolorum', or retellings of legends about the apostles adapted to hagiographic conventions.[89] He takes the opportunity presented by the names Simon Zelotes and Iudas Iacobi in Acts I.13 to comment,

> hos referunt historiae, in quibus passiones apostolorum continentur et a plurimis deputantur apocryfae, praedicasse in Perside ibique *a templorum pontificibus in ciuitate Suanir occisos* gloriosum subisse martyrium.[90]

He goes on to note that this detail is confirmed in Jerome's *Martyrology*, and M. L. W. Laistner places the phrase 'a templorum . . .occisos' in italics

---

[84] R. E. Kaske, '*Beowulf* and the Book of Enoch', *Speculum* 46 (1971), 421–31, at 422.

[85] *CCSL* 48.491.

[86] *CCSL* 121.341; 'whence, indeed, this same letter of Jude, because it has testimony from an apocryphal book at first was rejected by most; nevertheless it now deserves, by authority and antiquity and custom, to be reckoned certainly among holy scripture because Jude takes such testimony from apocrypha as is not apocryphal or doubtful but might be truly manifest in clear and true light'.

[87] 'Et quia de libro Enoch, qui apocryphus est, in ea assumit testimonium, a plerisque rejicitur, tamen auctoritatem vetustate jam et usu meruit, et inter sanctas Scripturas computatur', *PL* 23.615; 'and because in it he takes testimony from the Book of Enoch, which is apocryphal, it is rejected by many; however, now by age and use it has gained authority, and is reckoned among Holy scripture'. See also, *Commentarius in Epistolas Catholicas Scotti anonymi*, *CCSL* 108B.4.

[88] For Bede's comment on Jude 9, see the discussion below, p. 23.

[89] Five earlier acts, composed in the second or third centuries, concern Andrew (*CANT* 225), John (*CANT* 215), Paul (*CANT* 211), Peter (*CANT* 190) and Thomas (*CANT* 245); see Wilhelm Schneemelcher, 'Second and Third Century Acts of Apostles', in *New Testament Apocrypha*, ed. Schneemelcher, II.75–100; and J. K. Elliott, *Apocryphal New Testament* (1993; rev. Oxford, 1999), pp. 229–30.

[90] *CCSL* 121.106; 'histories, in which are contained passions of the apostles and which by most are reckoned apocryphal, relate that these preached in Persia, and there were killed by the temple priests in the city of Suanir'.

because Bede's wording corresponds to this source.[91] Laistner also provides a reference to the *Virtutes Apostolorum* (*CANT* 256), more commonly known in earlier scholarship as pseudo-Abdias, *Historiae Apostolicae*, a work compiled in Gaul in the sixth century.[92] This work does indeed contain the information Bede mentions,[93] and significantly, following the section on Simon and Jude, includes a discussion that identifies Abdias as the author of ten books on the acts of the apostles,[94] offering further evidence that it is to this source that Bede refers.

A second comment later in his *Retractio* should probably be connected to his discussion of apocryphal traditions concerning the death of Mary and does reveal his knowledge of a particular apocryphal text, the Transitus of Pseudo-Melito ($B^2$). In writing about Acts IX.29–30, Bede confronts a discrepancy between accounts of events following Paul's conversion in the Acts of the Apostles and Epistle to the Galatians: Acts (IX.26–8) suggests that Paul travels immediately to Jerusalem while in Galatians (I.17–18) Paul states that he spent three years in Arabia before returning to Damascus and then travelling to Jerusalem. While aware of these texts, Bede focuses on a mistaken belief in 'apocryphal books':

> Cum ergo constet quod Paulus post annos tres suae conuersionis uenerit Hierosolymam et apostolorum fuerit numero sociatus, existens adhuc, ut ipse scribit: *Ignotus facie ecclesiis Iudaeae quae erant in Chirsto*, errant multum qui apocryforum libros sectando putant eum secundo post passionem domini anno in apostolatum gentium cum Barnaba iam fuisse ordinatum.[95]

Shortly before this passage, in discussing Acts VIII.1, Bede had identified precisely such a book, although he does not use the term 'apocrypha' to describe it:

> Si dispersa ecclesia apostoli *remanserunt in Hierusalem*, ut Lucas ait, constat quia mendacium scripsit ille qui ex persona Militonis episcopi Asiae, librum exponens de obitu beatae genetricis dei,

---

[91] *Acta Sanctorum, Novembris*, 2.1, ed. Hippolyte Delehaye, Paul Peeters and Maurice Coens (Brussels, 1931), p. 2.

[92] Jean-Daniel Kaestli, 'Les principales orientations de la recherche sur les Actes Apocryphes des Apôtres', in *Les Actes Apocryphes des Apôtres: Christianisme et monde païen*, ed. François Bovon, and Michel van Esbroeck *et. al.*, Publications de la Faculté de Théologie de l'Université de Genève 4 (Geneve, 1981), p. 52.

[93] Johann Albert Fabricius, *Codex Apocryphus Novi Testamenti*, 2nd ed., 3 vols. in 2 (Hamburg, 1719), II.629.

[94] See *BHL* 7751; this section appears in the version printed in B. Mombritius, *Sanctuarium seu vitae sanctorum*, 2nd ed., 2 vols. (Paris, 1910), II.534–9. Fabricius, following the edition of W. Lazius (*Abdiae episcopi Babyloniae Historia certaminis apostolorum* [Basel, 1551]), moved this section to serve as a prologue to the work; Kaestli notes that the edition of F. Nausea (*Anonymi Philalethi Eusebiani in vitas, miracula passionesque apostolorum rhapsodiae* [Cologne, 1531]), which lacks this prologue, is closer to the manuscripts; 'Principales', p. 52.

[95] *CCSL* 121.139; 'Since, therefore, it may remain firm that three years after his conversion Paul went to Jerusalem and was united in the number of the apostles, being until then, as he himself wrote, *unknown by face to the churches of Judea, which were in Christ*, they err greatly who, following apocryphal books, believe that he was already ordained into the apostolic family with Barnabas in the second year after the passion of the Lord.'

dicit quod secundo post ascensionem domini anno apostoli fuerint omnes tota orbe ad praedicandum in suam quisque prouinciam diuisi.[96]

These and Bede's following remarks establish that he is alluding to Transitus B[2], and he concludes, 'haec ideo commemorare curaui quia noui nonnullos praefato uolumini contra actoritatem beati Lucae incauta temeritate adsensum praebere'.[97] While Bede's distrust of this source is clear, it may be significant that he does not use the term 'apocrypha' to describe it: Mary Clayton argues that by evading the central theme of the book, the corporal assumption of the virgin, Bede shows that he was 'equally unwilling to condemn or accept the belief and did not wish to assent to anything that had not been revealed in scripture'.[98] To have labelled it 'apocrypha' in this context might have cast too much doubt on a belief Bede wished to hold. In any case, his reference to those led astray by the mistaken chronology could include both Isidore's *De ortu et obitu patrum*,[99] and the pseudo-Isidorian work by the same name, believed to be an Irish composition (although perhaps written on the Continent) of the eighth century.[100]

Finally, a passage at the beginning of Bede's commentary on Luke raises the possibility that he knew a variety of apocryphal Gospels, although at the moment this seems unlikely. After quoting the opening four verses, he remarks:

> Quo manifestissime proemio signifcat eam sibi maxime causam euangelii fuisse scribendi ne pseudoeuangelistis facultas esset falsa praedicandi qui ut eorum hodieque monumenta testantur sub nomine apostolorum perfidiae conati sunt inducere sectas.[101]

While the 'hodieque' might suggest that this material circulated in Bede's circles, it could also recall Jerome's 'perseuerantia usque in praesens tempus monumenta' ('records surviving even to this present time'),[102] from the

---

[96] *CCSL* 121.134; 'If, when the church was scattered, the apostles remained in Jerusalem, as Luke says, it is evident that he wrote a lie who said, under the guise of Bishop Milito of Asia, in a book describing the death of the blessed mother of God, that in the second year after the Ascension of the Lord all the apostles were divided thoughout the world, each one preaching in his province', trans. Mary Clayton, *The Cult of the Virgin Mary in Anglo-Saxon England*, CSASE 2 (Cambridge, 1990), p. 18.

[97] *CCSL* 121.135; 'This, therefore, I have taken care to mention because I know that some, by heedless thoughtlessness, grant approval to the aforesaid volumes against the authority of blessed Luke', trans. Clayton, *Cult*, p. 18. See also *CCSL* 121.145.

[98] Clayton, *Cult*, p. 19.

[99] *PL* 83.150.

[100] *PL* 83.1287. See McNamara, *Apocrypha in the Irish Church*, p. 83; and Michael Lapidge and Richard Sharpe, *A Bibliography of Celtic-Latin Literature, 400–1200* (Dublin, 1985), p. 209.

[101] *In Lucae euangelium expositio*, *CCSL* 120.19; 'By this most clear beginning he makes known his greatest reason for writing the Gospel, lest there might be opportunity to preach for the pseudo evangelists, who, as their records even now testify, try under the name of the apostles to lead their sects to falsehood.'

[102] *CCSL* 77.1. The editor of Bede's commentary, D. Hurst, notes both this passage from Jerome and a passage from Ambrose's commentary on Luke (*CCSL* 14.7) as Bede's sources for lines 17–47.

beginning of his commentary on Matthew noted above. Bede's list of apocryphal texts, however, differs from Jerome's:

> Denique non nulli Thomae alii Bartholomei quidam Matthiae aliqui etiam duodecim apostolorum titulo repperiuntur falso sua scripta praenotasse. Sed et Basilides atque Apelles quorum unus trecentos sexaginta quinque caelos alter duos inuicem contrarios deos inter alia nefanda dogmatizabant euangelia sui nominis errore foeda reliquisse. Inter quae notandum quod dicitur euangelium iuxta Hebraeos non inter apocriphas sed inter ecclesiasticas numerandum historias.[103]

The main reason why this list appears so different is because Bede groups the Gospels associated with the apostles first,[104] before turning to Basilides (*CANT* 41) and Apelles (*CANT* 42). Virtually nothing survives of these two works,[105] and indeed Bede could have derived his information about the 365 heavens in one and the two gods in the other from Augustine's *De haeresibus* IV and XXIII.[106] Bede's final item, the Gospel according to the Hebrews (*CANT* 11), is not taken directly from Jerome, although it apparently replaces his Gospel according to the Egyptians (*CANT* 14). As yet, no source has been proposed for his comment, although it may have been motivated by one of Jerome's remarks elsewhere about this work, for example, in his *De uiris inlustribus* II: 'Evangelium quoque quod appellatur secundum Hebræos, et me nuper in Græcum Latinumque sermonem translatum est' ('the Gospel also which is called the Gospel according to the Hebrews, and which I have recently translated into Greek and Latin').[107] Bede simply may not have wished to label as apocryphal a work so clearly valued by Jerome.

A brief reference in Aldhelm's prose *De uirginitate* indicates that he probably knew the Apocalypse of Paul (*CANT* 325; also known as the Visio Pauli), but his comments here and elsewhere show little respect for this kind of material. In his section on Paul, he first recounts the hardships the saint endured, and then comments on his worthiness to receive a vision of heaven, 'licet revelatio quam dicunt Pauli in nave aurea florentis paradisi

---

[103] *CCSL* 120.19; 'And thereupon their writings were found marked with the false superscriptions, several of Thomas, of another Bartholomew [and] indeed of Matthew, even some of the twelve apostles. But both Basilides and Apelles, one of whom propounded, among other impious beliefs, three hundred and sixty-five heavens, the other two mutually opposing gods, left behind infamous gospels with the deception of their names. Among which is to be noted that what is called the Gospel of the Hebrews is not among the apocrypha, but to be numbered among the church histories.'

[104] He could have learned that there was more than one book associated with Thomas from the so-called Gelasian Decree, which lists a gospel as well as a revelation; see Schneelmelcher, *New Testament Apocrypha*, I.38–9.

[105] See Henri-Charles Puech, revised by Beate Blatz, 'Other Gnostic Gospels and Related Literature', in *New Testament Apocrypha*, ed. Schneemelcher, I.354–413, at 397–400.

[106] *CCSL* 46.291 and 300.

[107] *PL* 23.611, trans. Ernest C. Richardson, Nicene and Post-Nicene Fathers, 3.362. For Jerome's other remarks about this work, see Philipp Vielhauer and Georg Strecker, 'Jewish-Christian Gospels', in *New Testament Apocrypha*, ed. Schneemelcher, I.134–78.

dilicias eundem adisse garriat'.[108] The detail of the golden ship is itself revealing since, while Paul travels to see Christ's city in such a ship in chapter 23 of the Long Latin Versions,[109] it is placed within a quotation of II Corinthians XII.2 at the beginning of one of the shorter versions, Redaction XI:

> Scio hominem raptum usque ad tertium celum. in navi aurea erant quasi tres angeli hymnum dicentes ante me, uere sive in corpore siue extra corpus nescio, Deus scit.[110]

Even though this echo reveals that Aldhelm most likely knew the work, the rest of his comment makes it clear that he considers it of little value:

> Sed fas divinum vetat catholicae fidei sequipedas plus quppiam, quam canonicae veritatis censura promulgat, credere et cetera apocriforum deleramenta velut horrisona verborum tonitrua penitus abdicare et procul eliminare orthodoxorum patrum scita scriptis decretalibus sanxerunt.[111]

Later in this work, Aldhelm quotes Paul's description of Melchisedech as 'without father, without mother, without genealogy' (Heb. VII.3), and then comments,

> quamvis vulgata Ebreorum traditio hunc fuisse arbitretur Sem primogenitum Noe, tritavum Abrahae et Nachor et Aaron. Sed plurimum differt inter ambiguas fariseorum traditiones et elucubratam sacrae scripturae diffinitionem: apocriforum enim naenias et incertas fribulorum fabulas nequaquam catholica receptat ecclesia.[112]

With *nenia*, which he apparently drew from Jerome's Commentary on Matthew,[113] Aldhelm denigrates all biblical traditions outside the bible

---

[108] Ehwald, *Aldhelmi*, p. 256; 'even though the so-called *Revelatio Pauli* says foolishly that he came to the delights of flowering Paradise in a golden ship', trans. Michael Lapidge, *Aldhelm: The Prose Works*, ed. Lapidge and Michael W. Herren (Cambridge, 1979), p. 81.

[109] Theodore Silverstein and Anthony Hilhorst, *Apocalypse of Paul, A New Critical Edition of the Three Long Latin Versions* (Geneva, 1997), pp. 120–1; the detail appears in all four versions.

[110] M. E. Dwyer, 'An Unstudied Redaction of the *Visio Pauli*', *Manuscripta* 32 (1988), 125; 'I know a man caught up to the third heaven. In a golden ship were three like angels singing hymns before me, whether in the body or out of the body, I know not, God knows.' See also Charles D. Wright, 'Some Evidence for an Irish Origin of Redaction XI of the *Visio Pauli*', *Manuscripta* 34 (1990), 34–44.

[111] Ehwald, *Aldhelmi*, p. 256; 'but divine law forbids the followers of the catholic faith to believe more, in any respect, than what the judgement of canonical truth promulgates, and the decrees of the orthodox fathers in decretal writings have sanctioned the utter rejection and complete banishment of the other absurdities of the apocrypha as being a cacophonous thunder of words', trans. Lapidge, *Prose Works*, p. 81.

[112] Ehwald, *Aldhelmi*, p. 313; 'even though the popular tradition of the Hebrews declares that Sem was the first-born son of Noah, ancestor of Abraham, Nachor and Aaron. But there is considerable difference between the dubious traditions of the Pharisees and the elaborate exposition of Holy Scripture; for the catholic Church in no way accepts the trifles of apocryphal (books) and the uncertain tales of other absurdities' (I follow Lapidge's translation [*Prose Works*, p. 124], except for the first sentence where he adds 'that his father was').

[113] *CCSL* 77.4. This source suggests that it should be translated as 'a funeral song, song of lamentation, dirge'; Carlton T. Lewis and Charles Short, *A Latin Dictionary* (Oxford, 1879), s.v.

itself, echoing the phrasing of the Gelasian Decree *de libris recipiendis et non recipiendis* in the final clause. Indeed, 'apocriforum' is glossed in Old English in two manuscripts: 'tweogendlicra gewrita' (Brussels, Bibliothèque Royale 1650)[114]; and 'tweoniendlicra gewrita' (Oxford, Bodleian Library, Digby 146);[115] the sense is 'doubtful' or 'uncertain' writings.[116]

Before turning to other discussions of apocrypha in Old English, it is necessary to mention the Frankish scholar Frithegod, who served in the household of Archbishop Oda of Canterbury (941–58).[117] He refers to the apocrypha only in passing, as a way of denigrating the charges brought against Wilfred – who had travelled to Rome to try to regain his see in York – by the ambassadors of Berhtwald, archbishop of Canterbury.[118] Pope John judges the case,

> quicquid neutericis confinxit apocripha biblis
> cassetur priscis legatio, censeo, dictis.  (1210–11)[119]

The apocrypha are fabricated and then added to bibles. A gloss in the manuscripts reads 'scriptura (*or* scripta) non recipienda' ('scriptures not to be accepted'), again echoing the Gelasian Decree.

In addition to 'tweondlic gewrit' from the Aldhelm glosses, the *Thesaurus of Old English* offers one other Old English term for apocrypha,[120] *dyrngewritu*, that appears in a Latin–Old English glossary in BL, Cotton Cleopatra A.iii. Following 'sancta scriptura', which is glossed 'halig gewrit', 'apocrifa' is glossed 'dyrngewrita', recalling the Greek meaning of the word as 'hidden' or 'secret' writings. One other glossed text deserves consideration. In the preliminary matter of the Lindisfarne Gospels (BL, Cotton Nero D.iv), appears the opening of Jerome's Commentary on Matthew, already mentioned in connection with Bede's list of apocryphal Gospels and Aldhelm's use of *nenia*; here the phrase 'apocriforum nenias' is glossed 'wiðerweardra gedwola'.[121] The Toronto *Dictionary of Old English* cites this passage under 'gedwola', 'error, ignorance' (definition 1), and

---

[114] Louis Goossens, *The Old English Glosses of MS. Brussels, Royal Library 1650 (Aldhelm's De laudibus virginitatis)*, Brussels Verhandelingen van de koninklijke Academie voor Wetenschappen, Letteren en schone Kunsten van Belgie, Klasse der Letteren 36 (Brussels, 1974).

[115] Arthur S. Napier, *Old English Glosses, Chiefly Unpublished*, Anecdota Oxoniensia, Mediaeval and Modern Series 11 (Oxford, 1900), 130.

[116] See Joseph Bosworth, *An Anglo-Saxon Dictionary*, ed. Joseph Bosworth and T. Northcote Toller (Oxford, 1898), s.v. *tweogendlic*, and the *Supplement*, ed. Toller (Oxford, 1921), s.v. *tweonigendlic*.

[117] See Michael Lapidge, 'A Frankish Scholar in Tenth-Century England: Frithegod of Canterbury/ Fredegaud of Brioude', *ASE* 17 (1988), 45–65; repr. in *Anglo-Latin Literature 900–1066* (London, 1993), pp. 157–81 with addenda at p. 481.

[118] Frithegod's work relies on Eddius Stephanus's *Life of Bishop Wilfrid*, ed. and trans. Bertram Colgrave (Cambridge, 1927), chapters 50–5.

[119] *Frithegodi monachi Breuiloquium vitae beati Wilfredi et Wulfstani cantoris Narratio metrica de sancto Swithuno*, ed. Alistair Campbell (Zurich, 1950), p. 54; 'the embassy with its old charges may be, I judge, dismissed as one fabricated apocrypha for new bibles'.

[120] Jane Roberts and Christian Kay with Lynne Grundy, *A Thesaurus of Old English*, 2 vols., Kings College London Medieval Studies 11 (London, 1995), I.663.

[121] Walter W. Skeat, *The Holy Gospels in Anglo-Saxon, Northumbrian, and Old Mercian Versions*, 4 vols. (Cambridge, 1871–87), I.5–8, at 8. See Ker, *Catalogue*, 165.

more specifically under 1.a 'theological: error in matters of faith or dogma'; 1.a.ii is 'heresy' and this citation from the Lindisfarne Gospels is the only one given under 1.a.iii.[122] As a genitive plural, 'wiðerweardra' corresponds in grammatical form to 'apocriforum', but its meaning, 'adversary, enemy opponent, fiend',[123] does not fit particularly well. Instead the entire phrase may represent the glossator's attempt to render the idea 'apocrypha'. The choice of the term emphasizes the association of the apocrypha with heretical sects.

Several passages in the writings of Ælfric indicate that he used words related to *dwola*, as well as the expressions such as 'lease gesetnysse', 'false writings', to refer to the apocrypha. A telling example that includes both occurs at the beginning of his sermon on the Assumption of the Virgin (*Catholic Homilies* I.30). In his source, first identified by Max Förster,[124] Paschasius Radbertus, writing as if he were Jerome corresponding with Paula and Eustochium, offers his work 'ne forte si uenerit uestris in manibus illud apocryphum de transitu eiusdem uirginis, dubia pro certis recipiatis'.[125] Ælfric translates, 'þy læs ðe eow on hand becume. seo lease gesetnyss. þe ðurh gedwolmannum wide tosawen is. ⁊ ge ðonne þa gehiwedan leasunge for soðre race underfoð',[126] rendering 'illud apocryphum' as 'seo lease gesetnyss' and adding the phrase, 'þe ðurh gedwolmannum wide tosawen is'. At the beginning of another sermon on this feast in his Second Series of Catholic Homilies (II.29), he uses the phrase 'ða dwollican gesetnysse'[127] ('the heretical/apocryphal writings') to refer to accounts he had avoided in the earlier sermon, and in the conclusion of this sermon he returns again to the topic, referring to 'dwollican bec' ('heretical/apocryphal books') and 'dwollican leasunga' which he contrasts with true scripture.[128]

While there will be more detailed discussion of Ælfric's attitude toward the apocrypha later in this volume, recognizing his close association of these texts with the problem of heresy provides an insight into his particular understanding of both the apocrypha and the religious and literary world in which he wrote. For him, the apocrypha have an immediacy. These are not just texts written long ago by obscure sects seeking to advance arcane theological doctrines. Indeed in a section on the four evangelists added to a homily on St Mark (*Lives of Saints* 15) that draws on the beginning of Jerome's Commentary on Matthew noted earlier in connection with Bede

---

[122] *Dictionary of Old English*, Angus Cameron, Ashley C. Amos, Antonette diPaolo Healey, Sharon Butler, Joan Holland, David McDougall and Ian McDougall (Toronto, 1986), s.v. *dwola*.

[123] Bosworth and Toller, *An Anglo-Saxon Dictionary*, s.v. *wiðerweard*.

[124] *Über die Quellen von Aelfrics Homiliae Catholicae, I: Legenden* (Berlin, 1892), p. 28. See also the discussions in Clayton, *Cult*, pp. 235–44; and Godden, *Ælfric's . . .Introduction*, pp. 248–9.

[125] *De assumptione sanctae Mariae uirginis*, CCCM (Turnhout, 1966-), 56C.111–12; 'lest by chance were to come into your hands that apocrypha, *de transitu eiusdem uirginis*, to be received for certain when doubtful'.

[126] *Ælfric's Catholic Homilies, The First Series: Text* [hereafter cited as *CH I*], ed. Peter Clemoes, EETS ss 17 (Oxford, 1997), 430; 'lest into your hand should come the lying writing which is widely scattered by heretics, and you accept that feigned falsehood for the true account'.

[127] Godden, *CH II*, p. 255.

[128] Godden, *CH II*, p. 259.

and the Lindisfarne Gospels,[129] he does not repeat the list of apocryphal books; his concern is to stress that such works of heretics are to be rejected.[130] Instead, he views the apocrypha as the work of individuals who, if not simply misguided, seek to justify their own sinful lives and lead others astray. At the end of his sermon 'In natale sanctuarum uirginum' (*Catholic Homilies* II.39) he considers accounts of Mary's role at judgement:

> Sume gedwolmen cwædon þæt seo halige Maria cristes modor. and sume oðre halgan sceolon hergian æfter ðam dome ða synfullan of ðam deofle. ælc his dæl. Ac þis gedwyld asprang of ðam mannum. þe on heora flæscum lustum symle licgan woldon. and noldon mid earfoðnyssum ðæt ece lif geearnian.[131]

Moreover, his concern that he himself may fall into the error of writing apocrypha suggests that he perceives these texts as springing up all around him. He begins a short note on Mary in his *Catholic Homilies* II with a curt account of what can be said before explaining why he will say no more:

> Hwæt wylle we secgan ymbe Marian gebyrdtide. buton þæt heo wæs gestryned þurh fæder. and ðurh moder. swa swa oðre men. and wæs on ðam dæge acenned þe we cweðað Sexta Idus Septembris; Hire fæder hatte Ioachim. and hire moder Anna. eawfæste men on ðære ealdan æ. ac we nellað be ðam na swiðor awritan þy læs ðe we on ænigum gedwylde befeallon.[132]

While *gedwyld* here may be translated 'heresy' or 'false belief', it refers more generally to the error that arises from perverting the bible. Perceiving this concern may in turn clarify one theme in the Preface to the First Series of the *Catholic Homilies*: Ælfric hopes that his work, inspired as he says 'ðurh godes gife' ('by the grace of God'), may continue Christ's command to his disciples, and made through the prophets, to teach 'eallum þeodum ða ðing þe he sylf him tæhte' ('to all peoples the things that he himself had taught them').[133] He tellingly identifies this teaching as 'ða godspellican soðfæst-neysse þe he sylf gecwæð' ('the evangelical truth which he himself spoke').[134] If his writing is a continuation of the Gospels, the *gedwyld* that he has found 'on manegum engliscum bocum' ('in many English books'),[135] apparently

---

129  This use of Jerome's commentary as a prologue in the Lindisfarne Gospels explains Ælfric's identification of his source as Jerome's 'preface', *forespræc*; Skeat, *Ælfric's Lives of Saints*, I.329.

130  He concludes with the statement that the orthodox church, 'ne under-fehð þa gesetnyssa þe swilce gedwolan//ðurh he sylfe gesetton . buton soðfæstnysse'; Skeat, *Ælfric's Lives*, I.328; 'receives not the writings which such heretics wrote by themselves, without truth'.

131  Godden, *CH II*, p. 333; 'certain heretics said that saint Mary, Christ's mother, and certain other saints should plunder, after the Judgement, sinful men from the devil, each [according to] his portion. But this heresy/apocrypha arose from men who always wished to lie in their bodily pleasures and did not wish to win eternal life through hardships.'

132  Godden, *CH II*, p. 271; 'what shall we say about Mary's birthday except that she was conceived as others by her father and mother, and was born on the day we call 8 September. Her father was called Joachim, and her mother Anna, devout people according to the Old Law. But we wish not to write any more about this lest we fall into any heresy.'

133  Clemoes, *CH I*, p. 176.

134  Clemoes, *CH I*, p. 176.

135  Clemoes, *CH I*, p. 174.

being produced as well as disseminated by unlearned men, is non-canonical. While this definition of apocrypha differs from that of Bede, who like modern biblical scholars focused on texts written in the centuries around Christ's birth, it reveals Ælfric's awareness of the redaction and dissemination of older materials in his own day as well as the developing of new apocryphal traditions.[136]

*Circulation of the Apocrypha in Anglo-Saxon England*

While a full treatment of evidence for the knowledge of each apocryphal text in Anglo-Saxon England is beyond the scope of this essay, I would like to use this final section to call attention to some recent scholarship on the topic. The section on the apocrypha in the *Sources of Anglo-Saxon Literary Culture: A Trial Version*[137] attempted to provide a fuller treatment of the individual works than was available in J. D. A. Ogilvy's *Books Known to the English, 597–1066*;[138] this entry is currently being revised. A project closely related to *SASLC*, *Fontes Anglo-Saxonici*, has gathered much valuable information about the apocrypha in its sourcing of particular Anglo-Saxon texts. The database can be found at fontes.english.ox.ac.uk; individual works are listed in the general category 'source author' under either BS (for Biblia Sacra; IV Ezra, for example, is included here) or among the items grouped under ANON.

There have been a number of other publications in the field that deserve mention. Although the apocrypha is not the primary focus of either Charles D. Wright's *The Irish Tradition in Old English Literature*[139] or Bernhard Bischoff and Michael Lapidge's *Biblical Commentaries from the Canterbury School*,[140] these two studies raise, from different perspectives, the question of the early transmission of this material to England. As Martin McNamara's *The Apocrypha in the Irish Church* amply demonstrates, the Irish both preserved this material and adapted it freely in Latin and the vernacular.[141] Following the lead of Thomas D. Hill and James E. Cross,[142] Wright argues that the Irish tradition influences some Anglo-Saxon works, notably Vercelli Homily IX, but also poems such as *Christ III*. Some

---

[136] For Ælfric's use of 'passions' of the apostles, see the discussion of the Cotton-Corpus Legendary below. Also to be noted is his comment in his 'On the Old and New Testament' that Sapientia and Ecclesiasticus are not by Solomon, which explains his limited endorsement of them, 'swiðe micele bec, 7 man hig ræt on circan to micclum wisdome swiðe gewunelice'; Crawford, p. 40; 'very large books, and read in church, of long custom, for much good instruction'. See also his comments on Tobias and Macabees, pp. 48–9.

[137] Ed. Frederick M. Biggs, Thomas D. Hill and Paul E. Szarmach (Binghamton, 1990), pp. 22–70.

[138] (Cambridge, MA, 1967), pp. 66–74.

[139] CSASE 6 (Cambridge, 1993). See also Wright's 'The Irish Tradition', in *A Companion to Anglo-Saxon Literature*, ed. Phillip Pulsiano and Elaine Treharne (Oxford, 2001), pp. 345–74.

[140] CSASE 10 (Cambridge, 1994).

[141] See, too, McNamara's *Apocrypha Hiberniae, I: Euangelia infantia*, CCSA 13 and 14.

[142] Essays by each appear in *Sources of Anglo-Saxon Culture*, ed. Paul E. Szarmach (Kalamazoo, MI, 1986); Hill's contribution is 'Literary History and Old English Poetry: The Case of *Christ I, II*, and *III*' (pp. 3–22) and Cross's, 'Towards the Identification of Old English Literary Ideas – Old Workings and New Seams' (pp. 77–101).

apocrypha, such as the Apocalypse of Paul, play a particularly large role in
his argument, but also significant is his discussion of apocryphal motifs:

> the historical data available in Scripture often failed to satisfy Irish
> *curiositas* and was freely supplemented by apocryphal sources for
> minor literal details, particularly for numbers and names – the age
> of Adam, the number of the Holy Innocents or the names of the
> seven archangels and of the wives of Noah and his sons – and also
> for narratives of episodes in salvation history passed over in
> Scripture, such as the creation and fall of the angels and the
> childhood of Jesus.[143]

The Irish, then, pass on to the English both entire apocryphal texts and
specific information drawn from them. Their biblical commentaries, identified by Bernhard Bischoff,[144] and now appearing in the *Corpus Christianorum Continuatio Mediaevalis*,[145] become important witnesses in tracing
the transmission of this material.

Bischoff and Lapidge's study raises the possibility that apocrypha also
reached England through the appointment of Theodore to the see of
Canterbury in 668, but positive evidence is slight. While it seems likely
that this native of Tarsus, who studied extensively in several important
centres in the East before entering a monastery in Rome, must have known
a range of apocryphal works, there is little indication that he brought any
with him when, at the age of sixty-six, he set out for England with Hadrian,
who would become abbot of the monastery of SS Peter and Paul (later St
Augustine's) in Canterbury, and Benedict Biscop, first abbot of Monkwearmouth-Jarrow.[146] Bede speaks of the 'wholesome learning' that Theodore
and Hadrian taught in their new school: 'ita ut etiam metricae artis
astronomiae et arithmeticae ecclesiasticae disciplinam inter sacrorum
apicum uolumina suis auditoribus contraderent'.[147] The commentaries
themselves provide evidence of the knowledge of two apocryphal works,
the Book of Jubilees (*CAVT* 132) and the Assumption of Moses (*CAVT*
134), on the part of their author.[148] The Commentator, as Lapidge calls him,
cites Jubilees twice by name, first for the claim that Adam spent seven years

---

[143] *Irish Tradition*, p. 22; I have not included his notes.

[144] 'Turning-Points in the History of Latin Exegesis in the Early Irish Church: A.D. 650–800', in *Biblical Studies: The Medieval Irish Contribution*, ed. M. McNamara (Dublin, 1976), pp. 74–160 (trans. of 'Wendepunkte in der Geschichte der lateinischen Exegese im Frühmittelalter', in *Mittelalterliche Studien: Ausgewählte Aufsätze zur Schriftkunde und Literaturgeschichte*, 3 vols. [Stuttgart, 1966–81], I.205–73).

[145] See G. MacGinty, *Pauca problesmata de enigmatibus ex tomis canonicis. Praefatio – De Pentatucho Moysi*, CCCM 173.

[146] See Michael Lapidge, 'Benedict Biscop', in *Blackwell Encyclopaedia*, ed. Lapidge *et al.*, p. 60.

[147] *Bede's Ecclesiastical History of the English People*, ed. Bertram Colgrave and R. A. B. Mynors (Oxford, 1969), pp. 332–4; they translate: 'they gave their hearers instruction not only in the books of holy Scripture but also in the art of metre, astronomy, and ecclesiastical computation', pp. 333–5.

[148] Lapidge also considers the possibility that a translation of an acrostic poem from the Sibylline Oracles (see *CAVT* 274) known to Aldhelm was made at this time, but he doubts it is evidence for the knowledge of the complete Greek text. In his note on the commentary on Genesis II.8, he refers to the Acts of Andrew and Matthew (*CANT* 236) as one of a number of possible sources for the idea that paradise is located in the heavens.

less forty days in Paradise, and later in connection with Lamech's slaying of Cain.[149] Lapidge notes that, while the first detail does appear in the Ethiopic version of the apocryphon, the second has not been found; his suggestion, that 'possibly the Commentator had misremembered the text',[150] may indicate that he did not have it at hand to check. The references to the Assumption of Moses are not by name, and are complicated both by the loss of the end of the work and by an apparent borrowing from this lost conclusion in the canonical letter of Jude;[151] Jude 9 reads,

> cum Michahel archangelus cum diabolo disputans altercaretur de Mosi corpore
> non est ausus iudicium inferre blasphemiae
> sed dixit imperet tibi Dominus.[152]

In discussing the transfiguration, the Commentator remarks,

> sunt qui dicunt in hoc esse impletum quod ab angelo ad diabolum dicitur cum altercaretur de corpore Mosysi, 'Imperet tibi Deus, diabole'.[153]

Lapidge notes that 'the reference to the struggle of the archangel Michael with the devil over the body of Moses, and the quotation, is from Jude I.9' and that 'the "sunt qui dicunt" is perhaps a reference to the apocryphal "Assumption of Moses"'.[154] A remark by Bede on the verse in Jude in his commentary on the Catholic Epistles suggests that he is aware that it derives from an apocryphon, but from one that he does not have: 'de quibus scripturis Iudas hoc testimonium assumpserit non facile patet'.[155] This example, then, may suggest that while Theodore and Hadrian may have occasionally used apocrypha in their teaching, they apparently did not disseminate the actual texts in England.

In later Anglo-Saxon England, it is New Testament apocrypha – passions of the saints, texts related to Christ and Mary and apocalypses – that flourish. These works are often adapted to liturgical use and survive in collections referred to as legendaries and homiliaries; while it is possible in theory to distinguish between these as 'providing saints' legends for their specific days' and 'containing patristic sermons for certain occasions',[156] the

---

[149] *Biblical Commentaries*, pp. 310–11 and 445; and pp. 314–15 and 446.

[150] *Biblical Commentaries*, p. 200; here, he also suggests that Jubilees 'may have been the source of the Commentator's report that Enoch was transported to Paradise located on a mountain . . .as well as of the report that Abel was stoned by Cain'.

[151] Johannes Tromp, *The Assumption of Moses: A Critical Edition with Commentary*, SVTP 10 (Leiden, 1993), pp. 270–81.

[152] 'When Michael the archangel, disputing with the devil, contended about the body of Moses, he durst not bring against him the judgement of railing speech, but said: The Lord command thee.'

[153] *Biblical Commentaries*, p. 404; 'There are those who say that in this event was fulfilled that which was said by the angel to the devil when he was contending about the body of Moses: "the Lord command thee, o devil"', trans. Lapidge, p. 405. See also pp. 410–11.

[154] *Biblical Commentaries*, p. 517.

[155] *CCSL* 121.337; 'from what scriptures Jude has taken this testimony is not easily evident'.

[156] See Richard W. Pfaff, 'Liturgical Books', in *Blackwell Encyclopaedia*, ed. Lapidge *et al.*, p. 291; and Mary Clayton, 'Homiliaries and Preaching in Anglo-Saxon England', *Peritia* 4 (1985), 207–42; repr. in *Old English Prose*, ed. Paul E. Szarmach, Basic Readings in Anglo-Saxon England 5 (New York, 2000), pp. 151–98.

collections themselves, and thus the scholarship on them, are often more mixed. Two Latin collections have attracted much attention, the Pembroke Homiliary and the Cotton-Corpus Legendary. James E. Cross,[157] in particular, has called attention to Cambridge, Pembroke College 25, a late eleventh-century manuscript from Bury St Edmunds,[158] but representing a Carolingian collection known as the Homiliary of St Père de Chartres.[159] Cross's analysis indicates that this collection provides sources for some of the Old English homilies in the Vercelli Book, recently edited by Donald G. Scragg.[160] The significance of the Cotton-Corpus legendary (so named because it survives in its oldest form in BL, Cotton Nero E.i, parts i and ii, and Cambridge, Corpus Christi College 9)[161] for Ælfric's work was first demonstrated by Patrick Zettel in a 1979 Oxford D.Phil. thesis, that has, unfortunately, not been published. Malcolm Godden, however, draws on Zettel's work in his commentary on *Ælfric's Catholic Homilies*, as does Rohini Jayatilika in her entries on Ælfric's *Lives of Saints* in the database of *Fontes Anglo-Saxonici*. In contrast to his opposition to the apocrypha discussed earlier, Ælfric accepts this material – with the interesting exception of the legend of Thomas[162] – without question. Indeed Godden groups these works in his discussion of sources under the general category 'hagiography',[163] indicating that for Ælfric they would not have appeared to be apocrypha.[164]

A special case in this larger picture of the circulation of New Testament apocrypha in late Anglo-Saxon England is provided by James E. Cross's discovery of the significance of a Saint-Bertin manuscript, now Saint-Omer, Bibliothèque municipale 202, for some of the Old English translations of the *Gospel of Nicodemus* (*CANT* 62) and the *Vindicta salvatoris* (*CANT* 70).[165] The *Gospel of Nicodemus*, which provides information about Christ's death, descent into hell and resurrection, was previously known to have circulated in England in BL, Royal 5.E.XIII, a mid- to late ninth-century manuscript probably from Brittany, but in England by the

[157] *Cambridge Pembroke College Ms. 25: A Carolingian Sermonary used by Anglo-Saxon Preachers*, King's College London Medieval Studies 1 (London, 1987).

[158] Gneuss, *Handlist*, no. 131.

[159] Henri Barré, *Les Homéliaires Carolingiens de l'école d'Auxerre*, Studi e Testi 225 (Vatican, 1962), pp. 17–25.

[160] *The Vercelli Homilies and Related Texts*, EETS os 300 (Oxford, 1992).

[161] See P. Jackson and M. Lapidge, 'The Contents of the Cotton-Corpus Legendary', in *Holy Men and Holy Women: Old English Prose Saints' Lives and their Contexts*, ed. Paul E. Szarmach (Albany, NY, 1996), pp. 131–46.

[162] See M. R. Godden, 'Ælfric's Saints' Lives and the Problem of Miracles', *Leeds Studies in English* ns 16 (1985), 83–100, repr. in *Old English Prose*, ed. Szarmach, pp. 287–309.

[163] *Ælfric's . . .Introduction*, pp. lxi–lxii.

[164] For an opposing view, see Aideen O'Leary, 'An Orthodox Old English Homiliary? Ælfric's Views on the Apocryphal Acts of the Apostles', *NM* 100 (1999), 15–26.

[165] *Two Old English Apocrypha and their Manuscript Source: The Gospel of Nichodemus and the Avenging of the Saviour*, ed. J. E. Cross, with contributions by Denis Brearley, Julia Crick, Thomas N. Hall, and Andy Orchard, CSASE 19 (Cambridge, 1996). On Nicodemus, see also Zbigniew Izydorczyk, *Manuscripts of the 'Evangelium Nicodemi': A Census*, Subsidia Mediaevalia 21 (Toronto, 1993), and *The Medieval Gospel of Nicodemus: Texts, Intertexts, and Contexts in Western Europe*, ed. Izydorczyk, MRTS 158 (Tempe, AZ, 1997).

tenth century.[166] Cross and Julia Crick argue that the Saint-Omer manuscript is indeed the 'full spelboc wintres and sumeres' ('complete homiliary for winter and summer') recorded in Bishop Leofric's list of donations bequeathed at his death in 1072 to Exeter cathedral.[167] It includes both *Nicodemus* and the *Vindicta*, which relates the aftermath of the passion, Titus's avenging of Christ's death and his encounter with Veronica, and the trial of Pilate. Its texts of *Nicodemus* and the *Vindicta* are the sources for the Old English translations that survive in Cambridge, University Library Ii.2.11, itself recorded in the Exeter donation list;[168] the Old English translation of the *Vindicta* also appears in Cambridge, Corpus Christi College 196, another Exeter manuscript from around this time.[169] It seems likely, then, that these texts were not only known at Exeter during Leofric's time, but actively used. This information is all the more significant because of Leofric's reputation.[170] Educated in Lotharingia, he served in the royal court of Edward the Confessor before being appointed to the bishoprics of Devon and Cornwall, which then consolidated with a single seat at Exeter. He reformed the community at Exeter, seeing to the furnishings of the church and providing books for its library. The evidence of the *Gospel of Nicodemus* and the *Vindicta salvatoris* may not reveal a broader attitude toward the apocrypha, but does show that these specific texts were acceptable to at least one powerful clergyman in late Anglo-Saxon England.

It is perhaps appropriate to conclude with Mary Clayton's two studies of apocryphal texts and traditions concerning Mary. *The Cult of the Virgin Mary in Anglo-Saxon England* introduces the topic, surveying the range of literary, liturgical and art historical evidence. *The Apocryphal Gospels of Mary in Anglo-Saxon England*,[171] then, focuses on the non-canonical material, offering editions of the Old English texts as well as the important Latin sources. While some of the traditions that Clayton discusses are old – the *Protoevangelium of James* (*CANT* 50), for example, was compiled around 180–200 – others, such as *De nativitate Mariae* (*CANT* 52), date to the late tenth or early eleventh century. Moreover, as already noted in this essay, the reception of this material differs at different points in Anglo-Saxon England. While Mary presents a particularly complicated problem, our understanding of the circulation of each apocryphon in Anglo-Saxon England can only be enhanced by our growing knowledge of histories of individual manuscripts and texts as well as by our awareness of the field as a whole. While of interest to scholars of the apocrypha, this information also allows Anglo-Saxonists to map with greater precision the shifts in the religious and literary cultures of the period.

---

[166] See Thomas N. Hall, 'The *Euangelium Nichodemi* and *Vindicta saluatoris* in Anglo-Saxon England', in *Two Old English Apocrypha*, ed. Cross, pp. 36–81, at pp. 48–9.

[167] 'The Manuscript: Saint-Omer, Bibliothèque Municipale, 202', in *Two Old English Apocrypha*, ed. Cross, pp. 10–35, at pp. 31–5.

[168] Cross edits the text in *Two Old English Apocrypha*, pp. 139–247; see also p. 134 for the two other Old English translations of this work.

[169] Gneuss, *Handlist*, no. 62. See *Two Old English Apocrypha*, p. 8 and p. 135 for a third version.

[170] See Michael Lapidge, 'Leofric', in *Blackwell Encyclopaedia*, ed. Lapidge *et al.*, p. 282.

[171] CSASE 26 (Cambridge, 1998).

# 2

# *The Apocalypse of Thomas*: Some New Latin Texts and their Significance for the Old English Versions

CHARLES D. WRIGHT

*Table 1. Latin versions and manuscripts of* The Apocalypse of Thomas

*'Non-interpolated' version*

**B** Naples, Biblioteca Nazionale Vittorio Emanuele III, lat. 2 (Vindobon. 16), fol. 60, lower script (s. v[2]; *CLA* III.396) [fragment].

**N** Munich, Bayerische Staatsbibliothek Clm 4563 (s. xi[med.]), fol. 40.

*'Interpolated' version*

**M** Munich, Clm 4585 (s. ix[1]), 65v–67v.

**P** Vatican City, Biblioteca Apostolica, Pal. lat. 220 (s. ix[1]), 48v–53v.

**V** Verona, Biblioteca Capitolare I (1) (s. vi–vii), 403v, 404v (addition of s. vii; *CLA* IV.472) [fragment].

**W** Würzburg, Universitätsbibliothek M.p.th.f. 28 (s. viii[4/4]; *CLA* IX.1408), 57r–58v.

*Abbreviated versions*

**A** Munich, Clm 8439 (s. xv), fol. 191.

**T** Toronto, Collection of 190 pieces of vellum (current shelfmark 'MS 45'), fragment 24–25 (s. ix[2]).

**E** Einsiedeln, Stiftsbibliothek 319 (s. x[med.]), pp. 155–156.

**O** Vienna, Österreichische Nationalbibliothek 1878 [part B] (s. xii), 161v–162r.

**R** Vatican, Reg. lat. 49 (s. x[ex.]), 52v.

**H** Oxford, Bodleian Library, Hatton 26, part II (s. xiii[in.]), 88r.

THE *Apocalypse of Thomas* purports to be a letter of Christ to his famously doubting apostle concerning the travails that will usher in the last times and the cosmological signs that will occur on each of the seven days preceding the Day of Judgement. A lengthy historical-prophetic introduction found in some manuscripts, referring enigmatically to events of the first half of the fifth century, is generally regarded as an interpolation. The primitive apocalypse, then, would have consisted of a brief address by Christ to Thomas, warning generally of famine, wars, and pestilence as the end draws near, followed by the list of the signs of the final seven days. In addition to these 'interpolated' and 'non-interpolated' versions, there are also abbreviated versions that have only the list of signs. The existence of three distinct versions, together with a remarkable degree of variation even within the manuscripts of each version, makes the Latin textual tradition of *Thomas* an extremely complex one. It has never been adequately sorted out, and there has never been a complete critical edition, due in part to the circumstances of the twentieth-century rediscovery of the work. This was largely accomplished in a five-year span from 1907 to 1911, when a number of fragments and complete copies were independently discovered and edited by several scholars.

The first text discovered was the defective interpolated version **M**, published in 1907 by F. Wilhelm, who failed to recognize it as the lost early-Christian apocryphon.[1] Its significance was first noted in a 1908 review of Wilhelm's *Deutsche Legenden und Legendare* by Ernst von Dobschütz.[2] In that same year, J. Bick edited the fifth-century palimpsested fragments then in Vienna, now in Naples (**B**). Unaware of the recent discovery and identification of **M**, Bick believed that all these fragments belonged to another apocryphon, the *Epistola Apostolorum*;[3] but before the year was out, E. Hauler had demonstrated that one of the two folios was from *Thomas*.[4] In 1910, two more newly discovered texts were published: a seventh-century fragment in Verona, **V**, printed by M. R. James;[5] and a late abbreviated version, **A**, published by Walther Suchier in his edition of a medieval question-and-answer dialogue.[6] In the meantime, Dobschütz had discovered the complete interpolated text in **P**, and had begun work on a critical edition of *Thomas* for the series Texte und Untersuchungen zur Geschichte der altchristlichen Literatur. What is still the most important

---

[1] Ed. F. Wilhelm, *Deutsche Legenden und Legendare* (Leipzig, 1907), pp. 40*–42*. The text breaks off abruptly in the middle of the description of the sixth day. On the manuscript see Günter Glauche, *Katalog der lateinischen Handschriften der Bayerischen Staatsbibliothek München: Die Pergamenthandschriften aus Benediktbeuern: Clm 4501–4663* (Wiesbaden, 1994), pp. 140–2. In 1908 C. Frick, 'Die Thomasapokalypse', *Zeitschrift für die neutestamentliche Wissenschaft* 9 (1908), 172–3, drew attention to a reference to an apocryphal revelation of Christ to Thomas in a manuscript of Jerome's *Chronicon*, but he was not aware of the text published by Wilhelm. For this manuscript, Berlin, Staatsbibliothek Preußischer Kulturbesitz, Phillipps 1829 (Verona, s. ix$^{1/3}$), see now Bernhard Bischoff, *Katalog der festländischen Handschriften des neunten Jahrhunderts, I: Aachen–Lambach* (Wiesbaden, 1998), p. 91 (no. 435), and below, pp. 33 n. 9 and 47.

[2] *Theologische Literaturzeitung* 33 (1908), cols. 437–9. Dobschütz was already working on an edition of the *Decretum Gelasianum*, which mentions a *Reuelatio sancti Thomae* in its list of proscribed apocryphal books. See Dobschütz, *Das Decretum Gelasianum*, Texte und Untersuchungen zur Geschichte der altchristlichen Literatur 38/4 (Leipzig, 1912), p. 53.

[3] Bick, 'Wiener Palimpseste, I', *Sitzungsberichte der Wiener Akademie der Wissenschaften*, phil.-hist. Kl. 159, Abh. 7 (1908), pp. 90–100, at pp. 97–8. For a facsimile of 60r, see R. Beer, *Monumenta palaeographica Vindobonensia*, 2 vols. (Leipzig, 1910–13), II, pl. 33.

[4] Edmund Hauler, 'Zu den neuen lateinischen Bruchstücken der Thomasapokalypse und eines apostolischen Sendschreibens im Codex Vind. Nr. 16', *Wiener Studien* 30 (1908), 308–40. Hauler credits the identification to a private letter from Dobschütz. He provided a diplomatic edition of **B** on the basis of Bick's transcript, and a reconstructed text using Dobschütz's transcripts of **P** and **M**.

[5] M. R. James, 'Notes on Apocrypha, I: Revelatio Thomae', *Journal of Theological Studies* 11 (1910), 288–90; on this text see also below, n. 11.

[6] Suchier, *L'Enfant Sage (Das Gespräch des Kaisers Hadrian mit dem klugen Kinde Epitus)*, Gesellschaft für romanische Literatur 24 (Dresden, 1910), p. 272. The manuscript is a theological miscellany containing works attributed to Albertus Magnus, Bonaventure and Chrysostom, Alain de Lille's *Anticlaudianus*, pseudo-Cyprian *De duodecim abusiuis*, a tract on the three theological virtues, the *Adrianus et Epictitus* dialogue edited by Suchier, two homilies on the Virgin Mary, and an exposition of the Mass. See *Catalogus codicum latinorum Bibliothecae Regiae Monacensis*, 4 vols. in 7 parts, ed. C. Halm *et al.* (Munich, 1868–81), IV/1, 28.

publication to date took place in the following year, when P. Bihlmeyer published **N**, the only complete non-interpolated text.[7] Having collated **N** with the other manuscripts (using a transcript of **P** supplied to him by Dobschütz), Bihlmeyer realized that **N** and the fragmentary **B** represented a distinct version lacking the prophetic-historical introduction found in the other versions (aside from the abbreviated **A**, which Bihlmeyer did not know).[8]

Despite the flurry of discovery and editorial activity, no complete critical edition of the Latin versions was ever published. Dobschütz died in 1934 without having completed his edition, though part of it went as far as proof sheets that Max Förster was able to consult in his important 1955 study of the Old English versions.[9] The text of **P** has still never been fully collated or separately published,[10] and the published editions are not all reliable. Wilhelm was often at a loss to construe and punctuate the text he edited without benefit of any additional manuscripts; Hauler used Dobschütz's collation of the ninth-century interpolated manuscript **P** to fill in the blanks of the fifth-century non-interpolated **B**; and James was unaware of Wilhelm's text and of Hauler's reconstruction of **B** when he printed **V** from an incomplete and faulty transcript sent to him by Antonio Spagnolo, the librarian of the Biblioteca Capitolare in Verona.[11] One result of this dispersed and uncoordinated editorial activity is that some of the most important comparative critical analysis of the Latin texts has been submerged in composite translations published since 1911. M. R. James published English translations of both interpolated and non-interpolated versions in 1924.[12] These translations were the result of a careful collation

[7] P. Bihlmeyer, 'Un texte non interpolé de l'Apocalypse de Thomas', *Revue Bénédictine* 28 (1911), 270–82. On the manuscript see Glauche, *Katalog*, pp. 97–101.

[8] Marcel Dando, however, has suggested that the 'interpolation' was part of the original apocalypse, and would describe the two versions as 'long' and 'short' rather than 'interpolated' and 'non-interpolated': 'L'Apocalypse de Thomas', *Cahiers d'Études Cathares* 28 (1977), 3–58, at 5 and 42.

[9] Max Förster, 'A New Version of the Apocalypse of Thomas in Old English', *Anglia* 73 (1955), 6–36. I wish to thank Prof. Christoph Markschies, director of the project 'Neutestamentliche Apokryphen', for providing me with photocopies from Dobschütz's *Nachlass* of the proofs for 'Cap. II. Der Text' (paginated 1–17), and consisting of diplomatic transcripts of **BVMP** with some textual notes, and Prof. Jean-Daniel Kaestli, director of the 'Association pour l'étude de la littérature apocryphe chrétienne', for making available to me photocopies of Dobschütz's handwritten drafts of other chapters.

[10] Bihlmeyer had access to Dobschütz's collations, but naturally recorded only the variants for the non-interpolated text he edited. Förster quoted liberally from Dobschütz's unpublished edition, but only those passages or variants deemed relevant to the Old English versions. Hauler printed part of the 'interpolation' from Dobschütz's edition of **P** and **M**.

[11] See James's subsequent note, 'The *Revelatio Thomae* Again', *Journal of Theological Studies* 11 (1910), 569. The most serious error involves a phantom word (*nix*). According to Lowe, the modern interlinear transcript in the manuscript is in the hand of Scipione Maffei, but the word *nix* may be in a different hand. An accurate transcript of fol. 403v was given by E. Carusi and W. M. Lindsay in *Monumenti paleografici Veronesi*, fasc. II (Rome, 1934), p. 11 (with a facsimile of the entire page as plate 24; part of 403v is also reproduced in *CLA*). The text continues on 404v, but unfortunately only parts of a few words are legible (I have consulted a photograph supplied by the Biblioteca Capitolare). James was not able to consult an edition by G. G. Dionisi in his *Apologetiche Riflessioni* (Verona, 1755), p. 30, which also reads *nix*.

[12] James, *The Apocryphal New Testament* (Oxford, 1924; repr. with revisions in 1953), pp. 555–62. J. K. Elliott published a new edition of James's collection in 1993, but the translation of *Thomas*

and critical analysis of the texts available at that time, and are important scholarship in their own right; but due to the nature of the publication, James did not 'show his work'. Subsequent scholarly translations have had to rely on these same editions, without benefit of the abortive complete edition of Dobschütz, the only scholar who had access to all the manuscripts.

It is unfortunate that Dobschütz's edition of *Thomas* was never completed and published, but even if it had been, more recent discoveries would still necessitate a new critical edition. Another complete interpolated text (older than **P**) and two more abbreviated texts have been identified, but all remain unpublished, and have generally been overlooked since they were first noted.[13] These texts are published here for the first time, in parallel-column format together with three additional abbreviated texts whose existence has not, to my knowledge, previously been noted.[14] I will first discuss their manuscript contexts and briefly characterize their affiliations insofar as these can be determined. I will then focus on selected readings that have some bearing on the Old English translations. Although none of these new texts is an immediate source for any of the Old English translations of *Thomas* – some of which show significant divergence from all known Latin texts – they do provide parallels for a number of readings that previously had no Latin counterpart. In addition, some occur in manuscripts with concrete evidence of Insular associations, and so provide further confirmation of the special popularity of this work among the Irish and the Anglo-Saxons. Finally, I will offer some preliminary suggestions regarding the significance of *Thomas* for those who copied it in particular times – especially for those who copied it towards the end of what was reckoned as the sixth millennium, when apocalyptic countdowns such as that provided by *Thomas* were never more timely.

I begin with the oldest and fullest of the new texts, preserved in **W**, the so-called 'Homiliary of Burghard', dating from the last quarter of the eighth century.[15] In his 1984 catalogue of the Latin manuscripts formerly in the Würzburg Cathedral Library, Hans Thurn credited Bernhard Bischoff with the discovery that one of the anonymous items in the manuscript (57r–58v) has verbatim parallels with *Thomas*.[16] In fact, this tract on Antichrist and

---

(pp. 645–51) essentially follows that of James. An independent translation of the non-interpolated version by A. de Santos Otero is also valuable, but like James he provides only brief footnotes drawing attention to some of the most significant variant readings; see Edgar Hennecke and Wilhelm Schneemelcher, *New Testament Apocrypha*, 5th ed., trans. R. McL. Wilson, 2 vols. (Cambridge, 1991–93), II, 798–803. For translations into German and Italian, see *CANT*, p. 210.

[13] None of these versions is registered by Geerard, *CANT*.

[14] I am preparing a critical edition of all surviving versions.

[15] *CLA* IX.1408. On the manuscript see also B. Bischoff and J. Hofmann, *Libri Sancti Kyliani: Die Würzburger Schreibschule und die Dombibliothek im VIII. und IX. Jahrhundert*, Quellen und Forschungen zur Geschichte des Bistums und Hochstifts Würzburg 6 (Würzburg, 1952), pp. 10 and 100, and H. Thurn, *Die Handschriften der Universitätsbibliothek Würzburg*, III/1: *Die Pergamenthandschriften der ehemaligen Dombibliothek* (Wiesbaden, 1984), pp. 19–21. I follow the date given by Thurn (Lowe dates the manuscript s. viii², Bischoff s. viii$^{3/3}$).

[16] Thurn's reference (p. 20) seems not to have been noticed in subsequent scholarship. Bischoff's

the signs of Judgement incorporates a substantially complete interpolated text of *Thomas*. The manuscript contains some forty-six items, mostly sermons now attributed to Caesarius of Arles, though they are not so identified in the manuscript.[17] The copy of *Thomas* is not presented as a sermon in the formal sense, and is one of several items that were probably additions to an earlier homiliary. These include an apocryphal Letter of Titus, disciple of Paul;[18] pseudo-Jerome, *De septem ordinibus ecclesiae* (defective);[19] the spurious Acts of the Council of Caesarea (Recension A);[20] brief chronographical notes headed *Ratio orbis* and *Ratio mundi* (the first written in 604 and the second in 659);[21] and a Passion of St Christopher.[22] Two fragments now in Munich seem to have been copies of the same Caesarian homiliary, but unfortunately it is impossible to say whether they also would have included these supplementary items.[23]

Despite the manuscript's Dombibliothek provenance, there seems to be no concrete evidence to support its traditional association with Burghard, the Anglo-Saxon colleague of Boniface and, from 743, the first bishop of Würzburg.[24] The scriptorium that produced the manuscript has not been

partial handwritten transcript can be consulted in *Handschriftenarchiv Bernhard Bischoff*, ed. Arno Mentzel-Reuters, MGH Hilfsmittel 16 (Munich, 1997), fiche 29, 2.34–35.

[17] On the contents see, in addition to Thurn, G. Morin, 'L'Homéliaire de Burchard de Würzburg. Contribution à la critique des sermons de saint Césaire d'Arles', *Revue Bénédictine* 13 (1896), 97–111 and 193–214; Rainer Kurz, *Die handschriftliche Überlieferung der Werke des heiligen Augustinus*, V/2 (Vienna, 1979), p. 539.

[18] D. De Bruyne, '*Epistula Titi, discipuli Pauli, De Dispositione sanctimonii*', *Revue Bénédictine* 37 (1925), 47–72; Giulia Sfameni Gasparro, 'L'Epistula Titi discipuli Pauli de dispositione sanctimonii e la tradizione dell'enkrateia', in *Aufstieg und Niedergang der römischen Welt*, II: *Principat*, XXV/6, ed. Wolfgang Haase (Berlin, 1988), pp. 4551–664.

[19] PL 30, 148–57; see Roger Reynolds, 'The Pseudo-Hieronymian *De septem ordinibus ecclesiae*: Notes on its Origins, Abridgments and Use in Early Medieval Canonical Collections', *Revue Bénédictine* 80 (1970), 241–52, repr. with original pagination in his *Clerical Orders in the Early Middle Ages* (Aldershot, 1999), essay I; Bernard Lambert, *Bibliotheca Hieronymiana Manuscripta*, 4 vols. in 7 parts, Instrumenta Patristica 4 (Steenbrugge, 1969–72), IIIA, no. 312.

[20] Michael Lapidge and Richard Sharpe, *Bibliography of Celtic-Latin Literature 400–1200* (Dublin, 1985), no. 317. The manuscript is identified by C. W. Jones, *Bedae Pseudepigrapha: Scientific Writings Falsely Attributed to Bede* (Ithaca, 1939), p. 45.

[21] Bruno Krusch, 'Chronologisches aus Handschriften', *Neues Archiv der Gesellschaft für ältere deutsche Geschichtskunde* 10 (1885), 83–94, at 89–91, and MGH Scriptores rerum Merovingicarum, VII, 489–90 and 493–4.

[22] *BHL* no. 1766.

[23] The first is an eighth-century uncial manuscript from France, now Munich, Clm 14123 + 29386/1 (olim 29047; *CLA* IX.1330) for which see G. Morin, *Caesarii Arelatensis Sermones*, 2 vols., CCSL 103–4 (Turnhout, 1953), I, xlv; Bernhard Bischoff, *Die südostdeutschen Schreibschulen und Bibliotheken in der Karolingerzeit*, I: *Die bayrischen Diözesen*, 2nd ed. (Wiesbaden, 1960), p. 257. This manuscript eventually made its way to Regensburg; see Rosamond McKitterick, 'The Diffusion of Insular Culture in Neustria between 650 and 850', in *La Neustrie: Les pays au nord de la Loire de 650 à 850*, ed. Hartmut Atsma (Sigmaringen, 1989), pp. 395–432, at pp. 414–15; repr. with original pagination in McKitterick, *Books, Scribes and Learning in the Frankish Kingdoms, 6th–9th Centuries* (Aldershot, 1994), essay III. Another copy (Munich, Clm 29386/2, olim 29055) was made there in the early ninth century for Bishop Baturich (cf. Bischoff, *Schreibschulen*, p. 203, with Bischoff and Hofmann, *Libri Sancti Kyliani*, p. 10 and n. 28).

[24] Lowe rejected this association on palaeographical grounds, and Hans Thurn, in a recent survey of Würzburg manuscripts possibly or probably owned by Burghard, does not even mention the homiliary; see 'Irische und angelsächsische Handschriften auf dem Kontinent – am Beispiel der Würzburger Dombibliothek', in *Kilian, Mönch aus Irland aller Franken Patron 689–1989*, ed. Johannes Erichsen and Evamaria Brockhoff (Würzburg, 1989), pp. 313–27, at 322–4. Rosamond

pinpointed, but there are Insular features in the letter-forms and particularly in the ornamentation. E. A. Lowe, taking into account the presence of Old High German glosses whose oldest layer is in the Bavarian dialect,[25] states that it was 'written in a German centre where Anglo-Saxon influence was still alive, presumably in Bavaria'. According to Bischoff, its scripts are similar to the earliest scripts from Regensburg.[26] The two Munich fragments of this Caesarian homiliary are also connected with Regensburg. The earlier one, a Frankish product, has a Regensburg provenance, and the later copy was written there for Bishop Baturich. One case of a Würzburg–Regensburg link in the transmission of *Thomas* would not be particularly noteworthy, perhaps, but this is not the only such case. The interpolated text **M** was also copied by a scribe active at Regensburg during the episcopacy of Baturich (817–47), and was supplemented at Würzburg towards the end of the ninth century with the *Passio Sancti Kiliani*.[27] **M** eventually came to Benediktbeuern, where yet another manuscript of Thomas, the non-interpolated **N**, was written about the middle of the eleventh century.[28] Books have their own destiny, and manuscripts their wanderings and homes, but for whatever reasons, three of the relatively few surviving copies of the *Apocalypse of Thomas* can be located within a narrow triangle defined by Würzburg, Regensburg and Benediktbeuern. One of these (**W**) made its way from a scriptorium in or near the Regensburg diocese to Würzburg, and another one (**M**) wandered from St Emmeram in Regensburg, to the Dombibliothek in Würzburg, and finally to Benediktbeuern.

The earliest locus of dissemination of *Thomas*, however, seems to have been Italy. Our two earliest witnesses – representing both interpolated and non-interpolated recensions – are Italian. **B**, according to Lowe, was 'most likely' written in Italy, and was palimpsested at Bobbio in the eighth

McKitterick, in 'Anglo-Saxon Missionaries in Germany: Reflections on the Manuscript Evidence', *Transactions of the Cambridge Bibliographical Society* 9 (1989), 291–329, at 302–3 (repr. in McKitterick, *Books Scribes and Learning*, essay IV), has suggested that it might have been copied for Burghard by a Frankish or Bavarian scribe; but since Burghard died about 753, the date assigned to the manuscript by Bischoff and Thurn would rule this out as well. In any case, an Anglo-Saxon missionary context in southern Germany does seem likely.

[25] For the glosses see now Irmgard Frank, *Aus Glossenhandschriften des 8. bis 14. Jahrhunderts: Quellen zur Geschichte einer Überlieferungsart*, Quellen zur deutschen Sprach- und Literaturgeschichte 3 (Heidelberg, 1984), pp. 54–64, with a description of the manuscript and references at pp. 141–3.

[26] In his 'Panorama der Handschriftenüberlieferung aus der Zeit Karls des Großen', in Bischoff, *Mittelalterliche Studien: Ausgewählte Aufsätze zur Schriftkunde und Literaturgeschichte*, 3 vols. (Stuttgart, 1966–81), III, 5–38, at 26, Bischoff characterizes the manuscript as one of several from the dioceses of Freising, Regensburg and Passau that cannot be more precisely localized.

[27] Bischoff, *Schreibschulen*, p. 206; Hartmut Hoffmann, *Buchkunst und Königtum im ottonischen und frühsalischen Reich*, 2 vols., MGH Schriften 30/1–2 (Stuttgart, 1986), I, 356. The context of *Thomas* in Part I of the manuscript is hagiographical. The presence of Hugeburg's lives of Wynnebald and Willibald (*BHL* nos. 8996 and 8931) suggests that the compilation may have an ultimate origin in the Eichstätt-Heidenheim region.

[28] Paul Ruf, 'Kisyla von Kochel und ihre angeblichen Schenkungen', *Studien und Mitteilungen zur Geschichte des Benediktinerordens und seiner Zweige* 47 (1929), 461–76, at 465; Hoffmann, *Buchkunst*, I, 431.

century, while **V** was certainly written in north Italy.[29] There may also be a north Italian/south German link in the transmission of the Würzburg text on Antichrist, which conflates material from *Thomas* with several passages drawn from Lactantius's *Epitome diuinarum institutionum*, c. 66. The *Epitome* is itself a very rare work. There is only one complete manuscript, which dates from the end of the sixth or beginning of the seventh century, and there are only two further copies, both defective, prior to the fifteenth century – fewer even than *The Apocalypse of Thomas*.[30] Jerome already referred to it as 'the book without a head' (*De viris illustribus*, c. 80), and R. W. Hunt has stated flatly that 'The Epitome did not circulate in the Middle Ages . . .'.[31] There cannot have been many places where both these works were available. Bobbio is one candidate. Not only was the Naples fragment of *Thomas* palimpsested there but, according to Lowe, the oldest complete manuscript of the *Epitome* (Turin, Biblioteca Nazionale I. B.II.27; *CLA* IV.438) was also 'connected with Bobbio from the earliest times'. The brief extracts from Lactantius in the Würzburg text, however, agree more closely with a fifth-century north Italian manuscript now in Bologna (Biblioteca Universitaria 701; *CLA* III.280); according to Hunt, this manuscript may be from Nonantola, which had very close contacts with Bobbio. Again, since **B** is a non-interpolated text, there is no question of a connection with the interpolated text of **W**. Still, a north Italian centre such as Bobbio or Nonantola would be among the most likely to have held copies of both these works.[32] And since north Italian influences are evident in some of the earliest products of the scriptorium of St Emmeram in Regensburg,[33] the Würzburg text might well have been compiled in north Italy and transmitted across the Alps to a south-east German centre in or near Regensburg.

Although this conflation of Lactantius's *Epitome* and the *Apocalypse of Thomas* seems to have survived in complete form only in **W**, the opening of **W**, with the same incipit and including some of the material from *Thomas*, also survives in a pseudo-Augustinian tract *De Antichristo* found in six much later manuscripts:[34] Cologne, Stadtarchiv W f° 318 (s. xiv⁴/⁴), 257v–

---

[29] Cf. also the reference to an apocryphal book of Thomas in the Verona manuscript, Berlin Phillipps 1829 (n. 1 above). R. W. Burgess informs me, however, that the manuscript may have been written at Trier.

[30] *L. Caeli Firmiani Lactanti Epitome divinarum institutionum*, ed. E. Heck and A. Wlosok, Bibliotheca Teubneriana (Stuttgart, 1994), pp. 110–13; on the manuscripts, see pp. xxv–xxxiv.

[31] R. W. Hunt, 'The Medieval Home of the Bologna Manuscript of Lactantius', *Medievalia et Humanistica* 14 (1962), 3–6, at 3.

[32] Parallels with *Thomas* occur in a text found in a Novara manuscript (the *Apocrypha Priscillianistica*) and in the homilies *In nomine Dei summi* transmitted in manuscripts from the Lake Constance and Middle or Upper Rhine regions (see p. 40 and n. 77 below).

[33] Bischoff, *Schreibschulen*, pp. 173 and 185–6, and his 'Italienische Handschriften des neunten bis elften Jahrhunderts in frühmittelalterlichen Bibliotheken ausserhalb Italiens', in *Il Libro e il Testo: Atti del Convegno Internazionale, Urbino, 20–23 settembre 1982*, ed. Cesare Questa and Renato Raffaelli (Urbino, 1984), pp. 171–94, at p. 184.

[34] The Cologne and Karlsruhe manuscripts are listed in *Die handschriftliche Überlieferung*, ed. Kurz, p. 468; the Herzogenburg, Lilienfeld and Vienna manuscripts are listed in *Die handschriftliche Überlieferung*, VI/1, ed. Dorothea Weber (Vienna, 1993), p. 391; the Graz manuscript is registered in the database *In Principio: Incipitaire des textes latins*, Release 7 (Turnhout, 1999).

258v (**W**c);[35] Graz, Universitätsbibliothek 1133 (s. xiv), 68rb–69rb (**W**g);[36] Herzogenburg, Stiftsbibliothek 30 (s. xv), 296v–298v (**W**h);[37] Karlsruhe, Badische Landesbibliothek K. 405 (s. xiii), 57v–59r (**W**k);[38] Lilienfeld, Stiftsbibliothek 144 (s. xiii), 63rv (**W**l); and Vienna, Österreichische Nationalbibliothek 812 (s. xiii), 78rb-79rb (**W**v).[39] However, to judge from the three manuscripts I have thus far been able to consult (**W**cgv), this sermon subsequently focuses on the Antichrist, using material from other sources, and retains nothing from *Thomas* regarding the signs of the seven days.

W includes several passages paralleled in **M** that are not in **P**, the other main witness to the interpolated recension. Where all three texts overlap, **M** appears to occupy an intermediate position between **P** and **W**.[40] There is one long passage found in **P** and in abbreviated form in **W** that is not in **M**, but **M** is defective and breaks off before this point. The passage is an extended description of Christ's appearance at Judgement and the procession from Paradise of the souls of the saints, who are then clothed in garments of light and carried to heaven on a cloud. In both **P** and **W** these events are related as the conclusion of the signs of the eighth day, the Day of Judgement. Much of this also found in the non-interpolated text **N** (lines 48–71), but there it has been shifted to the end of the signs for the sixth day.

The other new texts of *Thomas* edited below are all abbreviated versions similar to **A**, reduced to the list of signs. With one exception, they preserve none of the introductory matter of the interpolated or non-interpolated recensions, but within the list of signs their textual affiliations are almost exclusively with the manuscripts of the interpolated recension, and primarily with **W** rather than with **M** or **P**.

The existence of an abbreviated text of *Thomas* in **T** was reported by Mary Swan in a recent survey of the Old English versions.[41] Its closest

[35] See Joachim Vennebusch, *Die theologischen Handschriften des Stadtarchivs Köln*, IV: *Die Sammlung Wallraf* (Cologne, 1986), p. 166.

[36] See Anton Kern, *Die Handschriften der Universitätsbibliothek Graz*, II (Vienna, 1956), pp. 238–9.

[37] See Hope Mayo, *Descriptive Inventories of Manuscripts Microfilmed for the Hill Monastic Microfilm Library: Austrian Libraries*, vol. 3 (Collegeville, MN, 1985), p. 103.

[38] See W. Brambach, *Die Handschriften der Hof- und Landesbibliothek in Karlsruhe*, IV: *Die Karlsruher Handschriften* (Karlsruhe, 1896), pp. 63–5.

[39] *Tabulae codicum manu scriptorum praeter graecos et orientales in Bibliotheca Palatina Vindobonensi*, 11 vols. (Vienna, 1864–1912), I, 137. Here the incipit is 'Cum cesserit in mundo finis'.

[40] While the main affiliation of **P** is clearly with the interpolated version, where both interpolated and non-interpolated versions overlap, **P** shares some distinctive readings with the non-interpolated text **N**, and **PN** also transmit some sentences that are not found at all in the other interpolated texts. On the other hand, there are very few cases of substantive agreement of other interpolated texts with **N** *against* **P**. The line of transmission represented by **P**, in other words, has not diverged as far from the common ancestor of both versions as have the other manuscripts of the interpolated version. A full analysis of the textual tradition will be given in my edition in preparation.

[41] Swan, 'The Apocalypse of Thomas in Old English', *Leeds Studies in English* ns 29 (1998), 333–46, at 340. Swan was alerted to this fragment by Claudine Conan, whose proposed date and origin (s. ix, north-east France) accords with that of Bischoff. A typewritten inventory headed 'A preliminary identification of the texts of some fragments in the collection of vellum fragments' by J. F. R. Coughlan, dated March 1976, correctly identifies the text on fol. 25 as an abbreviated version of Thomas, with reference to version **A** published by Suchier. (I am grateful to Edna

affiliation is with the fifteenth-century **A**. **T** begins defectively with part of a sentence paralleled only in **A**, where it is part of a question-and-answer sequence appended to an *Adrianus et Epictitus* dialogue. The surrounding material in **T** is from a similar dialogue text, the Alcuinian *Disputatio puerorum*. The version of *Thomas* transmitted by **AT**, then, has been adapted for an erotematic–catechetical context. **T** differs from **A** and from all the other abbreviated texts, however, in retaining a single sentence from the prologue of the interpolated version, in which Christ tells Thomas to hear what will happen on the Day of Judgement, as well as part of a rather confused description of the angels arriving to liberate the souls of the just.[42] Of all the abbreviated versions, the sub-group **AT** is textually the most closely related to **W**.

The next two abbreviated versions, though also closely related to **AT** and to **W**, show enough distinctive readings of their own to be regarded as another sub-group. The first of these, **E**,[43] is a composite manuscript containing a calendar and computistica, Einsiedeln annals, epitaphs of Einsiedeln abbots and a necrology.[44] To these were added Priscian's *Periegesis* (pp. 64–109); the abbreviated version of *Thomas*, represented as a letter of St Augustine (pp. 155–6); Hrabanus Maurus's *De computo* (pp. 157–274); and further computistica[45] and miscellaneous extracts, including two brief tracts on penitential commutations (pp. 276–80)[46] and

Hajnal of the Fisher Rare Book Library for providing me with a copy of this inventory.) Bischoff's dating and localization ('s. 2/2IX [northern France]') was reported by Roger E. Reynolds, 'Canon Law Collections in Early Ninth-Century Salzburg', in *Proceedings of the Fifth International Congress of Medieval Canon Law*, ed. Stephen Kuttner and Kenneth Pennington, Monumenta Iuris Canonici, Series C: Subsidia 6 (Vatican City, 1980), pp. 15–34, at p. 29, n. 92. Reynolds identifies the fragment as 'fols. 22/23', but as he specifies that it contains part of Alcuin's *Disputatio puerorum*, it is clear that it is the *Thomas* fragment, now fols. 24–25.

[42] The opening sentence, 'Audi Thomas quod oportet f(i)eri in die iudicii', is closely similar to the opening of **P** and **W**. The penultimate sentence, 'Tunc clamabunt . . . qui in me credunt . . .', parallels a passage in **PW** concerning the events of the eighth day; in **N** this passage concludes the non-interpolated text, but **PW** continue with material that **N** has transposed to the sixth day (see p. 34 above).

[43] See Gabriel Meier, *Catalogus codicum manuscriptorum qui in Bibliotheca monasterii Einsidlensis O.S.B. servantur* (Einsiedeln, 1899), p. 289. Bernhard Bischoff, in handwritten notes dated 21 June 1937, listed this text but identified it as 'd. XV signis'; see *Handschriftenarchiv Bernhard Bischoff*, fiche 65, 1.38. K. Halm, *Verzeichnis der älteren Handschriften lateinischer Kirchenväter in den Bibliotheken der Schweiz* (Vienna, 1865), p. 246, incorrectly states that this text also occurs in Einsiedeln 281, p. 37. On the manuscript see also A. Bruckner, *Scriptoria Medii Aevi Helvetica: Denkmäler schweizerischer Schreibkunst des Mittelalters*, 14 vols. (Geneva, 1835–78), I, 183–4; Odo Lang, *1050 Jahre Kloster und Bibliothek Einsiedeln* (Einsiedeln, 1984), p. 12.

[44] See MGH Scriptores, III, 137–49 for the annals; MGH Poetae, V/2, 331 for the epitaphs; and MGH Necrologiae Germaniae, I, 358–61 for the necrology. The computistica include two poems: *ICL*, nos. 12589 and 7612.

[45] These include two decennovenal cycles (pp. 19–62 and 111–56) and several poems: *ICL* nos. 1695, 12589, 12524, 8931, 151. On the ensemble of tables, annals and necrological entries see A. Bruckner, 'Zur Datierung annalistischer Aufzeichnungen aus Einsiedeln', in *Corolla Heremitana*, ed. A. Knoepli and M. Roesle (Olten, 1964), pp. 81–100, at pp. 92–9, with plates of pp. 27 and 99.

[46] For the incipits see Meier, p. 290. This material appears elsewhere as additions to the Penitential of Egbert, chs. 15 and 16, ed. F. W. H. Wasserschleben, *Die Bussordnungen der abendländischen Kirche* (Halle, 1851), pp. 246–7. Cf. August Nürnberger, 'Zur handschriftlichen Ueberlieferung der Werke des hl. Bonifatius', *Neues Archiv* 8 (1883), 299–325, at 317–20; Allen J. Frantzen, 'The

the earliest Western text about chess (pp. 298–99).[47] The core of the manuscript has previously been dated to about the middle (or early in the second half) of the tenth century,[48] but recently Matthias M. Tischler has argued for a date late in the tenth century.[49] A calculation of the *annus mundi* added at the end of Hrabanus's *De computo* (p. 274) gives the current date as 996, but additions to the necrology include the names of three persons who died in 997, and epitaphs of Einsiedeln abbots continued to be added down through Hermann (d. 1065), while Einsiedeln annals are recorded by many different hands down to 1569. The manuscript was certainly written at Einsiedeln, but according to Bischoff a rare metrical *probatio pennae* is indicative of the close connections between Einsiedeln and Regensburg.[50] Thus the Einsiedeln manuscript may be further evidence of a pivotal role for Regensburg in the transmission of *Thomas*. Einsiedeln, in turn, might have been a conduit for transmission of the work between England and the Continent, since the abbot from 964–996 was an Anglo-Saxon named Gregory, whose metrical epitaph is recorded on page two.[51]

Very closely related to **E** is the text found in the twelfth-century manuscript **O**. Here *Thomas* is part of a group of additions at the end of the second part (fols. 41–162) of a composite manuscript whose main texts are liturgical: the *Micrologus* of Bernold of Constance (41r–62v),[52] a litany (63r–67v) and a *Liber ordinum episcopalium* (68r–161v).[53] The added texts are a brief note on the mass for the dead,[54] the abbreviated text of *Thomas*

Penitentials Attributed to Bede', *Speculum* 58 (1983), 573–97, at 576 and n. 17; J.-P. Bouhot, 'Les pénitentiels attribués à Bède le Vénérable et à Egbert d'York', *Revue d'histoire des textes* 16 (1986), 141–69, at 164. None refers to the Einsiedeln copy.

[47] See Helena M. Gamer, 'The Earliest Evidence of Chess in Western Literature: The Einsiedeln Verses', *Speculum* 29 (1954), 734–50, at 741–2.

[48] Bruckner, 'Zur Datierung', p. 94.

[49] Tischler, 'Die ottonische Klosterschule in Einsiedeln zur Zeit Abt Gregors', *Festschrift zum tausendsten Todestag des seligen Abtes Gregor, des dritten Abtes von Einsiedeln 996–1996*, ed. Odo Lang (St Ottilien, 1996), pp. 93–181, at pp. 162–3.

[50] Bischoff, 'Elementarunterricht und Probationes Pennae in der ersten Hälfte des Mittelalters', *Mittelalterliche Studien*, I, 74–87, at 81–2. In 'Das griechische Element in der abendländischen Bildung des Mittelalters', *Mittelalterliche Studien*, II, 246–75, at 256 and n. 53, Bischoff suggests that the manuscript's use of Greek letters for the word '*EPITAΦION*' is an indication of Irish influence. For additional evidence of contacts with Regensburg, and specifically with Niedermünster, see Hagen Keller, *Kloster Einsiedeln im Ottonischen Schwaben*, Forschungen zur oberrheinischen Landesgeschichte 13 (Freiburg i.Br., 1964), pp. 71–3; Tischler, 'Die ottonische Klosterschule', pp. 116–18.

[51] See Daniel Rees, 'Abbot Gregory of Einsiedeln: A Link between Switzerland and England', in *Festschrift zum tausendsten Todestag*, ed. Lang, pp. 13–27.

[52] See Daniel S. Taylor, 'A New Inventory of Manuscripts of the *Micrologus de ecclesiasticis observationibus* of Bernold of Constance', *Scriptorium* 52 (1998), 162–91, at 190–1, who identifies the two main parts of the manuscript and assigns the letter B to the second. On its contents see also *Tabulae codicum*, II, 297–8.

[53] For the first *ordo* ('Mensis primi quarti septimi et decimi sabbatorum') see the index of incipits in vol. 1 of M. Andrieu, *Les ordines romani du haut moyen âge*, 5 vols., Spicilegium sacrum Lovaniense, Études et documents 11, 23–4, 28–9 (Louvain, 1960–74).

[54] The *In Principio* database lists copies (under the title 'De commemoratione defunctorum') in Orléans, Bibl. Munic. 174, Paris BN lat. 3531, Valenciennes, Bibl. Munic. 92, and Douai, Bibl. Munic. 345.

(without attribution or heading), a fragment of the *Somniale Danielis*,[55] and a papal decree from the year 1023.

The final two new abbreviated texts include the only English manuscript of *Thomas* yet discovered, and a Breton manuscript whose text is closely similar. The Breton manuscript, **R**, dating from the late tenth century, contains the collection known as the *Catechesis Celtica*. The Celtic connections of this manuscript were recognized by André Wilmart, who edited a selection of items from the manuscript in 1935, and by Paul Grosjean, who in 1954 argued for a specifically Irish origin for much of the collection.[56] In recent years the manuscript has been analysed by Martin McNamara and by Jean Rittmueller,[57] whose researches confirm that many of the items have Irish affiliations. Some of the materials in the collection were available to vernacular homilists in both Anglo-Saxon England and Ireland.[58]

The text of *Thomas* occurs on folio 52v.[59] In his unpublished typescript edition of the collection, R. E. McNally recognized this text's relation to the apocryphon, and its existence has been noted in Martin McNamara's inventory of the contents of the *Catechesis*.[60] But this too has not yet been published or compared with the other texts. Its closest affiliation is with a hitherto unknown abbreviated text in **H**. Part 2 of this composite manuscript, comprising folios 10–89, was written in England towards the beginning of the thirteenth century.[61] It contains a collection of sermons attributed to Maurice of Sully (10ra–54va) and Abbo of St-Germain-des-Prés (75vb–83ra)[62] as well as the *De uirtutibus et uitiis* of

---

[55] Lawrence T. Martin, ed., *Somniale Danielis: An Edition of a Medieval Latin Dream Interpretation Handbook* (Frankfurt a.M., 1981), with reference to this manuscript at p. 62.

[56] André Wilmart, 'Catéchèses Celtiques', in his *Analecta Reginensia*, Studi e Testi 59 (Vatican City, 1933), pp. 29–112; Grosjean, 'À propos du manuscrit 49 de la Reine Christine', *Analecta Bollandiana* 54 (1936), 113–36. I am grateful to Joseph F. Kelly for providing me with a copy of R. E. McNally's unpublished typescript edition of the *Catechesis*.

[57] McNamara, 'The Irish Affiliations of the *Catechesis Celtica*', *Celtica* 21 (1990), 291–334; 'Sources and Affiliations of the *Catechesis Celtica* (MS. Vat. Reg. lat. 49)', *Sacris Erudiri* 34 (1994), 185–237; and 'The Affiliations and Origins of the *Catechesis Celtica*: An Ongoing Quest', in *The Scriptures and Early Medieval Ireland*, ed. Thomas O'Loughlin, Instrumenta Patristica 31 (Steenbrugge, 1999), pp. 179–203. See also Jean Rittmueller, 'MS Vat. Reg. Lat. 49 Reviewed: A New Description and a Table of Textual Parallels with the *Liber questionum in euangeliis*', *Sacris Erudiri* 33 (1992–93), 259–305.

[58] See Charles D. Wright, *The Irish Tradition in Old English Literature* (Cambridge, 1993), pp. 80, 96–9, and 236.

[59] A brief citation actually appears earlier (35vb, ed. Wilmart, p. 58), at the conclusion of a tract on Easter, where we are told that there will be great signs on the seven days before Judgement, and that the first sign will be powerful thunder. Unfortunately, however, this tantalizing build-up is followed only by 'reliqua'. Wilmart referred in a footnote to Bihlmeyer's edition of the *Apocalypse of Thomas*, but he did not edit or even mention the fuller text of the signs later in the manuscript.

[60] McNamara, 'Sources and Affiliations', p. 234; the text is not mentioned in McNamara's entry on *Thomas* in *The Apocrypha in the Irish Church* (Dublin, 1975), pp. 119–21, or in his recent survey 'Some Aspects of Early Medieval Irish Eschatology', in *Irland und Europa im früheren Mittelalter: Bildung und Literatur*, ed. Próinséas Ní Chatháin and Michael Richter (Stuttgart, 1996), pp. 42–75.

[61] See F. Madan and H. H. E. Craster, *A Summary Catalogue of Western Manuscripts in the Bodleian Library at Oxford*, 7 vols. (Oxford, 1895–1953), II, 819–21.

[62] See Jean Longère, *Les sermons latins de Maurice de Sully Évêque de Paris (†1196). Contribution à l'histoire de la tradition manuscrite*, Instrumenta Patristica 16 (Steenbrugge, 1988), pp. 203–11.

Albuinus (58va–67rb),[63] supplemented by three groups of mainly anonymous and pseudonymous items on 54va–58va, 67rb–75vb, and 82va–89vb.[64] The last two of these groups (interrupted by the sermons of Abbo) include much material with Irish affiliations, beginning with a copy of the 'Three Utterances' sermon towards the end of the second group.[65] The third group, following the sermons of Abbo, includes a tract on fasting that corresponds to part of a sermon in the Hiberno-Latin compilation known as the *Catechesis Cracoviensis*;[66] an apocryphal text on the eight parts of Adam (86rb–va) that is found in many early Insular manuscripts;[67] a pastiche of homiletic and enumerative motifs that corresponds to part of a sermon in the so-called *Apocrypha Priscillianistica* (itself a pastiche of material that circulated in other putatively Irish compilations such as the *Liber de numeris* and the homilies *In nomine Dei summi*);[68] and a variant recension of a sermon by Columbanus on the vanity of human life.[69] Interspersed among these are a version of a pseudo-Isidorian sermon on the body and soul[70] and a popular pseudo-Augustinian

---

[63] Cf. Longère, pp. 206–8. The explicits, however, do not match those given by D. Verhelst, *Adso Deruensis, De ortu et tempore Antichristi*, CCCM 45 (Turnhout, 1976), pp. 75–89, or by H.-M. Rochais, 'Florilèges spirituels latins', *Dictionnaire de spiritualité, ascétique et mystique*, ed. M. Viller *et al.*, 17 vols. (Paris, 1937–95), V, cols. 452–4. The material on 60rb–66rb from Albuinus, together with two items ('Si nolumus timere' and 'Ubicumque humilitas regnat') from the group of texts on 67rb–75vb, is paralleled in Kremsmünster, Benediktinerstift 105, part IV (s. xiii², Bavaria or Austria). For this manuscript see Hauke Fill, *Katalog der Handschriften des Benediktinerstiftes Kremsmünster, Teil 1: Von den Anfängen bis in die Zeit des Abtes Friedrich von Aich (ca. 800–1325), Katalogband*, Denkschriften der Österreichischen Akademie der Wissenschaften, Philos.-hist. Klasse 166 (Vienna, 1984), pp. 138–9.

[64] The group of five texts on 54va–58va includes extracts from Julianus Pomerius, *De uita contemplatiua* II.x (PL 59, 454–5) and Gregory, *Homiliae in Euangelia* II.xl and I.i (PL 76, 1077–81; 1304C–1305C); two other items remain unidentified.

[65] 'Hic incipit sermo Domini summi. Primum quidem decet nos audire iusticiam', 75ra–vb. Cf. *CPPM*, I.1930.

[66] 'Modo incipit de ieiunio et quis primus ieiunauit. Interrogauerunt tractores quare ieiunauit dominus', 85va–86rb (not in *CPPM*). See the analysis of this collection from Karlsruhe, Badische Landesbibliothek Aug. perg. 196 (?eastern France, s. ix¹) by Thomas Amos, 'The *Catechesis Cracoviensis* and Hiberno-Latin Exegesis on the *Pater Noster*', *Proceedings of the Irish Biblical Association* 13 (1990), 77–107. The sermon is no. 14, which from 91r ('Interrogant tractatores quare ieiunauit istud ieiunium . . .') to the explicit (93v) parallels the text in **H**, though with significant variation.

[67] See Hildegard Tristram, 'Der "homo octipartitus" in der irischen und altenglischen Literatur', *Zeitschrift für celtische Philologie* 34 (1975), 119–53.

[68] 'Prima uirtus in baptismo', 86ra–87ra. The compilation in Karlsruhe, Badische Landesbibliothek Aug. perg. 254, fols. 72–213 (Novara, s. viiiᵉˣ·; *CLA* VIII.1110), at fols. 159–173, was edited by D. De Bruyne, 'Fragments retrouvés d'apocryphes Priscillianistes', *Revue Bénédictine* 24 (1907), 318–35. On the Irish affiliations of this material, see Wright, *The Irish Tradition*, pp. 64–9. The passage in **H** corresponds, with some variation and rearrangement, to De Bruyne, pp. 329–30, lines 66–79 and 86–104. Some of this, including a passage on the *cibus animae*, is also paralleled in the sermons edited by R. E. McNally, '"In nomine Dei summi": Seven Hiberno-Latin Sermons', *Traditio* 35 (1979), 121–43 (McNally's Document VI and beginning of Document VII, pp. 141–2), and in variant form in the *Liber de numeris*, PL 83, 1296D; cf. McNally, 'Der irische Liber de numeris: Eine Quellenanalyse des pseudo-isidorischen Liber de numeris' (diss. Munich, 1957), p. 38. For some further parallels see Wright, *The Irish Tradition*, p. 65 and n. 87; part of the *cibus animae* passage also occurs in the Toronto fragment of *Thomas* (see below, p. 40).

[69] 'De uita huius mundi qualis est. O uita tantos decepisti, tantos seduxisti', 87rab (*CPPM* I.1176).

[70] 'Omelia sancti Ysidori. Satis multum oportet nos timere', 83va-84rb (*CPPM* I.5306).

Doomsday sermon that often circulated with the Three Utterances (and that occurs just before *Thomas* in **W**).[71] Though preserved in a post-Conquest manuscript, the anonymous materials in **H** may well descend from a collection that circulated in Anglo-Saxon England. It is certainly representative of the type of compilation that anonymous Old English homilists made use of, with a high content of apocryphal and pseudonymous texts focused on eschatological themes that are often elaborated in listing passages with extended parallelism.

In any case, **H** is the only English manuscript known to date that contains a Latin version of *Thomas*. On folio 88r occurs an abbreviated text represented as the *dicta* or sayings of Saint Gregory. It is closely affiliated with the text of **R**, though it has a few distinctive readings of its own, and occasional agreement with other manuscripts. **H** is unusual, for example, in omitting reference to the *uox tenera et suauis* on the Day of Judgement – an omission that characterizes the Old English homilies as well. Instead, it substitutes another brief list of signs headed 'Effrem dicit'. This is followed by a description of angels blowing four trumpets, each of which summons forth a separate group: prophets first, martyrs second, good persons third, and sinners last. Yet another brief list of signs is added at the conclusion.

The Insular affiliations of manuscripts **R** and **H** are of interest in view of the evident popularity of *Thomas* in Ireland and Anglo-Saxon England, as witnessed by the vernacular adaptations. No early Latin manuscripts of *Thomas* from the British Isles have survived, but there is significant evidence of an Insular role in its transmission on the Continent. I have already noted the Insular palaeographical features of **W**. The evidence of **B** is somewhat double-edged: it was palimpsested at Bobbio in the eighth century, which proves that *Thomas* was available there, but also suggests that the Irish scribe who wrote over it preferred grammatical and patristic texts to apocryphal ones.[72] No such scruples troubled the scribe of **P**, which was written in Anglo-Saxon script in the Middle or Upper Rhine region in the early ninth century, and was at Lorsch by the tenth century.[73] Insular foundations such as Bobbio in north Italy (albeit without the participation of the Irish scribe who palimpsested **B**!) and Würzburg and Lorsch in Germany were likely conduits for transmission of the work between the Continent and the British Isles in the Carolingian era. By the tenth century, to judge from the inclusion of *Thomas* in **R**, Brittany may have been another

---

[71] 'De die iudicii incipit omelia sancti Augustini. Frates karissimi, quam timendus est', 87rb-va (Sermo App. 251; *CPPM* I.1036). The sermon was printed from **W** by Georg Baesecke, *Der Vocabularius Sancti Galli in der angelsächsischen Mission* (Halle, 1933), p. 134. For some manuscripts in which the Doomsday and 'Three Utterances' sermons appear together, see Charles D. Wright, 'Apocryphal Lore and Insular Tradition in St Gall, Stiftsbibliothek MS 908', in *Irland und die Christenheit: Bibelstudien und Mission*, ed. Próinséas Ní Chatháin and Michael Richter (Stuttgart, 1981), pp. 124–45, at pp. 136–7.

[72] For the upper script see *CLA* III.394.

[73] See Bernhard Bischoff, 'Lorsch im Spiegel seiner Handschriften', in *Die Reichsabtei Lorsch: Festschrift zum Gedenken an ihre Stiftung 764*, ed. F. Knöpp, 2 vols. (Darmstadt, 1973–77), II, 7–128, at 49 and 108–9; 'Paläographische Fragen deutscher Denkmäler der Karolingerzeit', *Mittelalterliche Studien*, III, 73–112, at 88. On the contents, see Wright, *The Irish Tradition*, p. 111.

important intermediary, as it was for other apocryphal materials as well as for Hiberno-Latin texts.[74] Moreover, **R** and **H** are not the only manuscripts that transmit *Thomas* along with Hiberno-Latin or Insular material. This is also the case with **W**, **P** and **T**. Among the supplementary items in **W** we find the spurious Acts of the Council of Caesarea, regarded as a seventh-century Irish forgery. **P** contains a unique Redaction (XI) of the *Visio Pauli* that quotes from the hymn *Te Deum* in the exclusively Irish textual tradition,[75] as well as the collection of Hiberno-Latin sermons *In nomine Dei summi*, to which I have already referred in connection with **H**. The fragmentary **T** transmits a portion of Alcuin's *Disputatio puerorum* on the Lord's Prayer, and part of the *cibus animae* motif found also in **H**.[76]

Analysis of the medieval transmission of *Thomas* must take into account briefer citations or adaptations in sermons and hymns on the Day of Judgement, and these also include texts that have been regarded as Irish or Irish-influenced. Bihlmeyer drew attention to a three-day sequence of signs, clearly based on a version of *Thomas* but with substantial variation, in the *Apocrypha Priscillianistica*, a compilation that transmits Hiberno-Latin material, and essentially the same sequence, in slightly fuller form, occurs in a sermon found in the manuscripts of the homilies *In nomine Dei summi*, including **P**.[77] The variants include a sign for the second day, *mare siccabitur*, that also occurs in the pseudo-Augustinian Doomsday sermon. Finally, a Hiberno-Latin hymn *De die iudicii* preserved in the *Collectanea Pseudo-Bedae* incorporates this sign within a list that has further parallels with *Thomas*.[78]

---

[74] See David Dumville, *Liturgy and the Ecclesiastical History of Late Anglo-Saxon England* (Woodbridge, 1992), pp. 112–16, and 'Ireland, Brittany and England: Transmission and Use of the Collectio canonum Hibernensis', in *Irlande et Bretagne, vingt siècles d'histoire: actes du colloque de Rennes (29–31 mars 1993)*, ed. Catherine Laurent and Helen Davis (Rennes, 1994), pp. 85–95; Helen Simpson McKee, 'Breton Manuscripts of Biblical and Hiberno-Latin Texts', in *The Scriptures*, ed. O'Loughlin, pp. 275–90. BL, Royal 5. E. XIII (Gneuss, *Handlist*, no. 459), a late ninth-century Breton manuscript that was in England by the middle of the tenth century, contains an extract from the Book of Enoch, a variant of an item in the *Apocrypha Priscillianistica* (for which see above, n. 66), a narrative on the siege of Jerusalem, and extracts from the *Collectio canonum Hibernensis*; see Dumville, 'Biblical Apocrypha and the Early Irish: A Preliminary Investigation, *Proceedings of the Royal Irish Academy* 73C (1973), 299–338, at 331; Pierre Petitmengin, 'La compilation "De vindictis magnis magnorum peccatorum": Exemples d'an-thropophagie tirés des sièges de Jérusalem et de Samarie', in *Philologia Sacra: Biblische und patristische Studien für Hermann J. Frede und Walter Thiele zu ihrem siebzigsten Geburtstag*, ed. Roger Gryson, 2 vols., Vetus Latina 24 (Freiburg, 1993), pp. 622–38; J. E. Cross, 'On Hiberno-Latin Texts and Anglo-Saxon Writings', in *The Scriptures*, ed. O'Loughlin, pp. 69–79, at pp. 72–4.

[75] See Charles D. Wright, 'Some Evidence for an Irish Origin of Redaction XI of the *Visio Pauli*', *Manuscripta* 34 (1990), 34–44.

[76] On the *cibus animae* passage, see above, n. 68. The Toronto fragment (24r, lines 1–8) parallels McNally, ' "In nomine Dei Summi" ', p. 142, lines 7–11. The Alcuin extract was identified by Reynolds, 'Canon Law Collection', and Coughlan, 'A preliminary identification'.

[77] See Bihlmeyer, p. 279; the passsage corresponding to *Thomas* is ed. De Bruyne, 'Fragments retrouvés', p. 325, lines 30–64. The sermon transmitted with the homilies *In nomine Dei summi* ('Predicatio carere tormenta. Peccatoribus autem et impiis homicidiis', 26v–28r in **P** [not in *CPPM*]) was not edited by McNally because it lacks the superscription shared by the others. Its text is slightly fuller than that edited by De Bruyne.

[78] 'Extinguetur sol et luna, stellae cadent in terram, coelum mouebit se de loco, et plicabitur ut liber. In tremendo die. / Fundamenta orbis terrae corruent cum ira grandi, montes liquescent, terra inarescet simul, et mare siccabitur'; *Collectanea Pseudo-Bedae*, ed. Michael Lapidge and Martha Bayless, Scriptores Latini Hiberniae 14 (Dublin, 1998), p. 186, with reference to biblical parallels,

More such citations will undoubtedly surface in other unpublished medieval texts *de die iudicii*.[79]

I turn now to the Old English versions and their relation to the Latin.[80] Four independent translations survive (see table 2). One immediate problem is that the sequence of days has been altered in three of the four Old English homilies. This has resulted from independent efforts to reconcile the eight-day sequence of the Latin versions with a seven-day sequence in Old English, presumably in order to make everything fit into one week, with Judgement falling on a Sunday. Table 3 shows how the Old English homilies adapt the eight-day sequence of the Latin, and how the days are identified in each homily. Two of them, Vercelli XV and the Corpus 41 homily, identify the days by their names, and sometimes also assign them an ordinal number. The Vercelli homilist fits the signs into seven days by skipping the signs of the fifth day. He assigns ordinal numbers to three of the first four days, but ceases numbering them after he has omitted the signs of the fifth. Judgement occurs on Sunday, but there is a lacuna after the opening sentence, and in what remains there is no specific correspondence with the eighth day in *Thomas*. The author of Blickling VII omits instead

---

p. 187. The first three signs are ultimately biblical (cf. Mt. XXIV.29, and with *montes liquescent* cf. Ps. XCVI.5, *montes sicut cera fluxerunt* [*ardebunt* pseudo-Augustine]). The non-biblical *mare siccabitur* is ultimately from the Doomsday sermon; for examples in Old English, see J. E. Cross, 'A Doomsday Passage in an Old English Sermon for Lent', *Anglia* 100 (1982), 103–8; Joyce Bazire and J. E. Cross, *Eleven Old English Rogationtide Homilies*, 2nd ed., King's College London Medieval Studies 4 (London, 1989), p. 139, n. 12. The sign *terra inarescet* is also closer to the Doomsday sermon's *terra ardebit usque ad inferos* than to II Peter III.10. The extension of *coelum . . . plicabitur* with *ut liber*, however, is ultimately from *Thomas*, probably by way of the Doomsday sermon (but compare Is. XXXIV.4, Apoc. VI.14); cf. also MGH Poetae, IV/2, 521 (*Caelum ut liber plicare*), and an Old English homily on the Harrowing of Hell in Cambridge, Corpus Christi College 41, ed. William H. Hulme, 'The Old English Gospel of Nicodemus', *Modern Philology* 1 (1904), 579–614, at 611 (*hefenas beoð gefealdene swa oðere béc*).

[79] A pseudo-Augustinian sermon in Würzburg, Universitätsbibliothek M.p.th.f. 80 (s. ix²/³, Bavaria; cf. Thurn, *Die Handschriften*, p. 67), 140r–144v, echoes *Thomas* in its references to a *uox suauis* and *angeli paciens* [*sic*] at Judgement. A *uox tenera et suauis* on the eighth day is mentioned in most versions of *Thomas*; **W** also refers to an *angelus paces* [= *pacis*, or *paciens*?]; cf. **T**'s *cum uirtute angelorum paxque* [*sic*] and **P**'s *angelus patris*. A fragmentary apocalypse in Avranches, Bibl. Munic. 108 (addition of s. x), in which Christ describes the end of the world and the Antichrist in response to questioning by his disciples, may echo the interpolated version in the phrase *inter se pacem non habebunt* (cf. **NV** *sacerdotes mei pacem inter se non habebunt*; **PW** *sacerdotes* [+ *dei* **P**] *in terre pacem non habebunt*), though due to lacunae the subject of *habebunt* is unclear, and there is no reference to *sacerdotes* in what can be deciphered. For the text see Bernhard Bischoff, 'Vom Ende der Welt und vom Antichrist (I); Fragment einer Jenseitsvision (II) (Zehntes Jahrhundert)', *Anecdota Novissima: Texte des vierten bis sechzehnten Jahrhunderts* (Stuttgart, 1984), pp. 80–4, at p. 81. As Bischoff notes, the description of the physical appearance of Antichrist has close parallels with Irish sources.

[80] Vercelli XV, ed. D. G. Scragg, *The Vercelli Homilies and Related Texts*, EETS os 300 (Oxford, 1992), pp. 250–65, earlier ed. Max Förster, 'Der Vercelli-Codex CXVII nebst Abdruck einiger altenglischer Homilien der Handschrift', *Festschrift für Lorenz Morsbach*, ed. F. Holthausen and H. Spies, Studien zur englischen Philologie 50 (Halle, 1913), pp. 116–28; Corpus 41, pp. 287–92, ed. Förster, 'A New Version', pp. 17–27; Blicking VII, ed. Richard Morris, *The Blickling Homilies of the Tenth Century*, EETS os 58, 63 and 73 (London, 1874–80; repr. in one vol., 1967), pp. 91–5; Bazire-Cross 3, ed. Bazire and Cross, *Eleven Old English Rogationtide Homilies*, pp. 47–54 (base text CCCC 162); earlier ed. Max Förster, 'Der Vercelli-Codex', pp. 128–37 (base text Hatton 116).

Table 2. *Old English versions of* The Apocalypse of Thomas

| DOE short title | Cameron no. | Manuscript(s) | Abbreviated name |
|---|---|---|---|
| HomU 6 | B.3.4.6 | Vercelli, Biblioteca Capitolare CXVII | Vercelli XV |
| HomU 12 | B3.4.12 | Cambridge, Corpus Christi College 41 | Corpus 41 |
| HomS 44; HomS 33 | B3.2.44; B3.2.33 | Cambridge, Corpus Christi College 162; BL, Hatton 116 | Bazire-Cross 3 |
| HomS 26 | B3.2.26 | Princeton Univ., Scheide Library 71 | Blickling VII |

Table 3. *The sequence of days in the Latin and Old English versions*

| Latin | Vercelli XV | Corpus 41 | Bazire-Cross 3 | Blickling VII |
|---|---|---|---|---|
| 1st | 1st/Monday | 1st/Sunday | 1st | 1st |
| 2nd | Tuesday | Monday | 2nd | 2nd |
| 3rd | 3rd/Wednesday | 3rd/Tuesday | 3rd | |
| 4th | 4th/Thursday | 4th/Wednesday | 4th | 3rd |
| 5th | | 5th/Thursday | 5th | 4th |
| 6th | Friday | 6th/Friday | 6th | 5th |
| 7th | Saturday | 7th/Saturday | 7th | 6th |
| | Sunday (Judgement) | [Sunday] (Judgement) | 7th/Sunday (Judgement) | Sunday (Judgement) |
| 8th (Judgement) | | | | |

most of the third-day signs of the Latin, assigning those of the fourth to his third day, and so on through his sixth day; but he seems to have salvaged one third-day sign by transferring it to his second day: his sign 'and seo heofon bið gefeallen æt þæm feower endum middangeardes' ('and heaven will fall from the four ends of the earth') may be based on a Latin third-day sign found in **M** and all the new texts edited below, according to which heaven will be folded up (*plicabitur*) like a book. (Förster suggested emending the Blickling homilist's *gefeallen* to *gefealden* to correspond to this sign.) The Corpus 41 homilist retains all seven days preceding Judgement, but begins them with Sunday rather than Monday so that Judgement can fall on the following Sunday. Bazire-Cross 3 retains signs from all seven days preceding Judgement in the Latin simply by conflating those of the seventh day with the Day of Judgement; but like all the Old English homilists he substitutes material from the Bible and other sources for the description of Judgement.

The basic affiliations of the Old English versions with the major Latin versions were identified by Förster,[81] who noted that both Vercelli XV and

---

[81] Förster, 'A New Version'. Förster had drawn attention to three of the Old English adaptations of *Thomas* in 'Der Vercelli-Codex', and Rudolf Willard noted the fourth in his *Two Apocrypha*

the homily in Corpus 41 have material corresponding to the interpolation. Vercelli XV translates most of the interpolation, while Corpus 41 translates just a few brief passages. Förster also stated that Blickling VII had 'a few general statements' from the interpolation, but he did not specify these and I find nothing in the homily that derives from it. Nor are there any traces of the interpolation in Bazire-Cross 3. But the absence of the interpolation is not the same thing as affiliation with the 'non-interpolated' version represented by **BN**. Whenever a reading in one of the homilies appears to reflect something in **N**, the same reading is usually found in the interpolated text **P**, and when it is not it always occurs in at least one of the other interpolated texts. There seem to be no readings in any of the Old English homilies that correspond exclusively with the non-interpolated version.[82] If Blickling VII and Bazire-Cross 3 lack anything corresponding to the interpolation, it is rather because these homilists chose to focus on the signs of the seven days, which occur in *both* versions, or because their Latin sources were abbreviated texts that had already removed the characteristic interpolation from the so-called 'interpolated version'. In effect, their sources were 'de-interpolated' rather than 'non-interpolated'.[83]

As a full analysis of the relation of the four Old English homilies to the

in *Old English Homilies*, Beiträge zur englischen Philologie 30 (Leipzig, 1935), p. 2. Subsequent studies include Milton McC. Gatch, 'Two Uses of Apocrypha in Old English Homilies', *Church History* 33 (1964), 379–91; Gatch, 'Eschatology in the Anonymous Old English Homilies', *Traditio* 21 (1965), 117–65; Graham D. Caie, *The Judgement Day Theme in Old English Poetry* (Copenhagen, 1976); Frederick Biggs, 'The Apocalypse of Thomas', in *Sources of Anglo-Saxon Literary Culture: A Trial Version*, ed. Biggs, Thomas D. Hill and Paul E. Szarmach (Binghamton, 1990), pp. 68–9; Robert Faerber, 'L'Apocalypse de Thomas en vieil-anglais', *Apocrypha* 4 (1993), 125–39, and 'Deux homélies de Pâques en anglais ancien', *Apocrypha* 6 (1995), 93–126; and Swan, 'The *Apocalypse of Thomas*'. See also M. Atherton, 'The Sources of Vercelli Homily XV (C.B.3.4.6)', 1996, *Fontes Anglo-Saxonici: World Wide Web Register*, http://fontes.english.ox.ac.uk/

[82] Förster (p. 13) suggested that the verb in Corpus 41's *steorran fleogaþ þas wiorld* (fifth day) renders **N**'s *cessabunt* (line 37) rather than the *uertentur* and *uertebuntur* in **A** and **M**, which correspond to Blickling VII's *yrnaþ wiþersynes* (fourth day). But *fleogaþ* does not correspond very precisely to *cessabunt*, and it is at least possible that it corresponds to **P**'s *uetabuntur*. Förster also connects Vercelli XV's *mycel þreatnes* (line 5) with the phrase *neccessitates multae* or *magnae* of the introduction in **N** and **B**. On the other hand, the phrase *necessitates multae* also occurs in **P** and **M** (p. *42, line 5), after the interpolation. When the Vercelli homilist arrives at the corresponding passage (lines 74–5), he does not translate this phrase, which suggests that it had been displaced in his source. In any case, his equivalent *mycel þreatnes* occurs within a sequence otherwise closer to the non-interpolated texts (compare lines 4–6 with **M**, p. *40, lines 4–6 and **N**, lines 6–8), and it is possible that the Vercelli homilist's source read *necessitas magna* for **M**'s *siccitas magna*. Again, Vercelli XV's *weallas* (line 94) if it corresponds to **N**'s *pinne* (line 25), is also paralleled in **P** (Scragg suggests it is a form of *wiellas*, translating *fontes* corrupted from *fortis*). So too Blickling's *for þara engla onsyne* (fifth day) corresponds to **NPT** (sixth day) *a conspectu . . . angelorum*, where **WRH** have *a uirtute(s) angelorum*.

[83] **RHEO**, at least, are related to the textual line of the interpolated versions and share nothing distinctive with **N**. **A** is somewhat anomalous, for it has some striking agreements with **N** alone. The evidence suggests that **N** stands apart from the interpolated texts not only in lacking the distinctive interpolation but also in the character of its readings in the list of the signs. The readings of **P** generally follow those of the other interpolated manuscripts, but **P** also has a significant number of agreements with **N** against the others. This could be explained in a number of ways, including scribal collation, memorial conflation, or convergent variation. But the broad patterns of agreement are sufficiently persistent to suggest that the interpolated manuscripts **MW** have simply diverged further than has **P** from the common ancestor of the two recensions.

Latin versions is beyond the scope of this essay, I will focus on selected readings in the new Latin texts that help to establish a composite approximation of their lost immediate sources. My first example is one in which the new texts provide much earlier attestations for a variant reading found otherwise only in the fifteenth-century manuscript **A**. All four Old English homilies list as one of the signs of the first day a 'great voice' (*stranglicu word* / *mycel stefn*; Corpus 41 has the plural *micela stefna*). In Bazire-Cross 3 this is the first sign, but in Vercelli XV, Corpus 41 and Blickling VII the great voice is preceded by a great mourning or lamentation (*geomrung* or *gnornung*). Only **A** among the previously published versions has a corresponding sign *murmor magnum*, but all the new texts also have this sign.

A few examples will illustrate why manuscript **P**, never printed in full and only partially collated, is important for establishing readings available to the vernacular homilists. In each of these cases **P**'s reading is paralleled in one or more of the new texts. The last sign of the first day in Vercelli XV, Bazire-Cross 3 and Blickling VII is a rain of blood (*blodig regn* / *blodegan rene*). Corpus 41, however, mentions a rain of blood *and* of fire. In **MNTREO** we find *pluuia* [*-m* **T**] *sanguinis* (**A** has *pluuia et sanguis*), but only **PWH** add *et ignis*.[84] One of the unparalleled signs added to the *second* day in Blickling VII, *blodig regn and fyren*, could possibly reflect this first-day variant sign as well.

At the beginning of the signs for the fourth day in Vercelli XV we find the curious expression *eorðan frymðe* ('origin [*frymðe* < *frum*, "first, original"] of the earth'?). Förster suggested that the phrase may translate 'a Latin *terrae oriens*, or rather *origo*', but preferred to emend to a postulated *\*hrympe*, 'noise'.[85] W. W. Heist would instead emend *frymðe* to *wynde*.[86] D. G. Scragg in his edition takes a different approach, suggesting that the word *hora* may have dropped out in the Latin sequence *Quarta die hora prima*, leaving *prima* to be construed with *terra*.[87] There is nothing in the surviving Latin texts for the fourth day to support the emendations of Förster or Heist, but Scragg's solution finds support in **PW**, where the word *primaria* ('first [rank], principal') in *primaria terra* seems to be a scribal error for *prima hora (maria et terra)*. **R**'s *prima maria et terrę* and **EO**'s *prima maria terra* show that this difficult passage was subject to other substitutions.

On the second day, according to the Corpus 41 homily, the gates of heaven will be opened (*heofenes geatu bioð ontynedu*). This corresponds to *et porte caeli aperientur* in **N** and **M**. Blickling VII, on the other hand, says that heaven will be opened *on sumum ende*. Another variant in **P** supplies a possible equivalent: instead of *porte caeli* **P** reads *parte celi*, which is hard to construe but may have been taken to mean that the heavens (with *celi* now

---

[84] This is one of the rare cases of a reading shared by **N** and one or more interpolated texts against **P**, and one of the few cases where **RH** agree with other manuscripts against each other. Förster had Dobschütz's collation of **P** but failed to note the correspondence with this reading in Corpus 41.

[85] Förster, 'A New Version', p. 24, n. \*54 (with reference to p. 30, line 25).

[86] Heist, *The Fifteen Signs before Doomsday* (East Lansing, MI, 1952), pp. 68–9, nn. 19–20.

[87] Scragg, *The Vercelli Homilies*, p. 263.

as subject of *aperientur*) were opened from or out of a certain part. The new versions all likewise substitute forms of *pars* for *port(a)e*, but instead of the ablative have easier nominatives, *pars* (**RHEO**) or *partes* (**WT**).

In some cases we have to conflate readings from several manuscripts to approximate what the homilists probably had in front of them. When Blickling VII goes on to say that 'mycel mægen forcymeþ þurh þone openan dæl' ('a great power will come through the open part'), we can approximate the Latin source by comparing *mycel mægen* with the nominative singular *potestas magna* of both **M** and **P** (though in **P** it is a *potestas ignis*; **TEO** have the ablative *potestate magna*); the verb *forþcymeþ* with *eruptuauit* of **P** and the related form *eruptus erit* of **N**; and the phrase *þurh þone openan dæl* with *per partes c(a)eli* of **WRHE**. Here again, Old English *dæl* presupposes a form of *pars* rather than *porta*. Vercelli XV and Corpus 41, on the other hand, read 'and great powers will belch forth (*uteðmiaþ/utæðmað*) through the gates of heaven', which presupposes the plural *potestates magn(a)e* of **WRH**, some form of *eructare* as in **W** and all the abbreviated texts, and the *per portas caeli* of **MNP**. None of the surviving Latin texts, however, matches exactly the sequence of any of the Old English homilies.

Some additional variants in the Old English find parallels *only* in the new texts. The first sign of the third day in the previously published texts is, once again, a *uox in caelo*, which stands behind Corpus 41's *stefn bið geworden of heofonum*.[88] But Vercelli XV has *þonne cymeð sigebeacen of heofonum*, and Bazire-Cross 3 has *on heofonum æteoweð fyrentacen*. The second elements *-beacen* and *-tacen* suggest Latin sources with *signum* instead of *uox*, and four of the new texts supply precisely that: **RHEO** speak of a *signum igneum*. This corresponds closely to Bazire-Cross 3's *fyrentacen*, and the addition *et solphureum/sulphureum* in **REO** (*et flummeum* **H**) may have suggested *sweflen lyg* in Bazire-Cross 3.[89] Vercelli XV's *sigebeacen* may reflect some other modification of *signum*, or may simply be the homilist's looser equivalent of *signum igneum*.

In the first sign of the fourth day, Vercelli XV and Corpus 41 specify two directions, north and east, as does Blickling VII for the third day, where the previously published texts have only *orientis* (Bazire-Cross 3 mentions only the north). But **W** and all the new abbreviated texts except **H** (which has a completely different first sign) add *aquilonis*. Corpus 41 has the north and east speak with each other (*sprecað tosomne / him betweonum*), presupposing a form of *loquor* as against **N**'s unique *liquabitur*;[90] but in the Latin this passage seems hopelessly corrupt and is scarcely translatable.

On the fourth day Vercelli XV, Corpus 41 and Blickling VII (third day) refer to 'all the power(s) of the earth' (*eal(le) eorðan mægen*) being shaken

---

[88] It is possible that the strange statement in Corpus 41 that the voice from heaven will 'kill [*acwelleð*] all this four-cornered world' reflects some conflation such as *\*uox in caelo necabit* [cf. **W**'s *negabunt*] *quattuor angulos mundi*.

[89] Though the Old English presupposes a connection of *solphureum* with the next sign in some such form as *\*et solphureum de abyssi terrae ascendit*.

[90] By contrast, *Saltair na Rann*, line 8081, *Legf(ait) fothai fudomnai* ('The deep foundations will melt'; ed. and trans. Heist, *The Fifteen Signs*, pp. 4–5), presupposes a source with *abyssi liquabuntur*.

(*onhrered* / *onstyred* / *onwended*), which presupposes a reading such as **R**'s *commouebuntur uniuerşe terrę uirtutes* (**EO** also read *commouebuntur uniuers(a)e uirtutes*, but construe the genitive *terr(a)e* with the following word *motus* rather than with *uirtutes*; **R** has *motus erit* alone, showing that its reading has resulted from misplacement of the word *terrę*). In the other versions it is through the power, literally 'by virtue' of an earthquake (*uirtute terrae moti*) that all the earth (not all the *powers* of the earth) will be shaken.

On the fifth day Corpus 41 says that the light of the moon and the sun will be taken away; Blicking VII (whose fourth-day signs correspond to those of the fifth day in the Latin) says that there will be no light at the setting (*setlgang*) of the sun and that the moon will be extiguished (*adwæsced*). The previously published versions refer only to the powers of light (*uirtutes luminis*) and the wheel of the sun (*rota solis*), although **N** does go on to say *et erit aer tristis sine sole et luna*. But **REO** refer to the *ortus* of both the sun *and* the moon being taken away.[91]

Finally, on the seventh day the previously published Latin texts present us with the curious spectacle of the angels fighting among themselves. Vercelli XV and Corpus 41 sensibly provide them with demons to fight against – as does the Middle Irish version appended to *Saltair na Rann*.[92] In **EO** there are four hosts of angels (*chori angelorum*; **T** has a single host) fighting among themselves, and unspecified agents destroy them for the sake of the elect (*necabunt* [+ *eos* **E**] *propter electos*). **WRH** specifically identify the parties as 'wicked angels' (*iniqui angeli*[93]) fighting among themselves and 'holy angels' who then destroy them (*pernecabunt*/*eradicabunt*).[94] In **N** and **P** no battle of wicked and holy angels is explicitly mentioned.

The new texts I have described further underscore how *The Apocalypse of Thomas* was subject to redaction, interpolation and abbreviation. It is hardly possible to reconstruct an original or archetypal text from the surviving witnesses, or even to critically edit just three primary recensions. As Thomas D. Hill has pointed out in his introduction to *Sources of Anglo-Saxon Literary Culture*, 'texts such as . . . the *Apocalypse of Thomas* did not circulate in a single authorized version, and . . . an edition of a single version . . . would misrepresent the way in which most medieval readers had access to [it]'.[95] An appropriate model for an edition of *Thomas*, I think, is the recent edition of the Long Latin versions of the *Apocalypse of Paul* by

---

[91] Cf. Is. XIII.10. *Saltair na Rann*, line 8164 (ed. and trans. Heist, *The Fifteen Signs*, pp. 8–9), similarly has 'the sun and moon will be quenched'.

[92] Ed. and trans. Heist, pp. 18–19 (lines 8313–30); cf. also pp. 64–65. Thomas D. Hill has noted that the motif of the strife between angels and devils occurs as a sign of Judgement in *Christ III*, lines 892–8: 'Further Notes on the Eschatology of the Old English *Christ III*', *NM* 72 (1971), 691–8, at 693–6.

[93] **W**'s independent genitive *iniquorum angelorum* may have been corrupted from a reading such as *\*impleatur .iiii.choris angelorum*.

[94] **W**'s *pernegabunt* is best taken as an orthographical variant of *pernecabunt* ('utterly destroy'), but **T**'s *subnegabunt* seems to imply a form of *nego* ('half-refuse').

[95] *Sources of Anglo-Saxon Literary Culture, Volume One: Abbo of Fleury, Abbo of Saint-Germaindes-Prés, and Acta Sanctorum*, ed. Frederick M. Biggs *et al.* (Kalamazoo, MI, 2001), p. xxii.

Theodore Silverstein and Anthony Hilhorst, who print all the surviving texts of three variant recensions in facing-page, parallel-column format.[96] Indeed, with the *Apocalypse of Thomas* this is the only practical way to sort out and make accessible for analysis the complex variations in the multiple signs of each of the seven days. If we want to clarify the interrelations of the Latin and the Old English versions, we need a new edition of this kind – in effect, a synoptic *Apocalypse of Thomas*.

The broader question of the significance of *Thomas* for those who copied, read or translated it in particular times and places must be reserved for fuller treatment in the context of a complete critical edition. But some preliminary suggestions can be made in view of the manuscript contexts I have described above. Most of the manuscripts fall into two broad categories: homiletic compilations, in which *Thomas* – shorn of its attribution to the apostle – is often accompanied by eschatological sermons such as the pseudo-Augustinian Doomsday and 'Three Utterances' sermons (**PWRH**); and chronological-computistical miscellanies (**ME**). **W**, a homiliary whose supplementary materials include chronological and computistical texts, straddles both categories. **A** and **T** form a third but seemingly marginal group, in which abbreviated versions of *Thomas* have been inserted into catechetical dialogues, while **N**, a legendary, and **O**, a liturgical miscellany, are anomalous (**B** and **V** are mere fragments).

The circulation of *Thomas* in chronological and computistical contexts is of special interest: as a countdown of the final seven days of the world it seems to have been regarded as, in effect, a tract *de temporibus*. In **M** *Thomas* follows the *Computus Helperici* (from an exemplar that gives the *annus praesens* as 946) in a section of the manuscript that also transmits computistica of Abbo of Fleury, who *c.* 970 opposed claims by certain priests in Paris that the world would end in the year 1000.[97] We know from a marginal citation attributed to Hydatius (d. *c.* 469) in a ninth-century manuscript of Jerome's *Chronicon* that a lost apocryphon ascribed to Thomas – presumably a version of our *Apocalypse of Thomas* – contained a calculation that the world would end nine Jubilees after the Ascension of Christ (i.e. in 482).[98] It would be facile to assume that the transmission of *Thomas* was always and everywhere associated with expectant fear of (or hope for) an imminent Parousia or the terrors of an approaching millennium; yet whoever was responsible for the fifth-century historical-prophetic interpolation – if it is indeed an interpolation – was certainly convinced that

---

[96] *Apocalypse of Paul: A New Critical Edition of Three Long Latin Versions*, ed. Silverstein and Hilhorst, Cahiers d'Orientalisme 21 (Geneva, 1997). It would be feasible to edit the closely related abbreviated texts **RH** and **EO** by choosing one of each pair as a base manuscript, but since none of these texts has previously been published, I have chosen to print them all in parallel. If more such abbbreviated versions come to light, however, it would soon become impractical to print them all individually.

[97] See Richard Landes, 'The Fear of an Apocalyptic Year 1000: Augustinian Historiography, Medieval and Modern', *Speculum* 75 (2000), 97–145, at 123–30.

[98] For this manuscript see n. 1 above. On Hydatius's citation see R. W. Burgess, 'Hydatius and the Final Frontier: The Fall of the Roman Empire and the End of the World', in *Shifting Frontiers in Late Antiquity*, ed. R. W. Mathisen and H. S. Sivan (Aldershot, 1996), pp. 321–32, at 329–32.

he was living in the last days, and used the time-honoured method of *vaticinia ex eventu* to prove it. In later centuries these (more or less) transparent historical allusions would become opaque, yet could still be taken seriously as prophecy. Or if this introduction were simply removed, the text would provide information about the signs immediately preceding Judgement without any clues as to whether those final seven days were imminent. Again, at some point after its uneventful expiration the explicit apocalyptic countdown by Jubilees dropped out of the manuscript tradition of the work. Thus rendered harmless as a long-term forecast of the end of the world, *Thomas* nonetheless retained its moral and emotional force as a warning of the terrors that would usher it in.

Since the notion that the world would last for six thousand years was so deeply ingrained – in spite of concerted efforts by the most well–informed ecclesiastical authorities to suppress it – the combination of *Thomas* with an *annus mundi* calculation in a manuscript written close to one of the projected millennial end-points could still be provocative.[99] The Old English version of *Thomas* in Blickling VII is followed closely in Homily XI by a passage declaring that 'ealla þa tacno 7 þa forebeacno þa þe her ure Drihten ær toweard sægde, þæt ær domes dæge geweorþan sceoldan, ealle þa syndon agangen, buton þæm anum þæt se awerigda cuma Antecrist nuget hider on middangeard ne com' ('all the signs and portents that our Lord forecast would come to pass have all happened except that the accursed visitant Antichrist has not yet appeared on earth').[100] The homilist then specifies the current year as 971, but – probably aware of projections of an apocalyptic year 1000 – he goes out of his way to stress that the ages of the world have been of varying length, and that the exact date of Doomsday cannot therefore be foreknown by anyone except God. As Richard Landes has demonstrated, combinations of *annus mundi* countdowns and disclaimers of apocalyptic forecasting (often with reference to Mt. XXIV.36, or Acts I.7, which the Blickling homilist cites) were a common pattern, notably in the decades preceding the end of the sixth millennium.[101] The Blickling homilist's remarks are reminiscent of Byhrtferth's in his *Enchiridion*, in

---

[99] For such calculations see Richard Landes, 'Lest the Millenium Be Fulfilled: Apocalyptic Expectations and the Pattern of Western Chronography, 100–800 CE', in *The Use and Abuse of Eschatology in the Middle Ages*, ed. Werner Verbeke *et al.* (Leuven, 1988), pp. 137–211, at pp. 169, nn. 128–9, and 210–11; Wolfram Brandes, '"Tempora periculosa sunt": Eschatologisches im Vorfeld der Kaiserkrönung Karls des Grossen', in *Das Frankfurter Konzil von 794: Kristallisationspunkt karolingischer Kultur*, 2 vols., ed. Rainer Berndt (Mainz, 1997), I, 49–79, at 52–7. A previously unpublished example from Venice, Biblioteca Nazionale Marciana Lat. II.46 (2400) (north Italy, s. xi) is cited by Charles D. Wright and Roger Wright, 'The *Joca monachorum* and Sermon *De dies malus*', forthcoming in *The Bobbio Missal: Liturgy and Religious Culture in Merovingian Gaul*, ed. Yitzhak Hen and Rob Meens (Cambridge Univ. Press).

[100] *The Blickling Homilies*, ed. Morris, pp. 117–19 (translation my own). As Morris notes, a later hand has added at the top of the page the words 'fif elddo sindon ahgan. On þam syxtan sceal beon dom deih'. Morris's translation of p. 117, lines 35–6 (*forþon fife þara syndon agangen on þisse eldo*) is seriously misleading. The homilist does not say that 'five of the [fore-tokens] have come to pass in this age' but that 'five of the [ages of the world] are past in this age', i.e. that the current age is the sixth. There is no reference to a specific number of signs. Cf. J. E. Cross, 'On the Blickling Homily for Ascension Day (No. XI)', *NM* 70 (1969), 228–40, at 233.

[101] Landes, 'Lest'.

which he associates the six ages with the number 1000, but then interprets the number spiritually, and similarly cautions that the first five ages were of unequal duration. By the time Byrhtferth completed the *Enchiridion* in about 1012, he had the further advantage of being able to point out that the literal millennial year after the birth of Christ had already passed (those who counted from the Passion instead of the Incarnation could, however, borrow another twenty-one years). That such disclaimers were necessary to combat or forestall literal interpretations of the number of years is clear from Byhrtferth's explicit acknowledgment that 'Manige men wenað þæt þes middaneard scyle standan on syx þusend wintrum, forþan þe God ælmihtig gesceop ealle þing binnan syx dagum, ac þæt getæl wise witan hyt on oðre wisan getrahtnodon' ('Many men believe that this earth will last for six thousand years, since God almighty made the earth in six days, but wise scholars have expounded the number in another manner').[102] Here Byrhtferth seems to echo Bede, who in his letter to Plegwine complained about ignorant persons who believed that the world would last for only 6000 years.[103] Despite Bede's authority, in the tenth and eleventh centuries we still find Anglo-Saxon and Irish texts that reckon six or seven ages of the world with a cumulative duration of 6000 (or 7000) years. Chronological notes in the 'Leofric-Tiberius Computus' (dating probably from 979×987) and *Ælfwine's Prayerbook* (1023×1031) specify that there are 999 years from the birth of Christ to the coming of Antichrist,[104] while a late Old English sermon states that world will end after seven ages totalling 7000 years.[105]

Even when not accompanied by an explicit disclaimer, an *annus mundi* calculation referring to the number of years remaining in the sixth millennium need not have been intended or understood as an apocalyptic countdown. Yet it would remain open to an apocalyptic interpretation by more literal-minded ecclesiasts such as those whom Bede, Abbo and Byrthferth denounced. **W** and **E**, written towards the end of the eighth and tenth centuries respectively, both transmit calculations of the *annus*

---

[102] *Byrhtferth's Enchiridion*, ed. and trans. Peter S. Baker and Michael Lapidge, EETS ss 15 (Oxford, 1995), pp. 236–7.

[103] Ed. Charles W. Jones, *Bedae Opera de Temporibus* (Cambridge, MA, 1943), p. 313, repr. in CCSL 123C (Turnhout, 1980), pp. 623–4.

[104] The Leofric-Tiberius computus survives in BL, Cotton Tiberius B.v (s. xi$^{2/4}$, Canterbury, Christ Church?, Winchester?; Gneuss, *Handlist*, no. 373), and in Oxford, Bodleian Library, Bodley 579 (2675) (this part probably 979×987, Canterbury or Glastonbury?; Gneuss, *Handlist*, no. 585), ed. F. E. Warren, *The Leofric Missal* (Oxford, 1883), p. 54. The parallel text in BL, Cotton Titus D.xxvi (Gneuss, *Handlist*, no. 380) is ed. Beate Günzel, *Ælfwine's Prayerbook*, Henry Bradshaw Society 103 (London, 1993), p. 144; as Günzel notes, the Roman numeral '.dccccxcx'. is here apparently an error for '.dccccxcix' (cf. also p. 72). For the chiliastic implications of these texts, see Hildegard L. C. Tristram, *Sex aetates mundi: Die Weltzeitalter bei den Angelsachsen und den Iren*, Anglistische Forschungen 165 (Heidelberg, 1985), pp. 38–9, 51–2 and 58–9.

[105] HomU 57 (B3.4.57), ed. Rubie D.-N. Warner, *Early English Homilies from the Twelfth Century MS. Vesp. D. XIV*, EETS os 152 (London, 1917), p. 140; Max Förster, 'Die Weltzeitalter bei den Angelsachsen', in *Neusprachliche Studien: Festgabe Karl Luick zu seinem sechzigsten Geburtstage*, ed. Friedrich Wild (Marburg, 1925), p. 199. Landes, 'The Fear', pp. 117, n. 79, and 118, n. 82, refers to essays by William Prideaux-Collins and Malcolm Godden on apocalyptic expectations and the millennium in Anglo-Saxon England as forthcoming in *The Apocalyptic Year 1000*, ed. Landes.

*mundi*. In **E** an addition giving the *annus praesens* as 996 *ab incarnatione domini* offers two alternative *annus mundi* calculations, both taken directly from Hrabanus's *De comupto*. The first, following Bede's calculations from the Vulgate (*secundum hębraicam ueritatem*), would place the end of the sixth millennium far into the future (AD 2044), while the second, based on the Septuagint (*secundum .lxx. uero interpretes*), would place it safely in the past (AD 801).[106] A generation earlier, however, Thietland of Einsiedeln (abbot 958–964) had specified in his commentary on II Thessalonians that the thousand-year final age had begun with Christ's passion, which implied that the loosing of the devil according to Revelation would take place in the year 1033.[107] During the second half of the tenth-century, then, there seems to have been uncertainty or difference of opinion within the Einsiedeln community as to the calculation of the age of the world and the relation of the *annus praesens* to the last times. In view of these alternative reckonings, the inclusion of *Thomas* in an Einsiedeln chronological miscellany is more readily explicable. Yet the first page of *Thomas* in the manuscript has been roughly crossed out. If this was an expression of disapproval, it was at best half-hearted, for the text remains fully legible; but the copying out and subsequent cancellation of *Thomas* may be a graphic record of ambivalence towards apocalyptic countdowns near the end of the first millennium after the birth of Christ.

For all the attention that has been given to the year 1000,[108] it is easy to overlook alternative medieval reckonings of the end of the sixth millennium. According to the *annus mundi* calculated by Eusebius in his *Chronicle* and perpetuated by Jerome's translation, the sixth millennium would run out not in the year 1000, but in the year 800.[109] Thus according to a reckoning that had not yet been wholly routed by Bede's alternative *anno Domini* method of dating, Charlemagne's coronation on Christmas Day 801 took place at the very turn of the new millennium. Leading up to this date,

---

[106] The text of the entry is printed by Meier, p. 290; I cite from the manuscript. The source for the alternative *annus mundi* dates in Hrabanus's *De computo* c. 65 is ed. W. M. Stevens, CCCM 44 (Turnhout, 1979), pp. 281–2.

[107] See Steven R. Cartwright, 'Thietland's Commentary on Second Thessalonians: Digressions on the Antichrist and the Beginning of the Millenium', forthcoming in *The Apocalyptic Year 1000*. I am grateful to Dr Cartwright for allowing me to see this paper in advance of its publication. The attribution to Thietland seems reasonably well founded, but is not beyond doubt; cf. Tischler, 'Die ottonische Klosterschule', pp. 170–1. See now the translation of the commentary by Steven Cartwright and Kevin L. Hughes, *Second Thessalonians: Two Early Medieval Apocalyptic Commentaries* (Kalamazoo, MI, 2001).

[108] For discussion and references see Landes, 'The Fear'; Johannes Fried, 'Endzeiterwartung um die Jahrtausendwende', *Deutsches Archiv für Erforschung des Mittelalters* 45 (1989), 381–473. Variations in the method of calculation would, however, admit of a range between 799 and 806 (Landes, 'Lest', p. 196). The re-emergence of the sermon 'Cum ceperit mundo finis' (with replacement of the signs of Judgement by a discourse on the Antichrist) in the thirteenth century might also be correlated with eschatological speculations of that era, for which see Hans Martin Schaller, 'Endzeit-Erwartung und Antichrist-Vorstellungen in der Politik des 13. Jahrhunderts', in *Festschrift für Hermann Heimpel*, 3 vols., Veröffentlichungen des Max-Planck-Instituts für Geschichte 36 (Göttingen, 1972), II, 924–47.

[109] In addition to the works of Landes and Brandes cited above, see Juan Gil, 'Los terrores del año 800', *Actas del Simposio para el Estudio de los Códices del 'Comentario al Apocalipsis' de Beato de Liébana* (Madrid, 1978), pp. 217–47.

in 786 and in several years during the 790s, ominous portents had been recorded by chroniclers in England and the Continent, including showers of blood, earthquakes and terrible thunder, all of which are signs of Judgement in *Thomas*.[110] The two *annus mundi* calculations in **W** (67r) both project the final year of the sixth millennium as 799. The first is merely implicit, but the one headed *Ratio mundi* specifies how many years are left: 'Et remanent de [MS dies] sexto miliario ut pro conpleatur anni C.XXXX tantum'.[111] For the author of this calculation, made in the year 659, the end of the sixth millennium was still well beyond his own lifetime; but for the scribe of **W**, copying the same text in the last quarter of the eighth century, it had nearly run its course. We cannot be sure that he would have interpreted the millennial endpoint in the apocalyptic sense warned against by Bede; but having just copied out the signs of Judgement from *Thomas* some ten folios earlier, he might have every reason to think that the final reckoning was close at hand.

*Appendix*

*Six New Latin Texts of* The Apocalypse of Thomas

The six texts below are printed in parallel-column format, except for the opening and closing parts of **W** (and the conclusion of **H**) that are not paralleled in the abbreviated versions **TRHEO**. **W** and **H** are edited from the manuscripts, the others from microfilms or printouts. Letters that are uncertain or hidden in the gutters are enclosed in angle brackets. I expand abbreviations silently and supply word-division and punctuation, but I do not emend or correct orthography or grammar except where necessary to make acceptable sense (in some of the more difficult passages and enigmatic signs 'acceptable' has to be defined liberally). The text of **W** is particularly corrupt, with frequent confusion of cases and verb forms due especially to the falling together of short *e* and *i*; but space does not permit a linguistic commentary, an apparatus comparing its readings with the previously

---

[110] See Brandes, ' "Tempora periculosa" ', pp. 70–5; Landes, 'Lest', pp. 191–2. Such *signa* are of course apocalyptic commonplaces, and not distinctive to *Thomas*. See Klaus Berger, 'Hellenistisch-heidnische Prodigien und die Vorzeichen in der jüdischen und christlichen Apokalyptik', in *Aufstieg und Niedergang der römischen Welt*, II: *Principat*, XXIII/2, ed. Wolfgang Haase (Berlin, 1980), pp. 1428–69, and Patrizia Lendinara's essay in this volume. The coincidence of reported natural disturbances and well-attested apocalyptic signs would, however, surely lend *Thomas* contemporary resonance and credibility. The D version of the *Anglo-Saxon Chronicle*, *s.a.* 793, refers to whirlwinds, lightning storms and fiery dragons in the sky as *forebecna* ('prodigies', 'fore-tokens'), the word used in Blickling XI for signs leading up to Doomsday; see *The Anglo-Saxon Chronicle: A Collaborative Edition*, vol. 6: *MS D*, ed. G. P. Cubbin (Cambridge, 1996), p. 17.

[111] Ed. Krusch, 'Chronologisches', p. 90.

published versions, or a complete collation with the overlapping material in the unpublished W*cgklv*. Parallel passages in the previously edited versions **BNMVA** are cited by line numbers for each section; parallels in **P** are cited from the manuscript, though much of **P** can be pieced together from variants and citations given by Hauler, Bihlmeyer, Förster and Scragg. Biblical sources are noted in the translations of **N** by de Santos Otero and of **M** and **N** by James (see n. 12, above), so are not listed here; for parallels with other apocryphal texts, see Bihlmeyer's notes on **N**.

The texts are published with the permission of the Universitätsbibliothek Würzburg; the Biblioteca Apostolica Vaticana, Vatican City; the Bodleian Library, Oxford; the Stiftsbibliothek, Benediktinerabtei Einsiedeln; the Österreichische Nationalbibliothek, Vienna; and the Thomas Fischer Rare Book Library, University of Toronto.

**W**: Würzburg M.p.th.f. 28:

[57r] Cum ceperit mundi[1] finis ultimus propinquare, malitia[2] inualescit et omnium uitiorum genera crebrescent, iustitiam[3] interibit; ingenia preualere, rariscere misericordiam, aduersa dominari, crescere nequitia, iniustitia propinquare, nefragare fidem, refrigescere caritatem, iniquitatem consurgere.

1 *corr. from* mundum      2 t *corr. from* c *(?)*; ti *seems to have been corrected (by the original scribe?) from* ci *in many instances, which will not be further specified*      3 *The hesitation between nominative and accusative forms and the infinitive construction in the following list is unique to* **W***;* W*cgv read* ingenium . . . inualescit, misericordia rarescit, *etc.*

Cf. Lactantius, *Epitome diuinarum institutionum* 66.1: cum coeperit mundo finis ultimus propinquare, malitia inualescet, omnia uitiorum et fraudum genera crebrescent, iustitia interibit, . . . uis et audacia praeualebit . . .

Erit famis, bella, et terrę motus per singula loca, gladius et siccetas[1] magna, plurimę discensiones populi, blasphemiae, iniquitas, zelus, nequitia, odium, superbiam. Et uniusquisque quod illi placit hoc loquatur. Sacerdotes in terre pacem non habebunt, ficto animo sacrificabunt. Videbunt populum de domo dei recedere. Erit enim turbatio populi; domus dei erit in desertum et altaria eorum abhominabuntur, ita ut aranea intexat in eis. Sanctitas conrumpitur,[2] sacerdotium adulterabitur, a⟨g⟩onia[3] effracuntur, uirtus deminuitur,[4] laetitia[5] periit, gaudium recedit, malum habundabit, hymni de domo dei cessabunt, ueritas non erit, auaritia habundabit, sacerdotium integrum minime inu⟨e-nie⟩tur.[6] Nauigium acessio[7] non erit in pelago, ut ⟨ne⟩mo[8] nemini noua referat, nec audaciter loquatur;[9] [57v] in pueris canas[10] uidebuntur, minor maiori aetati locum non dabit.

1 *corr. to* siccitas *(?)*      2 *corr. from* cumrumpitur      3 *possibly* aconia      4 *corr. from* teminuitur      5 *very light stroke over second* a; *read* laetitiam?      6 inu....tur *with 3–4 letters lost at end of line*      7 acersio      8 ut...mo *with 2–3 letters lost at end of line*      9 *first* u *added above line*      10 *for* cani

Cf. **M**.40*.2–41*.6, 27–30; **P**.48v.8–49r.12; **V**

Auaritia[1] et libido uniuersa cumrumpunt. Erunt[2] caedes et sanguis effusionis; omnis sexus et omnis aetas arma tractauit, et moris latrocinii depredabunt. Tunc erit tempus inlicitum et execrabilem[3] quo nemine libeat uiuere. Et uiuos lamentatio et mortuos gratulatio sequatur; ciuitates et oppidum interibunt modo ferro et igni, modo terrę motibus[4] crebris, modo aquarum inundatione, modo bestilentiae et fames.

| | | | |
|---|---|---|---|
| 1 ri *added above line* | 2 eorum | 3 *corr. from* exegrabilem | 4 *corr. from* montibus |

Cf. Lactantius, *Epitome* 66.2–3: auaritia et libido uniuersa corrumpet. erunt caedes et sanguinis effusiones, . . . omnis [*corr. from* omnes *B*] sexus et omnis aetas arma tractabit. . . . . more latrocinii depraedatio et uastitas fiet. . . . tunc erit tempus infandum et execrabile, quo nemini libeat uiuere [*om.* quo n. l. uiuere *T*] . . . uiuos lamentatio, mortuos gratulatio sequatur. ciuitates et oppida interibunt modo ferro et igni, modo terrae motibus crebris, modo aquarum inundatione, modo pestilentia et fame.

Et omnes fontes aquarum et putea in puluere et sanguinem conuertuntur.

Cf. **M**.41\*.34–5; Lactantius, *Epitome* 66.4: aqua omnis partim mutabitur in crurorem, partim in amaritudinem uitiabitur . . .

His malis accedunt prodigia[1] in caelo, et comites crebro apparebit, et anni et menses et dies breuitur, quia deus ad commotandum seculum reuertitur. Et erunt lacrimę et gemitus, nulla requies ad formidinem nec somnus ad requiem; dies cladem nox maetus semper augebit. Adpropinquante iam antichristum et duobus annis et quattuor[2] mensibus persequitur. Et deum se esse dicit, cum sit[3] antichristus; et qui ei crediderit accepit potestatem mirabilia faciendi, ut ignis discendant de cęlo, ut sol resistat ad cursu, ut imago quam posuerit loquatur. Quibus prodigiis inliciet[4] multos ut adorent eum, signumque eius in fronte suscipiunt. Et qui non susciperent exquisitis cruciatibus[5] moriuntur, ita ut uere duas partes hominum redigetur et tertia in deserta solitudine fugit.

| | | | |
|---|---|---|---|
| 1 gi *added above line* | 2 quarum | 3 *not in ms (cf. Lact., var. lect.)* | 4 inlicite |
| 5 *corr. from* cruciantibus | | | |

Cf. Lactantius, *Epitome* 66.5–10: his malis accedent etiam prodigia de celo, . . . cometae crebro apparebunt, . . . tunc et annus et mensis et dies breuiabitur; . . . quae cum euenerint, adesse tempus sciendum est, quo deus ad commutandum saeculum reuertatur. . . . tunc erunt lacrimae iuges et gemitus perpetes . . . nulla requies a formidine [ad formidinem *B*] nec somus ad quietem [requiem *T*]. dies cladem, nox metum semper augebit. . . . tunc et impius iustos homines ac dicatos deo duobus et quadraginta mensibus persequetur et se coli iubebit ut deum; se enim dicet esse Christum, cuius erit aduersarius. ut credi [esse deum cum sit antichristus qui ut erit aduersarius et ut credi *B*] ei possit, accipiet potestatem mirabilia faciendi, ut ignis descendat a caelo, ut sol resistat a cursu suo [*om.* suo *B* ], ut imago quam posuerit loquatur. quibus prodigiis inliciet multos, ut adorent eum signumque eius in manu aut fronte suscipiant. et qui non adorauerit signumque susceperit, exquisitis cruciatibus morietur. ita fere duas partes exterminabit, tertia in desertas solitudines fugiet [fugit *B*].

Haec sunt signa in finitionem seculi huius. Tunc captiuabuntur et cadent[1] in mucrone[2] gladii.

| | |
|---|---|
| 1 et cadent] dent | 2 *corr. from* motrone |

Cf. **M**.42\*.2–5; **N**.2–3, 9–10; **P**.50r.16, 50v.1–3; **B**.II.15–18

| **W**: Würzburg M.p.th.f. 28 | **T**: Toronto 190, frag. 24–25 | **R**: Vatican Reg. lat. 49 | **H**: Oxford Bodleian Hatton 26 | **E**: Einsiedeln 319 | **O**: Vienna 1878 |
|---|---|---|---|---|---|
| | . . . dies .xlv. in quibus est dominus atque saluator in maiestate uenturus. | | | INCIPIT EPISTOLA SANCTI AVGVSTINI DE VI DIEBVS ANTE DIEM IVDICII. | |
| | | De diebus .vii. ante diem iudicii. | Incipiunt dicta a sancto Gregorio .vii. dierum ante diem iudicii. | | |
| | Audi Thomas quod oportet f(i)eri in die iudicii. | | | | |

With **T** cf. **A**.234–7: 'Quod dies habebit? – Mille .cc.xx. tot sanctos persecuturus est et postea transiturus est in montem Olyueti, ubi aspectu saluatoris extinguitur. Postea erit spacium dierum .xlv., et post saluatoris uenturus est in sua maiestate. . .'; **N**.1–4; **M**.40*.3; **P**.48v.7–8; **B**.I.5–11

| **W**: Würzburg M.p.th.f. 28 | **T**: Toronto 190, frag. 24-25 | **R**: Vatican Reg. lat. 49 | **H**: Oxford Bodleian Hatton 26 | **E**: Einsiedeln 319 | **O**: Vienna 1878 |
|---|---|---|---|---|---|
| Prima die primum signum iudicii murmur [58r] magnus erit. | Primo die iudicii erit murmur magnus in cęlo. | Primo die primum signum iudicii mormur magnum erit in cęlo. | Prima die iudicii illud signum quod factum erit primum,[1] hoc erit murmor magnum in celo. | Primo die erit primum signum iudicii; murmur magnum erit. | Primo dei primum signum iudicii murmur magnum erit. |
| Ora tertia diei erit uox magna et fortis in firmamentum, | Hora .iii.a erit uox in cęl(o), | Hora tertia diei erit uox magna in firmamento cęli, | Hora tertia erit uox magna in firmamento cęli,[2] | Hora tertia diei erit uox magna in firmamento caeli, | Hora tercia diei erit uox magna in firmamento cęli, |
| nubus magna sanguinea ascendens ab aquilone. | et nubes sanguineę accedens ab aquilone, | nube magna sanguinea discendente ab aquilone. | et erit una nubes magna mixta cum sanguine ab aquilone. | nube magna sanguinea[1] descendente ab aquilone. | nube magna sanguinea descendentem ab aquilone. |
| Et tonitrua magna et fulgora fortia sequentur illa nube, et cooperiet totum caelum. | et t(o)nitrua magna et fulgora fortes, et secuntur illam nubem, et cooperit totum caelum | Et tonitrua magna erunt, et fulgora fortia sequentur illam nubem, et cooperient nubes cęlum. | Et tonitrua magna erunt, et fulgura magna secuntur illam nubem, et cooperiet nubes totum celum. | Tonitrua erunt; fulgura fortia sequentur illam nubem, cooperient nubes totum caelum. | Tonitrua erunt; fulgura forcia sequentur illam nubem, cooperientque nubes totum celum. |
| Et erit[1] pluuia sanguinea et ignis super totam terram. | pluuiam[1] sanguini(s). | Et erit pluuia sanguinis super terram. | Et erit pluuia sanguinis et ignis super terram. | Erit pluuia sanguinis super totam terram. | Pluuia sanguinis erit super totam terram. |
| | | | Tota ista signa erunt in primo die. | Ista sunt signa primo die. | |

**W**: 1 Et erit *not in ms*    **T**: 1 *read* pluuia (*abl.*)?    **H**: 1 signum primum *with signum cancelled*    2 *corr. from* celo    **E**: 1 *first* n *added above line*    **O**: 1 *first* n *added above line*

Cf. **M.**42*.5-9; **N.**12-17; **P.**50v.5-11; **A.**237-41; **B.**III.50017

| **W**: Würzburg M.p.th.f. 28 | **T**: Toronto 190, frag. 24-25 | **R**: Vatican Reg. lat. 49 | **H**: Oxford Bodleian Hatton 26 | **E**: Einsiedeln 319 | **O**: Vienna 1878 |
|---|---|---|---|---|---|
| Secundo autem die erit uox magna in firmamento[1] caeli, | Secundo autem die erit uox magna in firmament⟨o⟩ caeli, | Secunda die erit uox magna in firmamento cęli, | Secunda autem die erit uox magna in firmamento cęli, | Secundo autem die erit uox magna in firmamento cęli, | Secundo die erit uox magna in firmamento celi, |
| et mouetur terra de loco suo. | mouebuntur terrę de loco suo, | et mouebitur terra de celo suo. | et mouebitur de loco sancto suo terra. | et mouebitur terra a loco suo. | et mouebitur a loco suo. |
| Partes caeli aperientur ab orientem. | partes ape⟨ri⟩ant ab oriente; | Et pars aperietur in firmamento cęli ab oriente. | Et pars celi aperientur[1] in firmamento celi ab oriente. | Pars caeli aperietur in firmamento caeli ab oriente. | Pars cęli aperietur in firmamento cęli ab oriente. |
| Et potestates magnae eructuabuntur per partes cęli, et cooperiet totum cęlum usque in uespera. | potestate magna eructuabunt. | Et potestates magne eructabuntur per partes cęli, et cooperient totum cęlum. | Potestates magne eructabuntur per partes celi, et cooperient totum populum. | In potestate magna eructuabunt per partes caeli, et cooperient totum caelum. | In potestate magna eructuabunt partes cęli et cooperient totum cęlum. |
| | | | Ista signa erunt secunda die. | Ista sunt signa secundo die. | Ista signa sunt secundo die. |

**W**: 1 *corr. from* firmamentum

**H**: 1 *read* aperietur, *or* partes *for* pars

Cf. **M**.42*.10–14; **N**.18–23; **P**.50v.11–17; **A**.241–3; **B**.III.18–IV.1–7

| W: Würzburg M.p.th.f. 28 | T: Toronto 190, frag. 24–25 | R: Vatican Reg. lat. 49 | H: Oxford Bodleian Hatton 26 | E: Einsiedeln 319 | O: Vienna 1878 |
|---|---|---|---|---|---|
| Tercia autem die ora secunda erit uox in caelo, | Tertia autem die hora secunda erit uox in cęlo, | Tertia diei hora .ii. erit in cęlo signum igneum et solfureum, | Tercia die hora secunda in cęlo erit signum igneum et flummeum, | ⟨T⟩ertia autem die hora .ii.ʾaʾ erit in cęlo signum igneum et sulphureum; | Tercia autem die hora secunda erit in cęlo signum igneum et sulphureum; |
| et abyssi terrae[1] negabunt de quattuor angulos mire uoces. | et abyssi terre mugebunt a quattuor angulis terre. | et abissi terram rigabunt de .iiii. angulis mundi. | et abyssus terra rigabitur de .iiii.ʾorʾ angulis mundi. | abyssi terra ⟨r⟩egnabunt de .iiii.ʾorʾ angulis mundi. | abyssi terre regnabunt de quatuor angulis mundi. |
| Primum caelum[2] plicabitur uelud liber, | Primum cęlum plicabitur sicut liber, | Primum celum plicabitur ut liber, | Primum celum plicabitur ut liber, | Primum caelum plicabitur ut liber, | Primum cęlum conplicabitur ut liber, |
| et non apparebit continuo. Ab fumo et[3] putore[4] solphoris abyssi dies obscurabitur usque in ora .x. | usque horam decimam. | et non apparebit continuo, ut putei abissi obscurabuntur usque ad horam .x. | et non apparebit continuo, ut putei abyssi obscurabuntur usque ad horam decimam. | et non apparebunt continuo; putei abyssi abysso obscurabuntur usque ad horam .x.mam. | et non apparebit continuo; putei abissi obscurabuntur usque ad horam decimam. |
| Tunc dicent omnes: Puto finis adpropinquabit, ut pereamus. | Tunc dicent omnes homines[1]: Fines mundi adpropinquat. | Tunc dicent omnes angelici populi: Appropinqua nobis, domine, ne pereamus. | Tunc dicent omnes angeli et populi: Appropinqua nobis, deus, ut non pereamus. | Tunc dicent omnes angeli: Appropinquant nobis ut aperiamus. | Tunc dicent omnes angeli: Appropinquat ut aperiamus. |
| | | | Ista signa erunt tercia die.[1] | Ista sunt signa .iii. die. | |

W: 1 *read* terrae (?)  2 *corr. from* caelo  3 Ab fumo et *not in ms, cf.* N  4 putoris

H: 1 i *added below line*

T: 1 tercia die *not in ms*

Cf. **M**.42*.14–19; **N**.24–9; **P**.51r.1–7; **A**.243–7; **B**.IV.16–18

| **W**: Würzburg M.p.th.f. 28 | **T**: Toronto 190, frag. 24–25 | **R**: Vatican Reg. lat. 49 | **H**: Oxford Bodleian Hatton 26 | **E**: Einsiedeln 319 | **O**: Vienna 1878 |
|---|---|---|---|---|---|
| Quarta autem die primaria terra aquilonis et orientis loquitur | Quarta autem die hora .iiia. terra aquilonis orientis loquitur | Quarto die hora prima maria et terre aquilonis orientia loquentur | .iiii.ˈtaˈ die maria commouebuntur et terre simul commouebuntur | Quarta autem die hora i. maria terra aquilonis orientis loquentur; | [162r] Quarta autem die hora prima maria terra aquilonis orientis loquentur; |
| et abysus mugebit. | et abyssi inferni mugebunt. | et abissi mugebunt. | et abyssi mugient. | abyssi mugebunt. | abissi mugebunt. |
| Tunc mouetur uniuersa a uertutes terre motus. | Tunc mouebuntur uniuerse terre a uirtute sua. | Tunc commouebuntur uniuerse terre uirtutes. Et terrẹ¹ motus in illa die erit. | | Tunc commouebuntur uniuersae uirtutes. Terrae motus in illa die erit. | Tunc commouebuntur uniuerse uirtutes. Terre motus in illa die erunt. |
| In illa die cadent idola gentium et omnia aedifitia terre non stabunt. | In illa die cadent idola gentium et omnia aedificia terrẹ. | Et cadent idola gentium et omnia facta terrẹ. | Omnia ydola gentium in ipso die destructa erunt. | Cadent idola gentium, omnia effecta terrae. | Cadent ydola gentium, omnia fundamenta. |
| | | | | Ista sunt signa .iiii. die. | Ista signa sunt quarto die. |

**R:** 1 *not in ms*

Cf. **M**.42*.19–23; **N**.30–3; **P**.51r.7–12; **A**.247–50

| W: Würzburg M.p.th.f. 28 | T: Toronto 190, frag. 24–25 | R: Vatican Reg. lat. 49 | H: Oxford Bodleian Hatton 26 | E: Einsiedeln 319 | O: Vienna 1878 |
|---|---|---|---|---|---|
| Quinta autem die ora sexta erunt tonitrua magna in caelo. | Quinta autem die hora .vi.'ta' subito erunt tonitru⟨a⟩ magna | Quinta die hora .v. subito erunt tonitrua magna in cęlis. | Quinta autem die subito erunt tonitrua magna in celo. | Quinta die hora .v. subito erunt tonitrua magna in caelis. | Quinto die hora quinta subito erunt tonitrua magna in cęlis. |
|  | et fulgora fortissima. |  | Et splendor magnus erit. |  |  |
| Et uirtutes luminis et rota solis rapitur. | Virtutis luminis et[1] radia solis rapitur. | Ortus solis et ortus lunę rapietur. |  | Ortus solis et[1] ortus lunae nimis rapientur. | Ortus solis et[1] ortis lunę nimis rapientur. |
| Et erunt tenebre magnae in seculo usque in uespera, |  | Erunt tenebre magnę usque ad uesperum, | Et erunt tenebre magne usque ad uesperum, | Erunt tenebrae magnae in saeculo ad uesperam. | Erunt tenebrę magnę in seculo usque ad uesperam. |
| et stelle euertibunt a ministerio suo. | Stelle auertebuntur a ministerio suo. [f. 24v] | et stelle auertentur a ministeriis[1] suis. | et stelle uertentur a ministerio suo. | Stellę auertentur a ministerio suo. | Stelle auertentur a ministerio suo. |
| In illo die odent omnes seculo et contemnent uita seculi huius. |  | In ista die omnes gentes odient sęculum et condemnabunt uitam seculi huius. | In ista die omnes audient celum et condempnabunt uitam. | In isto die omnes gentes odient et contemnabunt uitam saeculi. | In isto die omnes gentes dicent et condempnabunt uitam seculi. |
|  |  |  |  | Ista sunt signa .v. die. |  |

T: 1 *not in ms*    R: 1 *misteris*    E: 1 *not in ms*    O: 1 *not in ms*

T: 1 *not in ms*

Cf. M.42*.23–8; N.34–9; P.51r.17–51v.1; A.250–3

| W: Würzburg M.p.th.f. 28 | T: Toronto 190, frag. 24-25 | R: Vatican Reg. lat. 49 | H: Oxford Bodleian Hatton 26 | E: Einsiedeln 319 | O: Vienna 1878 |
|---|---|---|---|---|---|
| Sexta autem die erunt signa ora quarta diei: | [f. 24v; text missing at top of page] | Sexta die hora .vi. diei | In sexto die hora sexta diei | [p. 156] Sexta autem die hora .vi. | Sexta autem die hora sexta |
| scinditur firmamentum caeli ab orientem usque ad[1] occidentem. | | scindetur cęlum in firmamento ab oriente parte usque ad occidentem. | scindetur celum a parte[1] orientis usque ab occidentem. | scindetur caelum a firmamento eius ab orientali parte usque ad occidentem. | scindetur cęlum a firmamento eius ab orientali parte usque ad occidentem. |
| Erunt angeli prospicientes super terram per aperturam caelorum. | | Erunt angeli prospicientes de cęlis. | Erunt[2] angeli prospicientes de celo. | Erunt angeli prospicientes super terram per aperturam caelorum. | Et per aperturam cęlorum |
| | . . debunt super terram exercitum angelorum prospicientem de caelo. | | | Omnes uidebunt super terram exercitus angelorum prospicientes de caelis. | omnis exercitus angelorum erunt prospicientes de cęlis super terram. |
| Tunc omnes homines fugient in montibus, et abscondent se a uertutes angelorum dicentes: Aperiat se terra et cooperiet nos. Fiunt enim talia qualia [58v] numquam facta sunt ex quo seculum creatum est. | Tunc omnes homines fugiunt in montes; abscondent se ⟨a con⟩spectu angelorum et dicent, Ap⟨eriat⟩ terram et cooperunt nos. Talia qualia f⟨a⟩cta sunt ex quo mundus creatus est non fuit. | Tunc fugient in montibus et abscondent se ante uirtutem angelorum dicentes: Aperiet se terra et deglutiet nos. Sunt et alia quae numquam facta sunt ex quo celum creatum est. | Tunc fugient homines in montes et abscondent se ante uirtutem angelorum dicentes: Aperiat se terra et decluciat nos. | Tunc omnes fugient in montes; abscondent se ante uirtutes caelorum dicentes: Aperiet se terra et conglutinat nos. Sunt namque alia que numquam facta sunt ex quo caelum creatum est.<br><br>Ista sunt signa .vi. die. | Tunc fugient ad montes et abscondent se ante uirtutes celorum dicentes: Aperiet se terra et conglutinat nos. Sunt namque alia quae numquam facta sunt. |

W:  1 ad ab      H:  1 perate      2 not in ms

Cf. M.42*.28–32; N.40–8; P.51v.1–13; A.253–60

| W: Würzburg M.p.th.f. 28 | T: Toronto 190, frag. 24–25 | R: Vatican Reg. lat. 49 | H: Oxford Bodleian Hatton 26 | E: Einsiedeln 319 | O: Vienna 1878 |
|---|---|---|---|---|---|
| Septima autem die ora secunda[1] per quattuor angulos caeli simul totum[2] caelum inplebitur,[3] | ⟨S⟩eptima ⟨a⟩utem die hora secunda per quattuor angulos caeli multum zelum implebitur | Septimo die hora .ii. per .iiii. angulos seculi simul totum celum plicabitur, | Septimo autem die hora secunda per angulos seculi simul totum celum plicabitur, | Septima die hora .ii. per .iiii. 'or' partes saeculi simul totum plicabitur, | Septima autem die hora secunda per quatuor partes seculi simul totum celum plicabitur,[1] |
| chori[4] iniquorum angelorum facientes bellum inter se tota die. | in choro angelorum faciens bella inter se tota die. | iniqui angeli facientes bellum inter se tota die. | iniqui angeli facientes bella intra se[1] tota die. | .iiii. 'or' chori angelorum facientes bellum inter se tota die; | .iiii. 'or' chori angelorum facientes bellum inter se tota die; |
| Angeli sancti pernegabunt eos propter electos dei. | Angeli subnegabunt eos propter electos meos. | Et angeli sancti pernecabunt eos propter electos meos. | Et sancti angeli eradicabunt eos. | necabunt eos propter electos. | necabunt propter electos. |
| Tunc uidebunt omnes gentes quia perditio eis aduenit. | Et tunc scient omnes gentes quia perditio eorum aduenit. | | | Tunc uidebuntur que aperienda erunt. | Tunc uidebuntur que aperienda erunt. |
| | | | | Ista sunt signa .vii. die. | Ista signa sunt septima die. |

W:  1 secunda erunt     2 tum     3 second i corr. from e ?     4 not in ms, cf. EOT

H:  1 see

O:  1 co(n)plicabitur with co *expunctuated*

Cf. N.72–7; P.51v.13–52r; A.260–3

| **W**: Würzburg M.p.th.f. 28 | **T**: Toronto 190, frag. 24–25 | **R**: Vatican Reg. lat. 49 | **H**: Oxford Bodleian Hatton 26 | **E**: Einsiedeln 319 | **O**: Vienna 1878 |
|---|---|---|---|---|---|
| In die autem octaua ora sexta erit¹ uox tenera et suauis in caelo ad orientem. | In die autem octauo hora vi.˥ta´ erit uox tenera et suauis in cẹlo ab oriente et occidente. | Post haec hora .vi. erit uox tenera, suauis, quando dicet pater sanctis et iustis: | Tunc audient omnes post dies istos hora sexta illud bonum uerbum quod pater dicet sanctis suis: | Post istos populos hora .vi. erit uox tenebrosa nimis qua dicet pater sanctis suis: | Post haec apparebit signum filii hominis qui iudicaturus est uiuos et mortuos et reddet unicuique iuxta opera sua. |
| Et tunc clamauit cum uirtute angelus paces qui habit potestatem super angelos sanctos. Exient cum illo uirtutes lumines in gaudio et currentis per aera sub caelo ut liberentur iusti, et gaudebunt de perditione seculi. | Tunc clamabunt cum uirtute angelorum, paxque habet potestatem super angelos sanctos. Et exeunt cum illo uirtutis luminis in gaudium sempiternum patris mei, currentes per aera sub caelo ut liberentur iusti mei qui in me credunt et ibunt in perpetuum. Impii autem in tenebras ubi finis numquam erit in saecula. | | | | |

**W**:  1  *added above line*

Cf. **N**.78–84; **P**.52r.2–8

| **W**: Würzburg M.p.th.f. 28 | **T**: Toronto 190, frag. 24–25 | **R**: Vatican Reg. lat. 49 | **H**: Oxford Bodleian Hatton 26 | **E**: Einsiedeln 319 | **O**: Vienna 1878 |
|---|---|---|---|---|---|
| | | Venite, benedicti patris mei possidete regnum quod uobis paratum ab[1] mundi. Aspera uox erit quando dicet impiis et peccatoribus: Ite, maledicti, in ignem eternum. In ista die iudicii . . .[2] | Venite benedicti patris mei, et reliqua. | Venite benedicti patris mei possidete regnum. | |
| | | | Effrem dicit. Dies domini in quo ostendit dominus mirabilia super terram. Ab hora mane usque ad horam terciam pluuia et ignis erunt, mare et terra transibunt, et timebunt omnes homines qui uidebunt. Ab hora tercia usque ad horam sextam[1] erit pluuia calida secundum similitudinem grandinis ut capud uiri. Ad hora autem sexta usque ad horam nonam ueniet pluuia sanguinis. | | |

**R**: 1 *supply* constitutione *or* origine (*Mt. XXV.34*)   2 *unrelated material omitted*

**H**: 1 a'd' horam [nonan *cancelled*] sextam

## H: Oxford Bodleian Hatton 26

Ad .iiii.`or´ uentis sonabunt montes ut tuba et uenient[1] .iiii.`or´ angelis cum tubis suis. Primus angelus[2] cantabit cum tuba et resurgent prophete. Secundus angelus cantabit cum tuba et resurgent martyres. Tercius angelus sonabit tuba et resurgent omnes boni homines simul cum gaudio in christo. Quartus angelus cantabit cum tuba et resurgent impii peccatores. Postea plicabitur celum et sol conuertetur in tenebris[3] et luna in sanguine, et stelle cadent de celo et omnes sancti regnabunt cum christo in regno celesti in secula seculorum amen.

**H:**   1 cum angelis *cancelled*      2 angelis      3 *corr. from* tenebras

## W: Würzburg M.p.th.f. 28:

Tunc uidebunt omnes uenientem dominum cum uirtutes sanctorum angelorum. Soluuntur clasure[1] ignis paradisi. Tunc spiritus et animę iustorum exient unusquisque ad corpus suum dicentes, Hic depositum est corpus meum. Tunc erit terrę motus per orbem terrarum; montes et petra scinduntur ab immo. Et reuertitur unusquisque spiritus in uaso suo. Tunc resurgent corpora sanctorum qui dormitionem ceperunt.

1 *corr. from* clusure

Cf. **N**.48–60; **P**.52r.8–52v.6

# 3

# Ælfric and the Epistle to the Laodiceans

## THOMAS N. HALL

EVEN the most cursory overview of the study of the Bible in medieval Britain would have to give serious attention to Ælfric, the most prolific translator of biblical texts into English before the fifteenth century and the most productive author of any kind to have emerged from the tenth-century Benedictine Reform centered at Winchester, where the reading and glossing of the Bible (particularly the Psalms) was a fundamental activity. Ælfric is one of our chief sources of information about how the Bible was used in the monastic Office in late Anglo-Saxon monasteries, and his homilies served as models for biblical preaching throughout the eleventh and twelfth centuries. A reader of Ælfric today would not have to venture far into the corpus before realizing that his writings are saturated with biblical quotations and paraphrases. Malcolm Godden has estimated that something in the neighborhood of 1135 separate biblical citations or quotations are embedded in Ælfric's *Catholic Homilies*, about half imported directly from Ælfric's sources, with the other half coming either from a Bible at Ælfric's disposal or from his own capacious memory.[1] The bible is thus an unmistakably central presence in Ælfric's work, and Ælfric scholarship has accordingly devoted a good deal of energy to probing the depths of his biblical knowledge and examining his methods of biblical interpretation.

An aspect of Ælfric's command of biblical literature that has come under repeated discussion since the 1960s is his attitude toward a number of texts and legends that are now classed as biblical apocrypha. Ælfric is not at all comfortable with these apocryphal texts and legends, even though they appear to have been well known and were evidently valued by some of his contemporaries. The texts and legends that come most immediately into play here are the apocryphal narratives of the Virgin's Nativity and Assumption, the *Vision of St Paul*, a legend on the passion of St Thomas, and a legend on the intercession of the Virgin at Judgement Day.[2] In most of the cases in which Ælfric protests against an apocryphal work, he does so

---

[1] Malcolm Godden, *Ælfric's Catholic Homilies: Introduction, Commentary and Glossary*, EETS ss 18 (Oxford, 2000), p. xliv.

[2] A nodal point for the discussions of these texts and legends is Mary Clayton's important essay, 'Ælfric and the Nativity of the Blessed Virgin Mary', *Anglia* 104 (1986), 286–315; see also her book, *The Cult of the Virgin Mary in Anglo-Saxon England*, CSASE 2 (Cambridge, 1990), pp. 244–53.

not only because he finds it doctrinally or theologically suspicious but because it fails to be included among the divinely inspired canonical scriptures as traditionally received. The problem has as much to do with authoritative reception as it does content. In his sermon for the Assumption of Mary in the second series of *Catholic Homilies*, for instance, Ælfric declines to tell the story which the feast is intended to commemorate because, as he says, 'if we say more about this feast day than we read in the holy books that have been written through the inspiration of God, then we would be like those heretics who have written many false traditions from their own imagination or from dreams'.[3] Ælfric will have nothing to do with these extra-biblical accounts of the Assumption, and he condemns those who have read them in Latin and Old English. Likewise, in a note appended to a homily in the second series, Ælfric explains that he has deliberately omitted a sermon for the Nativity of the Virgin because this story is known only from apocryphal sources, not from the Bible, and as Ælfric says, 'we will not write further concerning them lest we fall into any error'.[4] This apprehension of an unspecified error, coupled with a desire to uphold the canon of inspired scriptures as traditionally handed down, are key factors in Ælfric's stance on the question of acceptable versus unacceptable books, and they have contributed significantly to the portrayal of Ælfric in recent scholarship as a champion of patristic orthodoxy motivated by a firm allegiance to established ecclesiastical tradition.

I want to pick up where these discussions of Ælfric's attitude towards apocrypha have left off, and I want to redirect them to consider the factors that entered into Ælfric's thinking about the legitimacy, authenticity, and canonical authority of biblical literature in general with a particular emphasis on the Pauline epistles. On the face of it, this is not a set of issues that we might expect Ælfric to have become very exercised about since the debates over the formation of the biblical canon had been pretty much satisfactorily resolved centuries before Ælfric was born, and there were certainly very few questions left unanswered about the contents of the New Testament. But anyone who has investigated the history of the Bible in the Middle Ages will be aware that the transmission of the Bible, in Latin, in Greek, and in the medieval vernaculars, is not without its complications, and these complications extend to the content and arrangement of even the most familiar books of the Bible. This was true of the Bible in the age of Jerome, and it was still true in its own peculiar ways in pre-Conquest England. To consider how the decisions Ælfric makes in rejecting apocryphal texts relate to his criteria for accepting books of the New Testament, I will need to focus on a relatively narrow problem in Ælfric's reading of the Bible, but this relatively narrow problem has wider

---

[3] *Ælfric's Catholic Homilies, The Second Series: Text*, ed. Malcolm Godden, EETS ss 5 (London, 1979), p. 259, lines 119–23: 'Gif we mare secgað be ðisum symbeldæge þonne we on ðam halgum bocum rædað þe ðurh godes dihte gesette wæron. ðonne beo we ðam dwolmannum gelice. þe be heora agenum dihte oððe be swefnum fela lease gesetnyssa awriton'.
[4] *Ælfric's Catholic Homilies, The Second Series*, ed. Godden, p. 271, lines 5–6: 'we nellað be ðam na swiðor awritan þy læs ðe we on ænigum gedwylde befeallon'.

implications for the way Ælfric reads all of biblical and parabiblical literature.

The one piece of writing in which Ælfric sets down his thoughts concerning the contents and purpose of the entire Bible from beginning to end is his *Letter to Sigeweard* on the Old and New Testaments, an epistolary treatise written shortly after Ælfric arrived at Eynsham which one biblical scholar has called 'the most important treatment in English of the question of vernacular Scriptures before the Purvey tracts' of *c*. 1390.[5] To put this letter in context it will be helpful to recall that by the opening years of the eleventh century Ælfric had already translated the book of Joshua into English for Ealdorman Æthelweard,[6] and had either summarized or translated nearly a dozen other Old Testament books including Judges, I and II Kings, Daniel, Esther, Judith, I and II Maccabees, and substantial portions of Genesis, Numbers, and Job.[7] Now, partly in response to these translations, a layman named Sigeweard from Eastheolon,[8] who may be identifiable with one of the signatories to the foundation charter of Eynsham abbey,[9] had asked Ælfric to preach to him in his house and requested copies of Ælfric's writings, especially his biblical translations. In 1005 or 1006, Ælfric complied with Sigeweard's request by writing an epistolary essay that has come down to us in only one complete copy rubricated as the *Libellus de veteri testamento et novo*, although it is often simply referred to, as I will here, as the *Letter to Sigeweard*.[10] In it Ælfric summarizes the contents of the Bible, narrates the

[5] Geoffrey Shepherd, 'English Versions of the Scriptures before Wyclif', in *The Cambridge History of the Bible, Volume 2: The West from the Fathers to the Reformation*, ed. G. W. H. Lampe (Cambridge, 1969), pp. 362–87, at p. 375.

[6] As Ælfric himself informs us in his *Letter to Sigeweard*, ed. S. J. Crawford, *The Old English Version of the Heptateuch, Ælfric's Treatise on the Old and New Testament and his Preface to Genesis*, EETS os 160 (London, 1922; repr. with additions by N. R. Ker, 1969), p. 32, lines 405–7. Subsequent references to Ælfric's *Letter to Sigeweard* will be noted parenthetically within the text of this essay, keyed to line numbers in Crawford.

[7] The extent and nature of Ælfric's scriptural translations are most thoroughly and reliably examined by J. Raith, 'Ælfric's Share in the Old English Pentateuch', *Review of English Studies* ns 3 (1952), 305–14; Minnie Cate Morrell, *A Manual of Old English Biblical Materials* (Knoxville, TN, 1965), pp. 3–18; Richard Marsden, 'Ælfric as Translator: The Old English Prose *Genesis*', *Anglia* 109 (1991), 319–58; Marsden, 'Old Latin Intervention in the Old English *Heptateuch*', *ASE* 23 (1994), 229–64; Marsden, 'Translation by Committee? The "Anonymous" Text of the Old English Hexateuch', in *The Old English Hexateuch: Aspects and Approaches*, ed. Rebecca Barnhouse and Benjamin C. Withers (Kalamazoo, MI, 2000), pp. 41–89, at pp. 41–6 and 74; and Jonathan Wilcox, 'A Reluctant Translator in Late Anglo-Saxon England: Ælfric and Maccabees', *Proc. of the Medieval Association of the Midwest* 2 (1993), 1–18.

[8] On the probable identity of Eastheolon with the present-day village of Asthall, about eight miles from Eynsham, see Margaret Gelling, *The Place-Names of Oxfordshire*, 2 vols., English Place-Name Society 23–4 (Cambridge, 1953–54), II.299.

[9] P. H. Sawyer, *Anglo-Saxon Charters: An Annotated List and Bibliography*, Royal Historical Society Guides and Handbooks 8 (London, 1968), no. 911.

[10] Oxford, Bodleian Library, Laud Misc. 509 (s. xi$^{3/4}$ or xi$^2$), 120v–141v. A shorter, incomplete version which omits Ælfric's discussion of the New Testament survives in Oxford, Bodleian Library, Bodley 343 (s. xii$^2$), 129r–132r. There are also two partial witnesses in BL, Cotton Vitellius C. v (this part s. xi$^1$), 33r–35r (lines 1017–1153 only); and BL, Harley 3271 (s. xi$^1$), 125v–126r (lines 1227–61). See the useful discussion of this letter and its transmission by Jonathan Wilcox, *Ælfric's Prefaces*, Durham Medieval Texts 9 (Durham, 1994), pp. 37–44. Some brief remarks on the letter are given by Caroline Louisa White, *Ælfric: A New Study of his Life and*

principal events of the eight ages of the world, and shows how each Old
Testament patriarch and prophet foreshadowed, either by words or deeds,
the advent and mission of Christ. This letter has received very little
scholarly attention, in part I suspect because its approach to the organization and interpretation of the Bible has been perceived as so thoroughly
conventional (by early eleventh-century standards) that it reveals little of
Ælfric's own independent thought. The letter offers no original exegesis
and, as Michael Lapidge has remarked, its sole guiding purpose was
evidently to serve as 'a practical and straightforward introduction to the
various books of the Bible'.[11] There is, however, one point at which Ælfric
departs from this adherence to conventional wisdom to make a claim about
the contents of the Bible that is in stark conflict with the majority view
among the church fathers. This point comes when, in the process of
enumerating and commenting on the books of the New Testament, he
lists the epistles of St Paul and includes the apocryphal Epistle to the
Laodiceans among them, numbering it fifteenth, after Philemon:

> Paulus se apostol awrat manega pistolas, for þan þe Crist hine
> gesette eallum þeodum to lareowe, 7 on soþre eufæstnysse he gesette
> ða þeawas, ðe þa geleafullan folc on heora life healdað, þa þe hig
> sylfe gelogiað 7 heora lif for Gode. Fiftyne pistolas awrat se an
> apostol to þam leodscipum, þe he to geleafan gebigde; þa syndon
> micele bec on þære bibliothecan 7 þa fremiað us to ure rihtinge, gif
> we þæs leoda lareowes lare folgiað. He awrat to þam Romaniscum
> anne, to Corinthios ii., eac to Galathas anne, to Ephesios anne, to
> Philipenses anne, to Thesalonicenses twegen, to Colosenses anne,
> eac to Ebreos anne, 7 to his agenum discipulum Timotheum twegen,
> 7 Titum anne, to Philemonem anne, to Laodicenses anne; ealles
> fiftyne, swa hlude swa ðunor, geleafullum folcum. (lines 938–49)[12]

To those of us who are accustomed to thinking of Ælfric as the supreme
authority on biblical matters in the late Anglo-Saxon period, a man steeped
in tradition and bound to the principles of orthodoxy and ecclesiastical
custom, this passage may come as a surprise, and in discussing its implica-

---

*Writings* (London, 1898), pp. 66–7; Virginia Day, 'The Influence of the Catechetical *narratio* on
Old English and Some Other Medieval Literature', *ASE* 3 (1974), 51–61, at 57–8; and Paul
G. Remley, *Old English Biblical Verse: Studies in 'Genesis', 'Exodus' and 'Daniel'*, CSASE 16
(Cambridge, 1996), pp. 87–90 and 201–5. On the date of the letter's composition, see P. A. M.
Clemoes, 'The Chronology of Ælfric's Works', in *The Anglo-Saxons: Studies in Some Aspects of
their History and Culture Presented to Bruce Dickins*, ed. Peter Clemoes (London, 1959), pp. 212–
47, at p. 245, repr. in *Old English Prose: Basic Readings*, ed. Paul E. Szarmach (New York and
London, 2000), pp. 29–72, at p. 57.

[11] Michael Lapidge, *Anglo-Latin Literature 600–899* (London and Rio Grande, OH, 1996), p. 90.

[12] 'The apostle Paul wrote many epistles, for Christ appointed him to be a teacher of all peoples,
and in true righteousness he established the customs which the faithful observe in their life who
devote themselves and their life to God. This one apostle wrote fifteen epistles to the nations he
converted to the faith. These are great books in the Bible, and they will help us improve ourselves
if we follow the instruction of this teacher of nations. He wrote one to the Romans, two to the
Corinthians, also one to the Galatians, one to the Ephesians, one to the Philippians, two to the
Thessalonians, one to the Colossians, as well as one to the Hebrews, and two to his own disciple
Timothy, and one to Titus, one to Philemon, one to the Laodiceans – fifteen in all, as loud as
thunder to the faithful.'

tions for Ælfric's understanding of the constitution of the biblical canon, I should begin by commenting on the checkered career of this fifteenth Pauline epistle, which turns out to be important enough to the history of the Latin Bible that it is printed as an appendix to Weber's edition of the Vulgate, where its twenty verses take up just over half a page.[13] The epistle is so short, in fact, that it can be reproduced here in its entirety, in an English translation by J. K. Elliott, followed by some source notes that I will comment on momentarily:

> 1. Paul, an apostle not of men and not through man, but through Jesus Christ, to the brethren who are in Laodicea: 2. Grace to you and peace from God the Father and the Lord Jesus Christ. 3. I thank Christ in all my prayer that you continue in him and persevere in his works, in expectation of the promise at the day of judgement. 4. And may you not be deceived by the vain talk of some people who tell tales that they may lead you away from the truth of the gospel which is proclaimed by me. 5. And now may God grant that those who come from me for the furtherance of the truth of the gospel (. . .) may be able to serve and to do good works for the well-being of eternal life. 6. And now my bonds are manifest which I suffer in Christ, on account of which I am glad and rejoice. 7. This to me leads to eternal salvation, which itself is brought about through your prayers and by the help of the Holy Spirit, whether it be through life or through death. 8. For my life is in Christ and to die is joy. 9. And his mercy will work in you, that you may have the same love and be of one mind. 10. Therefore, beloved, as you have heard in my presence, so hold fast and work in the fear of God, and eternal life will be yours. 11. For it is God who works in you. 12. And do without hesitation what you do. 13. And for the rest, beloved, rejoice in Christ and beware of those who are out for sordid gain. 14. May all your requests be manifest before God, and be steadfast in the mind of Christ. 15. And do what is pure, true, proper, just and lovely. 16. And what you have heard and received, hold in your heart, and peace will be with you. 17. Salute all the brethren with the holy kiss. 18. The saints salute you. 19. The grace of the Lord Jesus Christ be with your spirit. 20. And see that (this epistle) is read to the Colossians and that of the Colossians to you.[14]

1 = Gal. I.1.    2 = Gal. I.3; Phil. I.2.    3 = Phil. I.3.    4 cf. Col. II.4; Gal. I.11.    5 cf. Phil. I.12.    6 = Phil. I.13, 18.    7 = Phil. I.19–20.    8 = Phil. I.21.    9 = Phil. II.2.    10 = Phil. II.12.    11 = Phil. II.13.    12 cf. Phil. II.14.    13 cf. Phil. III.1.    14 = Phil. IV.6; cf. I Cor. XV.58, II.16.    15 = Phil. IV.8.    16 = Phil. IV.9.    17 = I Thess. V.26.    18 = Phil. IV.22.    19 = Phil. IV.23; Gal. VI.18.    20 cf. Col. IV.16.

By far the shortest of the New Testament apocrypha, the Epistle to the Laodiceans was probably composed in the second or third century as an attempt to substantiate Paul's admonition toward the close of his epistle to

---

[13] *Biblia Sacra iuxta Vulgatam versionem*, ed. R. Weber *et al.*, 3rd ed. (Stuttgart, 1983), p. 1976.

[14] J. K. Elliott, *The Apocryphal New Testament: A Collection of Apocryphal Christian Literature in an English Translation* (Oxford, 1993), p. 546.

the Colossians that 'once this epistle has been read by you, have it read also in the church of the Laodiceans, and see to it that you also read the one to the Laodiceans' (Col. IV.16).[15] The letter's eventual acceptance as a canonical Pauline epistle by some medieval readers was thus encouraged by Paul himself, as well as by the fact that the language of this letter is lifted almost entirely from true Pauline epistles (especially Philippians), which lends to it an air of authenticity. I have attempted to indicate the extent of this debt to legitimate Pauline epistles in the source notes just above, which show that every single verse of this apocryphal epistle either repeats verbatim or adapts a verse from one of the true Pauline epistles. To an early reader of the Bible familiar with the language of the fourteen authentic Pauline epistles, then, Laodiceans would have read and sounded unmistakably like one of the divinely inspired writings of St Paul. It is evidently due both to the antiquity of the Epistle to the Laodiceans and to its stylistic similarity to real Pauline letters that this epistle is found in a large number of medieval bibles. The earliest surviving copies of the Epistle to the Laodiceans are preserved in Old Latin manuscripts of the New Testament, but over a hundred medieval Vulgate manuscripts transmit this letter as well, including the oldest extant copy of the Vulgate, the Codex Fuldensis, written for Victor of Capua in 546.[16]

These claims to authenticity notwithstanding, condemnations of the Epistle to the Laodiceans, or of an epistle by the same name, appear as early as the second or third century and continue throughout the Middle Ages. A Marcionite epistle to the Laodiceans was condemned in the Muratorian Fragment at the end of the second century,[17] and an epistle to the Laodiceans was likewise condemned at the Second Council of Nicea in 787.[18] Jerome was probably familiar with the same Latin Epistle to the Laodiceans that Ælfric knew, though he explains in his *De viris illustribus* that it is rejected by everyone he knows who has read it ('Legunt quidam et ad Laodicenses, sed ab omnibus exploditur').[19] Later writers, however, occasionally quote from Laodiceans and acknowledge it as a genuine

---

[15] Important editions and studies of the Epistle to the Laodiceans begin with R. Anger, *Über den Laodicenerbrief: Eine biblisch-kritische Untersuchung* (Leipzig, 1843); J. B. Lightfoot, *Saint Paul's Epistles to the Colossians and to Philemon: A Revised Text*, 7th ed. (London, 1884), pp. 274–300, who includes a critical edition of the Epistle on pp. 287–9; *Apocrypha IV: Die apokryphen Briefe des Paulus an die Laodicener und Korinther*, ed. A. von Harnack, 2nd ed., Kleine Texte für Vorlesungen und Übungen 12 (Berlin, 1931), pp. 2–6; F. Stegmüller, *Repertorium Biblicum Medii Aevi*, 11 vols. (Madrid, 1950–80), I.214–15 (no. 233); A. von Harnack, *Marcion. Das Evangelium vom fremden Gott: Eine Monographie zur Geschichte der Grundlegung der katholischen Kirche: Neue Studien zu Marcion*, 2nd ed., Texte und Untersuchung zur Geschichte der altchristlichen Literatur 44.4 (Leipzig, 1924; repr. Darmstadt, 1996), pp. 134*–49*; E. Hennecke, *New Testament Apocrypha*, ed. W. Schneemelcher, English translation ed. R. McL. Wilson, revised ed., 2 vols. (Cambridge, 1991), II.42–6; and Elliott, *The Apocryphal New Testament*, pp. 543–6, who provides additional bibliography.

[16] B. M. Metzger, *The Canon of the New Testament: Its Origin, Development, and Significance* (Oxford, 1987), p. 239.

[17] Hennecke, *New Testament Apocrypha* I.36; G. M. Hahneman, *The Muratorian Fragment and the Development of the Canon* (Oxford, 1992), pp. 196–200.

[18] Lightfoot, *Saint Paul's Epistles*, p. 787.

[19] *Hieronymus de viris inlustribus*, ed. E. C. Richardson, Texte und Untersuchung zur Geschichte der altchristlichen Literatur 14.1 (Leipzig, 1896), p. 11, lines 4–5 (ch. 4).

Pauline composition. In the late fourth and early fifth centuries, it was included in the reading of the Priscillianist circles in Spain,[20] and it is quoted in the fifth- or sixth-century pseudo-Augustinian *Liber de divinis scripturis*.[21] Haymo of Auxerre deemed this epistle to have some use even though he thought it should be excluded from the canon ('in canone non habeatur, aliquid tamen utilitatis habet').[22] And in the twelfth century, John of Salisbury likewise accepted Laodiceans as a legitimate work of Paul.[23] During the thirteenth and fourteenth centuries, vernacular translations of the Epistle to the Laodiceans were incorporated into Albigensian, Bohemian, and Flemish versions of the Bible, and English translations began appearing in the fifteenth century.[24] Although today the Epistle to the Laodiceans tends to be dismissed by biblical scholars as a 'tendentious fabrication'[25] and a 'vacuous forgery',[26] it clearly achieved a wide enough circulation in Old Latin, Vulgate, and vernacular versions of the Bible to convince many medieval readers that it was genuine.

It is also clear that several copies of the Epistle to the Laodiceans were in circulation in the British Isles before and during Ælfric's lifetime. Two centuries before Ælfric composed his *Letter to Sigeweard*, the Epistle to the Laodiceans was copied into the Book of Armagh (Dublin, Trinity College Library, 52, datable to *c.* 807), which is the only complete extant Old Latin version of the Pauline epistles. The Armagh copy of Laodiceans is among the earliest known and is prefaced by the caveat 'incipit aepistola ad laudicenses sed hirunimus eam negat esse pauli' (recalling Jerome's dismissal of it in the *De viris illustribus*).[27] A second copy of Laodiceans

---

[20] E. C. Babut, *Priscillien et le priscillianisme*, Bibliothèque de l'École des Hautes Études, Sciences Historiques et Philologiques 169 (Paris, 1909), pp. 231–40. B. Vollmann summarizes evidence for knowledge of the apocryphal texts read and authored by the Priscillianist circle in his article 'Priscillianus' in *Paulys Realencyclopädie der klassischen Altertumswissenschaft*, ed. G. Wissowa *et al.*, 34 vols. with 15 supplements (Stuttgart and Munich, 1894–1972), Supplementband XIV, cols. 527–36. In his treatise *De apocryphis*, Priscillian endorses the canonicity of the Epistle to the Laodiceans by insisting that this epistle must be authentic since the apostle Paul enjoined the Colossian church to read it: *Priscilliani quae supersunt*, ed. G. Schepss, CSEL 18 (Vienna, 1889), p. 55, lines 12–22.

[21] *S. Aureli Augustini Hipponensis Episcopi liber qui appellatur speculum et liber de divinis scripturis sive speculum quod fertur s. Augustini*, ed. F. Weihrich, CSEL 12 (Vienna, 1887), p. 516, lines 16–18.

[22] Haymo, *In Epistolam ad Colossenses* iv (PL 117, col. 765A).

[23] John of Salisbury, *Ep.* cxliii (PL 199, col. 126C). This letter was composed *c.* 1165.

[24] Vernacular translations of the Epistle to the Laodiceans are surveyed by Anger, *Über den Laodicenerbrief*, pp. 66–166; and Lightfoot, *Saint Paul's Epistles*, pp. 297–300.

[25] D. N. Penny, 'The Pseudo-Pauline Letters of the First Two Centuries' (unpubl. Ph.D. dissertation, Yale Divinity School, 1979), p. 321.

[26] D. G. Meade, *Pseudonymity and Canon: An Investigation into the Relationship of Authorship and Authority in Jewish and Earliest Christian Tradition*, Wissenschaftliche Untersuchungen zum Neuen Testament 39 (Tübingen, 1986), p. 159. R. Bauckham, 'Pseudo-Apostolic Letters', *Journal of Biblical Literature* 107 (1988), 469–94, captures the thrust of much modern criticism of the Epistle to the Laodiceans when he writes that Laodiceans 'is nothing but a patchwork of Pauline sentences and phrases from other letters, mainly Philippians. The result is a series of highly generalized exhortations which address no particular situation and reveal no intention by the author to communicate any clear message. It seems as though he may really have been motivated only by the desire to produce something that would look as though Paul could have written it' (p. 485).

[27] *Liber Ardmachanus: The Book of Armagh*, ed. J. Gwynn (Dublin, 1913), p. 271. Laodiceans

appears in the so-called 'Royal Bible' (BL, Royal 1. E. VII + VIII), a two-volume bible produced in southern England toward the end of the tenth century, during Ælfric's lifetime.[28] This deluxe bible is, apart from the Codex Amiatinus, the most complete bible surviving from Anglo-Saxon England, and it is also the earliest bible of any origin or provenance in which the Epistle to the Laodiceans is capitulated – that is, divided into chapters consisting of just a few sentences each – a sign that the text has undergone editorial scrutiny. (The text of the Epistle to the Laodiceans from the 'Royal Bible' is reproduced in the Appendix to this essay.) Two other English bibles of the late eleventh and early twelfth century also include copies of Laodiceans among the Pauline epistles, in each case placing it immediately after Hebrews. These are the two-volume 'Gundulf Bible' (San Marino, California, Huntington Library, HM 62), copied in the late eleventh century by a Norman scribe working at Rochester or Canterbury;[29] and the New Testament portion of a multi-volume Vulgate (Baltimore, Maryland, Walters Art Gallery, 18), produced at either Christ Church, Canterbury, or Rochester during the first half of the twelfth century.[30] At least one other pre-twelfth-century English Bible may have originally included a copy of the Epistle to the Laodiceans as well, though nothing of the text remains. In his catalogue of the manuscripts in Trinity

---

follows Colossians. For a detailed description of the manuscript's contents, see M. L. Colker, *Trinity College Library Dublin: Descriptive Catalogue of the Mediaeval and Renaissance Latin Manuscripts*, 2 vols. (Dublin, 1991), I.93–7.

[28] On the contents, date, and provenance of the 'Royal Bible', with a detailed analysis of the Old Testament portion, see Richard Marsden, 'The Old Testament in Late Anglo-Saxon England: Preliminary Observations on the Textual Evidence', in *The Early Medieval Bible: Its Production, Decoration and Use*, ed. Richard Gameson, Cambridge Studies in Palaeography and Codicology (Cambridge, 1994), pp. 101–24, at pp. 109–19; see also Marsden, *The Text of the Old Testament in Anglo-Saxon England*, CSASE 15 (Cambridge, 1995), pp. 321–78; and Marsden, ' "Ask What I am Called": The Anglo-Saxons and their Bibles', in *The Bible as Book: The Manuscript Tradition*, ed. J. L. Sharpe III and K. Van Kampen (London, 1998), pp. 145–76, at p. 160. Laodiceans appears in Vol. 2 (Royal I. E. VIII), 198r, following Hebrews (see the Appendix below). D. N. Dumville, 'On the Dating of Some Late Anglo-Saxon Liturgical Manuscripts', *Transactions of the Cambridge Bibliographical Society* 10 (1991), 40–57, at 47–8, classifies the main script as Style-I Anglo-Caroline minuscule of the late tenth century. The bible's twelfth-century corrections and revisions are briefly commented on by Teresa Webber, 'Script and Manuscript Production at Christ Church, Canterbury, after the Norman Conquest', in *Canterbury and the Norman Conquest: Churches, Saints and Scholars 1066–1109*, ed. R. Eales and Richard Sharpe (London and Rio Grande, OH, 1995), pp. 145–58, at 155–6.

[29] Seymour De Ricci and W. J. Wilson, *Census of Medieval and Renaissance Manuscripts in the United States and Canada*, 2 vols. (New York, 1935–7; repr. 1961), I.48; Helmut Gneuss, *Handlist of Anglo-Saxon Manuscripts: A List of Manuscripts and Manuscript Fragments Written or Owned in England up to 1100*, MRTS 241 (Tempe, AZ, 2001), p. 143 (no. 934); Richard Gameson, *The Manuscripts of Norman England (c. 1066–1130)* (Oxford, 1999), nos. 899 and 900.

[30] De Ricci and Wilson, *Census of Medieval and Renaissance Manuscripts* I.760; Gameson, *The Manuscripts of Norman England*, no. 7. This manuscript is a companion volume to BL, Royal I. C. VII. I have had difficulty confirming the claims of Mary P. Richards, *Texts and their Traditions in the Medieval Library of Rochester Cathedral Priory*, Transactions of the American Philosophical Society 78.3 (Philadelphia, PA, 1988), pp. 61–84, especially at pp. 63–5 and 80–3, that these two bibles and the 'Royal Bible' all make use of a distinctive Franco-Saxon text type that was imported from Saint-Germain-des-Prés to Canterbury during the Benedictine Reform in the late tenth century. For a similar statement, see Richards, 'A Decorated Vulgate Set from 12th-Century Rochester, England', *Journal of the Walters Art Gallery* 39 (1981), 59–67, at 64.

College, Cambridge, M. R. James observed that the late eleventh-century bible in Trinity College B. 5. 2 (148), from Lincoln, 'must have contained the Epistle to the Laodiceans' since an explicit following the Epistle to the Hebrews identifies Hebrews as the *fifteenth* Pauline epistle.[31]

At certain points in the ninth, tenth, eleventh, and early twelfth centuries, therefore, there were bibles and part-bibles in Ireland and England that included Laodiceans among the epistles of Paul. Yet even if Ælfric gained access to such a manuscript and read the epistle himself, as his comment in the *Letter to Sigeweard* seems to indicate, his conviction that it was a legitimate Pauline epistle is difficult to understand. How can it be that the Ælfric who casts doubt on the most widely read apocrypha in tenth- and early eleventh-century England accepts as canonical a work that had been denounced by Jerome and conciliar legislation? And how are we to reconcile Ælfric's acceptance of Laodiceans here in the *Letter to Sigeweard* with the suspicion he voices elsewhere about works that have false or dubious claims for being included in scripture?

The answer, I think, has partly to do with numbers. Toward the end of the *Letter to Sigeweard*, at the conclusion of his survey of the contents of the Old and New Testaments, Ælfric makes a point of emphasizing that the Bible contains seventy-two books, the same number as there were of nations and languages dispersed at the Tower of Babel, and the same as the number of disciples sent forth by Christ to preach to the world (Luke X.1, 17):

> Twa 7 hundseofontig boca sind on bibliothecan, for þan þe hig sume sind tosette on twa for heora langnysse on geleafulre ciricean: þæt mæg sceawian þe ða gesetnisse cann. 7 swa fela þeoda wurdon todælede æt þære wundorlican byrig, þe þa entas woldon wircean mid gebeote æfter Noes flode, ær þan ðe hi toferdon. And swa fela leorningcnihta asende ure Hælend mancinne to bodienne þæra boca lare mid þam cristendome, þe þa com on þas woruld þurh ðone Hælend sylfne 7 þurh his bydelas. Syndon swa þeah gesette oðre bec ðurh halige lareowas, þe man hæfð wide gehwær on cristendome Criste to lofe. (lines 1176–84)[32]

---

[31] M. R. James, *The Western Manuscripts in the Library of Trinity College, Cambridge: A Descriptive Catalogue*, 4 vols. (Cambridge, 1900–4), I.186. This manuscript is the second volume of the part bible preserved in Lincoln, Cathedral Library, 1 (A. 1. 2) (Lincoln, s. xi[ex] or xi/xii), containing Genesis through Job; see R. M. Thomson, *Catalogue of the Manuscripts of Lincoln Cathedral Chapter Library* (Cambridge, 1989), p. 3. I have not been able to substantiate M. R. James's remark in *The Apocryphal New Testament* (Oxford, 1924), p. 478, that the Epistle to the Laodiceans 'is commoner in English MSS. than in others', save through the supporting claim of B. Carra de Vaux, 'L'Épitre aux Laodicéens en Arabe', *Revue Biblique* 5 (1896), 221–6, at 221–2, that Laodiceans survives 'surtout dans les Bibles latines et anglaises, entre le sixième et le quinzième siécle'. B. F. Westcott, *The Bible in the Church: A Popular Account of the Collection and Reception of the Holy Scriptures in the Christian Churches* (London, 1913), pp. 209–10, similarly states that '[i]n England and France it [the Epistle to the Laodiceans] seems to have been especially popular', though he offers nothing to back this up. Other medieval bibles that include Laodiceans are noted by S. Berger, *Histoire de la Vulgate pendant les premiers siècles du moyen âge* (Paris, 1893; repr. New York, 1958), pp. 16, 23, 99, 127, and 341–2; E. Jacquier, *Le Nouveau Testament dans l'église chrétienne*, 2 vols. (Paris, 1911–13), I.345–51; and H. J. Frede, *Altlateinische Paulus-Handschriften*, Vetus Latina: Die Reste der altlateinische Bibel 4 (Freiburg, 1964), pp. 51, 159 and 169.

[32] 'There are seventy-two books in the Bible (for some are divided into two parts in the orthodox

In enforcing this parallel between the number of biblical books and the number of nations and disciples, Ælfric is making use of an idea he has already raised earlier in the *Letter to Sigeweard*. The number of nations and languages at Babel is a detail he mentions first in his synopsis of the book of Genesis:

> Nu segð us seo boc be Noes ofspringe, þæt his suna gestrindon twa 7 hundseofontig suna; þa gebunnon to wircenne þa wundorlican burh 7 þone heagan stipel, þe sceolde astigan upp to heofenum, be heora unræde; ac God silf com þærto 7 sceawode heora weorc 7 sealde heora ælcum synderlice spræce, þæt heora ælcum wæs uncuð hwæt oþer sæde, 7 hi swa geswicon sona þære getimbrunge, 7 hi ða toferdon to fyrlenum lande on swa manegum gereordum swa þæra manna wæs. (lines 212–27)[33]

The number of Christ's disciples is also mentioned earlier in the *Letter to Sigeweard* in Ælfric's discussion of the contents of the four Gospels, where after naming the twelve apostles he remarks that 'Æfter þisum he geceas twa 7 hundseofonti to his lareowdome him to leorningcnihtum, þa he tosende geond eall to ælcere birig þider þe he towerd wæs, þæt mann wiste his cyme . . .' (lines 906–9).[34] The passage toward the end of the *Letter to Sigeweard* which pulls these ideas together is thus meant to stress the correspondence of narrative details from both the Old and New Testaments with a numerical principle that governs the size of the biblical canon. The seventy-two peoples and languages from the Old Testament corresponds to the seventy-two disciples from the New Testament, which in turn corresponds to the seventy-two books of the Bible.

This numerical formula equating the number of books, nations, languages, and disciples was of course very popular in the early Middle Ages, and it is paralleled in several other Old English texts, including the prose *Solomon and Saturn* dialogue,[35] the poem known as *Lord's Prayer*

---

churches on account of their length; anyone who knows their arrangement will observe this). And the same number of nations came to be divided at the magnificent city which the giants boastingly planned to build after Noah's flood until they were dispersed. And our Lord sent the same number of disciples to proclaim to mankind the teaching of these books throughout Christendom, which came to the world through the Lord himself and through his messengers. However, other books have been composed by holy teachers which have been distributed everywhere throughout Christendom to the glory of Christ.' Elsewhere, in the opening of his homily for the Assumption of the Virgin (*CH* I.30), Ælfric explains that the Bible as he knew it was made up of the seventy-two books translated by Jerome from Hebrew and Greek into Latin: 'twa 7 hundseofontig boca þære ealdan æ 7 þære niwan he [Jerome] awende on leden to anre bibliothecan' (*Ælfric's Catholic Homilies, The First Series: Text*, ed. Peter Clemoes, EETS ss 17 (Oxford, 1997), p. 429, lines 13–14). On Ælfric's use of the term *bibliotheca*, see n. 42 below.

[33] 'Now the book tells us concerning Noah's descendants that his sons begat seventy-two sons, who started building that wonderful city and high tower which in their foolishness they expected to reach up to heaven. But God himself came there and beheld their work and gave every one of them a different language, so that they could not understand what each other said, and they immediately ceased construction, and they then scattered to distant lands with as many languages as there were men.'

[34] 'After these he chose seventy-two to instruct as his disciples, whom he sent forth to each town that he wished to visit, so that his coming should be known.'

[35] *The Prose 'Solomon and Saturn' and 'Adrian and Ritheus'*, ed. James E. Cross and Thomas D. Hill,

*II*,[36] an Old English gloss to an *adiuratio* formula for trial by fire in the tenth-century 'Durham Collectar',[37] the entry on St Jerome in the list of relics donated to Exeter by King Athelstan,[38] and several anonymous homilies,[39] as well as a number of additional examples by a variety of patristic and medieval authors.[40] Just as earlier exegetes had justified the canonicity of four and only four gospels by associating each of the four evangelists with one of the four beasts in Ezechiel's vision (an association which Ælfric himself makes in lines 882–90 of the *Letter to Sigeweard*),[41] so Ælfric's enumeration of seventy-two books, nations, languages, and disciples rests on the assumption that the number of books in the Bible is typologically determined by a set of internal criteria and is not open to negotiation. This method of typological determinism, linking Old Testament figures and events with their New Testament parallels to show how certain biblical texts anticipate and fulfil and thereby confirm others, is in fact the governing interpretive mode of the *Letter to Sigeweard*. Throughout this letter, as Ælfric summarizes the important stories in each book of

---

McMaster Old English Studies and Texts 1 (Toronto, 1982), pp. 34 and 123–4 (*SS* 59); cf. pp. 28 and 74–5 (*SS* 14).

[36] *The Lord's Prayer II*, ed. Elliott van Kirk Dobbie, *The Anglo-Saxon Minor Poems*, ASPR 6 (New York, 1942), p. 71, lines 20–1.

[37] *Die Gesetze der Angelsachsen*, ed. F. Liebermann, 3 vols. (Halle, 1903–16; repr. 1960), I.411 (no. V.1, Latin text and OE gloss); *The Durham Collectar*, ed. Alicia Corrêa, HBS 107 (London, 1992), p. 225 (Latin text only).

[38] Max Förster, *Zur Geschichte des Reliquienkultus in Altengland*, Sitzungsberichte der Bayerischen Akademie der Wissenschaften, Phil.-hist. Abteilung 8 (Munich, 1943), p. 76, lines 152–5.

[39] E.g. pseudo-Wulfstan Homily XLIII, ed. Arthur Napier, *Wulfstan. Sammlung der ihm zugechriebenen Homilien nebst Untersuchung über ihre Echtheit*, Sammlung englischer Denkmäler 4 (Berlin, 1883; repr. with a supplement by Klaus Ostheeren, Dublin, 1967), p. 214, line 30. Other examples are noted in the two articles by Hans Sauer cited in the following note.

[40] Examples from the writings of Augustine, Isidore, Alcuin, Hrabanus Maurus, Honorius Augustodunensis and others are assembled by W. Haubrichs, *Ordo als Form: Strukturstudien zur Zahlenkomposition bei Otfrid von Weißenburg und in karolingischer Literatur*, Hermaea: Germanistische Forschungen, Neue Folge 27 (Tübingen, 1969), pp. 98–9; H. Meyer, *Die Zahlenallegorese im Mittelalter: Methode und Gebrauch*, Münstersche Mittelalter-Schriften 25 (Munich, 1975), pp. 98 and 168; H. Meyer and R. Suntrup, *Lexikon der mittelalterlichen Zahlenbedeutungen*, Münstersche Mittelalter-Schriften 56 (Munich, 1987), col. 761; and Charles D. Wright and Richard Marsden in *Collectanea Pseudo-Bedae*, ed. Martha Bayless and Michael Lapidge, Scriptores Latini Hiberniae 14 (Dublin, 1998), p. 214 (note to no. 62). Marguerite-Marie Dubois, *Ælfric: Sermonnaire, docteur et grammarien* (Paris, 1943), p. 91, once proposed that Ælfric based his enumeration of the books of the Bible on a specific passage in Isidore, *De vetere et novo testamento questiones* (PL 83, col. 155), but this idea was of course widely available, as Haubrichs and others make clear. The closely allied tradition concerning the number of languages and peoples in the world is surveyed by H. J. Weigand, 'The Two and Seventy Languages of the World', *Germanic Review* 17 (1942), 241–60; Hans Sauer, 'Die 72 Völker und Sprachen der Welt: Ein mittelalterlicher Topos in der englischen Literatur', *Anglia* 101 (1983), 29–48; Sauer, 'Die 72 Völker und Sprachen der Welt: Einige Ergänzungen', *Anglia* 107 (1989), 61–4; and Marijane Osborn, 'The Seventy-Two Gentile Nations and the Theme of the Franks Casket', *NM* 92 (1991), 281–8. The total of seventy-two candles lit and extinguished during Nocturns and Lauds on Maundy Thursday, Good Friday, and Holy Saturday within the Divine Office are said to signify either the number of biblical books or the number of human languages in the ninth-century Amalarian liturgical commentary (a work evidently known to Ælfric) recently recovered by Christopher A. Jones, ed. and trans., *A Lost Work by Amalarius of Metz: Interpolations in Salisbury, Cathedral Library, MS. 154*, HBS Subsidia 2 (London, 2001), pp. 190 and 236 (§ 3.2.8).

[41] The analogy goes back to Irenaeus: see Metzger, *The Canon of the New Testament*, p. 263.

the Bible, he persistently identifies Old Testament types that find their ultimate meaning in the New Testament, usually in the life of Christ. Adam's creation on the sixth day, for instance, betokens the advent of Christ in the sixth age of the world (lines 166–71). Eve, who was created out of Adam's side, represents God's church, which emerged from Christ's side when the mingled blood and water poured forth from the wound in his side as he hung on the cross (lines 171–6). The slaughter of Abel by Cain signifies the death of Christ at the hands of the Jews, our wicked brothers (lines 176–9). Adam's third son, Seth, whose name means 'seed', a symbol of rebirth, represents Christ's resurrection from death on the third day (lines 180–3). Noah, who was preserved from the flood when he entered the ark and whose name means 'rest' (*requies*), is another type of Christ, who has rescued us from the stormy billows of the ocean of this world and invites us to seek eternal rest in him (lines 195–203). Joshua leading the Israelites into the promised land likewise anticipates Christ, who will lead us all into the kingdom of heaven if we believe in him and do good works (lines 414–21). David's triumph over the giant Goliath anticipates Christ's ultimate defeat of Satan (lines 476–83), and so forth. These and other instances of typological anticipation and fulfilment invoked by Ælfric affirm the organic interrelatedness of biblical narratives spanning the two testaments, and the correspondences he asserts and reasserts between the seventy-two nations, languages, disciples, and books operate in an identical manner to demonstrate the fundamental unity and consistency of the Bible, a masterfully organized work whose every detail is in its right place.[42]

The chief complication for this argument Ælfric raises concerning the typologically based numerical integrity of the canon is that several patristic authorities known to him accept only seventy-one books in the Bible. In his famous discussion of the biblical canon in Book 2 of *De doctrina christiana*, Augustine enumerates forty-four books of the Old Testament and twenty-seven books of the New Testament (including only fourteen Pauline epistles), yielding a total of seventy-one.[43] This is the same number and

---

[42] This view of the Bible is reinforced by Ælfric's repeated use in the *Letter to Sigeweard* (lines 448, 486, 503, 931, 943, 1014 and 1018) of the Latin loan *bibliotheca* to refer to the Bible, a term that promotes the concept of the Bible as a complete, self-contained library. On medieval use of the term *bibliotheca* to denote a unified collection of sacred scriptures, see A. Mundó, '"Bibliotheca": Bible et lecture du Carême d'après saint Benoît', *Revue Bénédictine* 60 (1950), 65–92, especially 71–8; M. Duchet-Suchaux and Y. Lefèvre, 'Les noms de la Bible', in *Le Moyen Age et la Bible*, ed. P. Riché and G. Lobrichon, Bible de tous les temps 4 (Paris, 1984), pp. 13–23, at 13–15; *Dictionary of Old English*, fasc. *B*, ed. Antonette diPaolo Healey *et al.* (Toronto, 1991), s.v. *bibliopece, bibliopeca*. Ælfric's use of this term as a synonym for the Bible is remarked by O. H. Funke, *Die gelehrten lateinischen Lehn- und Fremdwörter in der altenglischen Literatur von der Mitte des X. Jahrhunderts bis um das Jahr 1066* (Halle, 1914), pp. 81–2, 110, 115, 151 and 168; and E. G. Stanley, 'Ælfric on the Canonicity of the Book of Judith: "hit stent on leden þus on ðære bibliothecan"', *Notes and Queries* ns 32 (1985), 439. The term is similarly employed by Byrhtferth of Ramsey, who refers to Genesis as 'liber primus bibliothece': *Byrhtferth's Enchiridion*, ed. Peter S. Baker and Michael Lapidge, EETS ss 15 (Oxford, 1995), p. 8 (i.I.82–3); cf. Michael Lapidge, *Anglo-Latin Literature 900–1066* (London and Rio Grande, OH, 1993), p. 128.

[43] Augustine, *De doctrina christiana* II.8 (13), ed. J. Martin, CCSL 32 (Turnhout, 1962), pp. 39–40. See C. J. Costello, *St. Augustine's Doctrine on the Inspiration and Canonicity of Scripture*

selection of books approved by the Council of Hippo in 393 and the Third Council of Carthage in 397, the same promulgated in the Pseudo-Gelasian Decree (which Ælfric knew through a copy in the Boulogne manuscript), and the same number and order adopted by Cassiodorus in the *Institutes* and by Isidore in the *Etymologies*.[44] For anyone in the Christian Latin West who took the trouble to count the books in the Bible as they had been inventoried by Augustine, Cassiodorus, and Isidore, the correct number of books was seventy-one, not seventy-two. I think Ælfric was more than capable of counting, but I think he was more strongly persuaded by the symbolism of the number seventy-two than he was by the less interesting number seventy-one, and I think his commitment to the idea that the Bible must contain seventy-two books had an influence on his decision to add Laodiceans to the list of canonical Pauline epistles. In the terms of simple biblical math, the received Augustinian canon of seventy-one books plus Laodiceans equals the typologically satisfying number of seventy-two.

There are difficulties with this explanation, however. One is that, in spite of his insistence that there are seventy-two books in the Bible, the books Ælfric actually names in his inventory do not add up to seventy-two. In the *Letter to Sigeweard*, as Ælfric walks us through the contents of the Bible, he is careful to tell us which books make up certain numbered groups such as the five books of the Pentateuch, the four books of kings, the twelve minor prophets, the three books of wisdom written by Solomon, the four gospels, and the seven catholic and fifteen Pauline epistles. But he does not give us a book-by-book accounting of the entire Bible. Instead his main interest lies in the principal figures and events whose stories are told in these books, all mapped onto the chronological framework of the eight ages of the world from creation to eternity. The books themselves come in and out of focus as Ælfric moves from story to story, and his preoccupation with the stories rather than the books helps explain why in discussing the Old Testament he mentions only forty-two books by name, omitting Lamentations, and counting I and II Chronicles as a single book. So even though Ælfric is quite specific about the overall number of books in the Bible, he makes little effort to show that the books in his survey add up to that number.

An additional complication is that an author whom Ælfric knew well had his own method for symbolically determining the correct number of Pauline epistles, and that number is not fifteen but fourteen. In Book 35 of the *Moralia in Job*, Gregory the Great explains that there is a reason why the

---

(Washington, DC, 1930), p. 48. There is a good chance Ælfric knew this passage: for a brief parallel between *De doctrina christiana* II.xxix.9–13 and Ælfric's sermon for St Bartholomew's day (*CH* I.31), see Godden, *Ælfric's Catholic Homilies: Introduction, Commentary and Glossary*, p. 266.

[44] Cassiodorus, *Institutiones* I.13, ed. R. A. B. Mynors (Oxford, 1937; repr. 1963), pp. 38–9; Isidore, *Etymologiae* VI.ii.34–50, ed. W. M. Lindsay (Oxford, 1911). On the conciliar pronouncements regarding the size of the biblical canon, see F. F. Bruce, 'Tradition and the Canon of Scripture', in *The Authoritative Word: Essays on the Nature of Scripture*, ed. D. K. McKim (Grand Rapids, MI, 1983), pp. 59–84, at pp. 66–7. For the copy of the Pseudo-Gelasian Decree in Boulogne-sur-Mer, Bibliothèque municipale, 63 (England, s. xi¹), 26r–29r, and its connection with Ælfric, see Enid M. Raynes, 'MS. Boulogne-sur-Mer 63 and Ælfric', *MÆ* 26 (1957), 65–73, at 71.

church accepts fourteen and only fourteen Pauline epistles, and that is that the number fourteen denotes the mystical perfection of the church since it is the sum of the number of gospels and commandments. This argument falls right in line with the general trend of numerical symbolism which we find throughout Gregory's writings, where special significance is often assigned to the numbers four and ten, which can be added or multiplied to yield the biblically significant numbers fourteen and forty. In his sixteenth Gospel homily, for instance, Gregory explains that the period of Lent is forty days long because in the Lenten fast the ten commandments are fulfilled by the four gospels; one simply has to multiply one by the other to realize their combined application to Lent.[45] If the equation Gregory developed in Book 35 of the *Moralia* to justify the number of Pauline epistles were this clear and straightforward, it probably would have served as a powerful deterrent to any attempt to extend the canon of Pauline epistles beyond fourteen. The problem is that, in the process of explicating this bit of sacred arithmetic, Gregory admits that in actuality the apostle Paul did write a total of fifteen epistles; it's just that we only accept fourteen of them:

> Et recte uita sanctae Ecclesiae permultiplicata decem et quattuor computatur, quia utrumque testamentum custodiens, et tam secun-dum legis decalogum, quam secundum quattuor euangelii libros uiuens, usque ad perfectionis culmen extenditur. Vnde et Paulus apostolus quamuis epistolas quindecim scripserit, sancta tamen Ecclesia non amplius quam quattuordecim tenet, ut ex ipso episto-larum numero ostenderet quod doctor egregius legis et euangelii secreta rimasset.[46]

The effect of this passage from Gregory is that it gives licence to more than one way of counting Paul's letters, and sure enough, later readers of the *Moralia* took it either way depending on their preference. One twelfth-century biblical commentator named Hervé of Bourg-Dieu (d. 1149) in his commentary on Colossians quotes Gregory's explanation of the mystical perfection of the number fourteen and uses it to condemn Laodiceans as a non-canonical epistle.[47] Yet Gregory's unmistakable assertion that Paul wrote *fifteen* epistles in all can just as easily be taken as an implicit endorsement of the authenticity of Laodiceans, even though he does not

---

[45] *Gregorius Magnus. Homiliae in Evangelia*, ed. R. Étaix, CCSL 141 (Turnhout, 1999), p. 113, lines 87–9: 'Cur ergo in abstinentia quadragenarius numerus custoditur, nisi quia uirtus decalogi per libros quatuor sancti euangelii impletur?' On similar instances of numerical symbolism in Gregory's writings, see G. R. Evans, *The Thought of Gregory the Great* (Cambridge, 1986), p. 10.

[46] Gregory, *Moralia in Iob* XXXV.xx.48, ed. M. Adriaen, *S. Gregorii Magni Moralia in Iob Libri XXIII–XXXV*, CCSL 143B (Turnhout, 1985), p. 1808, lines 16–24. 'And truly the life of the holy church can be reckoned by adding ten and four, each number from a different testament, one from the decalogue of the law and one from the four books of the living gospel, the sum of which is indicative of perfection. Thus even though the apostle Paul wrote fifteen epistles, the holy church has received no more than fourteen, so that through this number of epistles that illustrious teacher revealed the secrets of both the law and the gospel.'

[47] Hervé of Bourg-Dieu, *In Epistolam ad Colossenses* iv (PL 181, cols. 1354–5). On the career of this little-known biblical commentator, see G. Oury, 'Hervé de Bourg-Dieu', in *Dictionnaire de Spiritualité*, ed. M. Viller *et al.*, 17 vols. (Paris, 1937–95), VII.1, cols. 373–7.

name Laodiceans as the mysterious fifteenth epistle written by Paul but not accepted by the church.[48] I think I know how Ælfric would have been inclined to read this passage, and I will add that this passage was certainly known to Ælfric since he adapted portions of the same chapter for his sermon on Job in the second series of *Catholic Homilies* (*CH* II.30).[49]

This brings us to a point where I can at least say what I think the main issues are in Ælfric's acceptance of Laodiceans as a canonical Pauline epistle and in how his view of Laodiceans relates to the larger question of his understanding of how one distinguishes between acceptable and unacceptable books. To begin with, I think Ælfric had access to a bible that included Laodiceans among the Pauline epistles. I think he read this epistle and recognized in it its pervasively Pauline diction, and on these grounds I think he embraced it as an authentic Pauline composition. We have no way of knowing how many copies of the New Testament Ælfric owned or consulted during his lifetime, but his acceptance of Laodiceans as canonical would make most sense if this epistle appeared in every New Testament Ælfric ever knew, or at least the ones he paid close attention to, including the one or ones he came into contact with while studying under Æthelwold at Winchester. I cannot imagine Ælfric naming this epistle among Paul's letters and twice emphasizing that Paul wrote *fifteen* letters ('as loud as thunder to the faithful') unless Laodiceans was part of the Bible as he had come to know it over a long period of time, probably in multiple bibles, and probably in the bibles he read at Winchester and at Cerne and at Eynsham. A lifetime of reading bibles that included Laodiceans would have given Ælfric reason to ignore the patristically sanctioned enumeration of twenty-seven New Testament books with only fourteen Pauline epistles. This is not to say, however, that the bibles in which Ælfric read the Epistle to the Laodiceans would necessarily have shielded him from the vagaries of this epistle's erratic reception history. The copy in the 'Royal Bible', which is the closest thing we have to a bible surviving from late tenth-century Ælfrician England, is preceded by two traditional prefaces to the Pauline epistles, one of which announces twice that Paul wrote fourteen and only fourteen epistles, even though in listing those epistles by name it then proceeds to identify Laodiceans as the fifteenth and final Pauline epistle, right after Hebrews.[50] If Ælfric's bible included a similar set of prefatory materials

---

[48] As Bishop Lightfoot remarks, even though Gregory 'does not mention the Epistle to the Laodiceans by name, there can be little doubt that he intended to include this as his fifteenth epistle, and that his words were rightly understood by subsequent writers as affirming its Pauline authorship' (*Saint Paul's Epistles*, p. 295).

[49] Godden, *Ælfric's Catholic Homilies: Introduction, Commentary and Glossary*, p. 600.

[50] The 'Argumentum' immediately following the epistle of Jude at 174rb, which serves as the first of two prefaces to the Pauline epistles, includes an inventory of the Pauline epistles that reads as follows: 'Pauli apostoli aepistolae numero .xiiii.: Ad Romanos .i., Ad Corinthios .ii., Ad Galathas .i., Ad Ephesios .i., Ad Philipenses .i., Ad Colosenses .i., Ad Thesalonicenses .ii., Ad Timotheum .ii., Ad Titum .i., Ad Phylemonem .i., Ad Hebreos .i., Ad Laudicenses .i. Omnis textus uel numerus epistolarum ad unius hominis perfectionem proficiunt.' Then follows a brief summary of the contents of all fourteen (!) epistles, which includes the reiterated statement at 174va22–3 that 'Omnes ergo epistole Pauli sunt numero .xiiii.' For the full text of this preface (but without the mention of Laodiceans), see D. de Bruyne, *Préfaces de la Bible latine* (Namur, 1920), pp. 217–18. Additional manuscripts of this preface are listed by S. Berger, 'Les préfaces

accompanying the text of Laodiceans, he may have found himself having to choose between the conflicting message of the preface and the self-evident Pauline authorship of the epistle as revealed by its own language.

I do think it is a factor that Ælfric's *Letter to Sigeweard* was intended to serve as a set of elementary instructions on how to read the Bible for a non-scholarly lay reader and as such is calculated to present a simplified and uncomplicated account of scripture, a basic set of facts about the Bible. But I do not think Ælfric would have used this simplified presentation to mislead Sigeweard by smoothing over a controversy regarding the make-up of the biblical canon or the number of Pauline epistles. If anything, his desire to provide Sigeweard with a primer of fundamental biblical know-ledge would have led him to include only his most unshakeable convictions about the contents of the Bible. I think Ælfric believed what he wrote.

I do think Ælfric knew Gregory's *Moralia*, and in particular I think he had at least at one point read the passage in Book 35 where Gregory seems simultaneously to affirm the Pauline authorship of Laodiceans and exclude it from the canon. But I think Ælfric must have read this passage selectively, seizing on Gregory's assertion that Paul wrote a total of fifteen epistles but dismissing Gregory's qualification that the church accepts only fourteen of them (a contradiction that is mirrored in the preface to the Pauline epistles in the 'Royal Bible'). The idea of Ælfric dismissing Gregory's qualification is discomforting because it is utterly uncharacteristic of Ælfric to reject any teaching by Gregory, and equally uncharacteristic of him to reject a statement that purports to represent longstanding Christian tradition. But in this case, I think Ælfric was forced to make a decision, and the factor that weighed most heavily upon him in his forging of that decision was not patristic authority but his own experience reading the Bible. If he had read Laodiceans and took it to be Pauline, then he could find a way to excuse the oversight of those who had miscounted and those (including Augustine, Jerome, and Gregory) who had neglected to accept Laodiceans as a canonical book. In the age-old war between experience and authority, Ælfric in this rare instance comes down solidly on the side of experience.

At the same time, I think Ælfric was won over by the symbolic power of the number seventy-two and relied on its symbolism to justify his belief that Laodiceans was a real Pauline letter that must be counted among the books of the Bible. His choice to deviate from the count of seventy-one books advocated by Augustine, Cassiodorus, Isidore and others put Ælfric in the uncomfortable position of defying patristic tradition, but it had the over-riding advantage of affirming the far-reaching truths of numerical typology, which was after all something he had learned from Gregory and Augustine.

It might be argued that the Epistle to the Laodiceans is such a small and inconsequential text that surely not a great deal hangs on what Ælfric thought about it. It has very little spiritual or doctrinal value, in fact virtually no substantive message at all. But in Ælfric's mind this little epistle

---

jointes aux livres de la Bible dans les manuscrits de la Vulgate', *Mémoires présentés par divers savants à l'Académie des Inscriptions et Belles-Lettres* 1st ser. 11 (1904), 1–78, at 61 (no. 254).

was an inspired work of Paul, a book of the New Testament, and recommended reading for educated laymen in eleventh-century Oxford-shire. Its place in the early debates over the contents of the biblical canon reminds us that the books we now refer to as 'apocrypha' were subject to several different patterns of reception and methods of categorization in the early Middle Ages, some of which may not have been recognized by Ælfric. If I am right about the variables that went into Ælfric's thinking about this epistle, then its presence in his survey of scriptures also shows that his views on advisable Christian reading practices were not always dominated by strict adherence to ecclesiastical tradition. Past discussions of Ælfric's attitude towards apocrypha have conditioned us to think of Ælfric as a writer whose views on just about everything were profoundly determined by orthodox patristic teaching, and to a great extent this is no doubt true. But the profundity of that debt does not carry over to the *Letter to Sigeweard*. For if the views expressed in this letter can be taken to represent an advanced stage in Ælfric's intellectual career, a period after he had settled at Eynsham when his other writings such as the *Letter to the Monks of Eynsham* and his *Life of St Æthelwold* are mature and confident and summative in nature, reflecting decades of patient scholarship and analysis, then the final arbiter for Ælfric in his decisions about acceptable versus unacceptable books is not the judgement of the church fathers, and not conciliar legislation or the Pseudo-Gelasian Decree, but the insight that derives from his own individual experience as a reader.

## *Appendix*

### The Epistle to the Laodiceans from the 'Royal Bible' BL, Royal I. E. VIII (S. England, s. x/xi), 198r

Because the text of the Epistle to the Laodiceans in the 'Royal Bible' is the closest surviving copy in time and place to Ælfric, I reproduce it here along with the set of *capitula* that precedes it. The text is corrupt or idiosyncratic in several places. As the variants listed by J. B. Lightfoot, *Saint Paul's Epistles to the Colossians and to Philemon: A Revised Text*, 7th ed. (London, 1884), pp. 284 and 287–9, indicate, other manuscripts correctly read 'De manifestis uinculis' rather than 'De manifesta uincula' in the second *capitulum*, and 'et Deum Patrem omnipotentem, qui suscitauit eum a mortuis' is a rare addition to verse 1. The second half of verse 4, beginning 'sed peto ne uos auertant', is paralleled in most other manuscripts by 'ut uos auertant'. Verse 13 in other manuscripts begins 'Et quod est reliquum' or 'Et quod est optimum' rather than the seemingly incomplete 'Et quod est' here. The 'Royal Bible' is one of only two manuscripts listed by Lightfoot (the other being Cambridge, Trinity College B. 5. 1 (s. xii)) that include the benedictional conclusion after verse 20. Many manuscripts omit verse 17 entirely.

The epistle is divided into four chapters. There are no verse divisions in the manuscript, but to facilitate comparison with modern editions and translations, I have added the by-now conventionalized verse numbers as given in *Biblia Sacra iuxta Vulgatam versionem*, ed. R. Weber *et al.*, 3rd ed. (Stuttgart, 1983), p. 1976. Scribal additions are enclosed within angled insertion marks (` ´). I have regularized the capitalization of *nomina sacra*, added modern punctuation, left grammatical irregularities unaltered, and preserved instances of *e-caudata* (ę). An English translation follows.

⟨198ra⟩ Incipiunt capitula in epistola ad Laudicenses.
I      Paulus apostolus per Laudicensibus Domino gratias refert et hortatur eos ut a seductoribus `non´ decipiantur.
II     De manifesta uincula apostoli in quibus laetatur et gaudet.
III    Monet Laudicenses apostolus ut sicut sui audierunt presentiam, ita retineant et sine retra`ctatu´ faciant.
IV     Hortatur apostolus Laudicenses ut fide sint firmi et que (*corr. from* quem) integra et uera et Deo sunt placita faciant. Salutatio fratrum in osculo sancto.
Expliciunt capitula.


Incipit epistola ad Laudicenses.
⟨I⟩ [1]Paulus apostolus non ab hominibus neque per hominem sed per Iesum Christum et Deum Patrem omnipotentem, qui suscitauit eum a mortuis, fratribus qui sunt Laudiceae. [2]Gratia uobis et pax a Deo Patre et Domino nostro Iesu Christo. [3]Gratias ago Deo meo et Christo Iesu per omnem orationem meam, quod estis permanentes in eo et perseuerantes in operibus eius, sperantes promissum in die iudicationis. [4]Neque enim destituant uos quorundam uaniloquia insinuantium, sed peto ne uos auertant (*corr. from* auartanta) `a´ ueritate euangelii quod a me praedicatur. [5]Et nunc faciet Deus ut qui sunt ex me ad perfectum ueritatis euangelii Dei seruientes et facientes benignitatem eorum quae sunt salutis uitae aeternę.

II [6]Et nunc palam sunt uincula mea quę patior in Christo in quibus laetor et gaudeo. /198rb/ [7]Et hoc mihi est ad salutem perpetuam, quod ipsum factum orationibus uestris administrante Spiritu sancto siue per uitam siue per mortem. [8]Est enim mihi uere uita in Christo et mori gaudium. [9]Et ipse in uobis faciet misericordiam suam ut eandem dilectionem habeatis et sitis unanimes.

III [10]Ergo, dilectissimi, ut audistis praesentia mei, ita retinete et facite in timore Dei, et erit uobis pax et uita in aeternum. [11]Est enim Deus qui operatur in uobis. [12]Et facite sine retractatu quaecumque facitis.

IIII [13]Et quod est, dilectissimi, gaudete in Christo, et praecauete sordidos in lucrum. [14]Omnes sint petitiones uestrae palam apud Deum. Et estote sensu firmi in Christo Iesu. [15]Et quae sunt integra et uera et iusta et pudica et amabilia et sancta, facite. [16]Et quae audistis et accepistis, in corde retinete, et erit uobis pax. [17]Salutate omnes fratres in osculo sancto. [18]Salutant uos omnes sancti in Christo Iesu. [19]Gratia Domini nostri Iesu Christi cum spiritu uestro. [20]Et facite legi Colosensibus hanc epistolam, et Colosensibus uos legite. Deus autem et Pater Domini nostri Iesu Christi custodiat uos inmaculatos in Christo Iesu, cui est honor et gloria in secula seculorum. Amen. Explicit epistola ad Laudicenses.

### Translation

Here begin the chapter headings of the Epistle to the Laodiceans.

I    The apostle Paul conveys the grace of the Lord to the Laodiceans and urges them not to be deceived by seducers.

II   Concerning the apostle's manifest bonds in which he is glad and rejoices.

III  The apostle admonishes the Laodiceans that just as they have heard in his presence, so should they persist and work without hesitation.

IV   The apostle exhorts the Laodiceans to be of firm faith and to do what is pure and true and pleasing to God. He greets the brothers with the holy kiss.

Here end the chapter headings.

Here begins the Epistle to the Laodiceans:

I [1]Paul, an apostle not of men and not through man but through Jesus Christ and God the Father almighty, who has raised him from the dead, to the brothers who are in Laodicea: [2]Grace to you and peace from God the Father and our Lord Jesus Christ. [3]I give thanks to my God and Jesus Christ in all my prayer that you remain steadfast in him and persevere in his works in expectation of the promise at the day of judgement. [4]And may the idle talk of some who gossip not lead you astray, but I pray that they not divert you from the truth of the gospel that is proclaimed by me. [5]And now may God grant that those who come from me for the fulfilment of the truth of the gospel may serve God and do their good works for the salvation of eternal life.

II [6]And now my bonds are made manifest which I suffer in Christ, for which I am glad and rejoice. [7]And this leads to my eternal salvation, which itself is brought about through your prayers and with the help of the Holy Spirit, whether through life or through death. [8]For truly my life is in Christ and to die is joy. [9]And he will work his mercy in you so that you may have the same love and be of one mind.

III [10]Therefore, most beloved, as you have heard in my presence, so hold fast and work in the fear of God, and peace and eternal life will be yours. [11]For it is God who will work in you. [12]And do without hesitation what you do.

IV [13]And so, most beloved, rejoice in Christ and beware of those who are out for sordid gain. [14]May all your requests be manifest before God, and be steadfast in Jesus Christ. [15]And do what is pure and true and just and proper and lovely and holy. [16]And what you have heard and received, hold in your heart, and peace will be with you. [17]Greet all the brothers with the holy kiss. [18]All the saints salute you in Jesus Christ. [19]The grace of our Lord Jesus Christ be with your spirit. [20]And see that this epistle is read to the Colossians, and you read the one to the Colossians. And now may God the Father of our Lord Jesus Christ keep you faultless in Jesus Christ, to whom is honor and glory forever. Amen. Here ends the epistle to the Laodiceans.

# 4

# The *Versus Sibyllae de die iudicii* in Anglo-Saxon England

PATRIZIA LENDINARA

THE Sibylline tradition is a significant aspect of medieval discourse and its influence is widespread. The original text of the earliest prophecies is lost, but a large corpus of oracular pronouncements known as *Oracula Sibyllina*,[1] consisting of several books of Greek hexameters, is preserved. The corpus under examination[2] consists of a mass of early material, continually reworked, added to and interpolated – so complex that it is hard to assign a date to each of the *Oracula*. The *Oracula*, which show a blend of early Jewish and Hellenistic material as well as of pre-Christian and Christian elements, were written between the mid-second century BC – Book III is the oldest of the oracles – and approximately AD 300: in the sixth century they were assembled as a collection and provided with an introduction.[3] The most ancient books date from the time of the reign of Ptolemy Philometor (180–145 BC) – who fostered the dialogue between the Jews and the Greeks – and originated in the town of Alexandria.[4]

As extant, the *Oracula Sibyllina* can be divided in two groups: collection A consists of eight oracles or *logoi* (Books I–VIII in Geffcken's edition) and was probably compiled by the author of the Sibylline preface. The preface contains an exhortation to read the oracles and adds further information about the Sibyls (such as the list of the Sibyls and the story of the meeting between the Cuman Sibyl and Tarquinius Priscus). Collection B of the *Oracula*[5] includes oracles 9 and 10, the content of which is also found in other oracles (and therefore was excluded from Geffcken's edition). Oracles 11–14 contain dynastic prophecies which are quite different from the ethical

[1] Ed. J. Geffcken, *Die Oracula Sibyllina,* Die griechischen christlichen Schriftsteller der ersten drei Jahrhunderte 8 (Leipzig, 1902) (Books I–IX); for the text of Books I–XI with German translation and commentary, see A. Kurfess, *Sibyllinische Weissagungen. Urtext und Übersetzung* (Berlin, 1951); English translation by J. J. Collins in J. H. Charlesworth, *The Old Testament Pseudoepigrapha*, I, *Apocalyptic Literature and Testaments* (Garden City, NY, 1983), pp. 317–472.
[2] The first edition of the Greek text is that by X. Betuleius or Sixtus Birck (Basel, 1545).
[3] J. Geffcken, *Die Komposition und Entstehungszeit der Oracula Sibyllina* (Leipzig, 1902).
[4] Book III ends with a prophecy on what is going to happen after the Last Judgement (lines 741–808).
[5] In the nineteenth century, Cardinal A. Mai discovered four further books of the *Oracula* of Jewish origin, which are found only in some manuscripts and date from the first to the fourth centuries AD.

and eschatological oracles of the earlier collection and oracles 12–13 provide a summary of the history of Rome from Augustus to the victory of Odenato, and date from the middle of the third century AD.

The whole corpus of the *Oracula Sibyllina* was put together by a Byzantine scholar in about the sixth century AD. The eight books were quoted by both Greek and Latin patristic authors and parts were translated into Latin. The text which circulated in the medieval West, including the British Isles was, with a few probable exceptions, the Latin translation of the Sibylline books. A still larger influence was exerted all through the Middle Ages[6] by different aspects of the Sibylline tradition.[7] Those affecting Anglo-Saxon England are considered below.

The Greek Sibylline prophecies have been ranked among the Old and New Testament apocrypha[8] because their vision incorporated the Jewish apocalyptic perception dominated by a monotheistic belief, which strove toward a final Judgement, bringing about a division of good and evil.[9] The Jews tried to communicate their apocalyptic visions through the medium of oracular language, using a literary style which was familiar to the Greeks and adopting the literary conventions which one would expect from a pagan Sibyl, though the content of the sayings was rather more fit for a Jewish prophet. The author of the preface emphasised their edifying content and set them against pagan literature. The *Oracula* responded to the needs of both Greek and Roman people in the first centuries of the Christian era, giving an indication of what they expected from the conversion and providing what was presented as a series of divine revelations; in their own style, the *Oracula* offered judgement of past events treated as future events.

The prophetic dimension is a fundamental element of religious experience and features prominently in the Bible, especially in the Old Testament books of the prophets, as well as in the Acts of the Apostles, the Pauline epistles (Thessalonians, Corinthians) and Revelation. Several episodes of the Old Testament, such as the Ascension of Isaiah, verged on heterodoxy and were to be marginalized as heretical. On the other hand the *Oracula*, which were to be regarded as apocryphal writings, drew part of their content from the Bible: in Book III, the history of the Tower of Babel is told (III.97) and the Exodus is foretold (III.248).

---

[6] See Bernard McGinn, '*Teste David cum Sibylla*: The Significance of the Sibylline Tradition in the Middle Ages', in *Women of the Medieval World: Essays in Honour of J. M. Mundy*, ed. J. Kirschner and S. F. Wemple (Oxford, 1985), pp. 7–35; M. Le Merrer, 'Des Sibylles à la sapience dans la tradition médiévale', *Mélanges de l'école française de Rome, Moyen Âge* 98 (1986), 13–33.

[7] Ursula Dronke, '*Voluspá* and Sibylline Traditions', in *Latin Culture and Medieval Germanic Europe*, ed. R. North and T. Hofstra, Germania Latina I (Groningen, 1992), pp. 3–21.

[8] A. M. Denis, *Introduction aux Pseudépigraphes Grecs d'Ancien Testament* (Leiden, 1970), pp. 111–22 and E. Hennecke, *Handbuch zu den Neutestamentlichen Apocryphen* (Tübingen, 1904), pp. 339–50.

[9] H. W. Parke, *Sibyls and Sibylline Prophecy in Classical Antiquity*, ed. B. C. McGing (London and New York, 1988), p. 11: 'The Jews had long conceived the picture of a Day of the Lord, when Yahweh would reveal himself in justification of Israel and confutation of the Gentiles.'

*Book VIII of the* Oracula

The oracles of Collection A offer the best image of the Sibylline prophecy as it was accepted by the Christian tradition: the earliest strata of Books VI–VIII date from the second century. Book VIII, the best known of the Christian *Oracula*, dates from the reign of Marcus Aurelius and is remarkable for its violently anti-Roman tone.[10] It is made up of two parts: the former (lines 1–216) is a Jewish survey of the history of the world and the impending doom; the latter (lines 217–500) contains Christian prophecies beginning with a section of 34 lines,[11] whose initial letters spell out the acrostic '*ΙΗΣΟΥΣ ΧΡΕΙΣΤΟΣ ΘΕΟΥ ΥΙΟΣ ΣΩΤΗΡ ΣΤΑΥΡΟΣ*' that is 'Jesus Christ, Son of God, Saviour, Cross':[12]

Ἰδρώσει δὲ χθών, κρίσεως σημεῖον ὅτ' ἔσται.
Ἥξει δ' οὐρανόθεν βασιλεὺς αἰῶσιν ὁ μέλλων,
Σάρκα παρὼν πᾶσαν κρῖναι καὶ κόσμον ἅπαντα.
Ὄψονται δὲ θεὸν μέροπες πιστοὶ καὶ ἄπιστοι
Ὕψιστον μετὰ τῶν ἁγίον ἐπὶ τέρμα χρόνοιο.
Σαρκοφόρων δ' ἀνδρῶν ψυχὰς ἐπὶ βήματι κρίνει,
Χέρσος ὅταν ποτὲ κόσμος ὅλος καὶ ἄκανθα γένηται.
Ῥίψουσιν δ' εἴδωλα βροτοὶ καὶ πλοῦτον ἅπαντα.
Ἐκκαύσει δὲ τὸ πῦρ γῆν οὐρανὸν ἠδὲ θάλασσαν
Ἰχνεῦον, ῥήξει τε πύλας εἱρκτῆς Ἀίδαο.
Σὰρξ τότε πᾶσα νεκρῶν ἐς ἐλευθέριον φάος ἥξει
Τῶν ἁγίων· ἀνόμους δὲ τὸ πῦρ αἰῶσιν ἐλέγξει.
Ὁππόσα τις πράξας ἔλαθεν, τότε πάντα λαλήσει·
Στήθεα γὰρ ζοφόεντα θεὸς φωστήρσιν ἀνοίξει.
Θρῆνος δ' ἐκ πάντων ἔσται καὶ βρυγμὸς ὀδόντων.
Ἐκλείψει σέλας ἠελίου ἄστρων τε χορείαι.
Οὐρανὸν εἱλίξει· μήνης δέ τε φέγγος ὀλεῖται.
Ὑψώσει δὲ φάραγγας, ὀλεῖ δ' ὑφώματα βουνῶν,
Ὕψος δ' οὐκέτι λυγρὸν ἐν ἀνθρώποισι φανεῖται.
Ἴσα δ' ὄρη πεδίοις ἔσται καὶ πᾶσα θάλασσα
Οὐκέτι πλοῦν ἕξει. γῆ γὰρ φρυχθεῖσα τότ' ἔσται
Σὺν πηγαῖς, ποταμοί τε καχλάζοντες λείψουσιν.
Σάλπιγξ δ' οὐρανόθεν φωνὴν πολύθρηον ἀφήσει
Ὠρύουσα μύσος μελέων καὶ πήματα κόσμου.
Ταρτάρεον δὲ χάος δείξει τότε γαῖα χανοῦσα.
Ἥξουσιν δ' ἐπὶ βῆμα θεοῦ βασιλῆος ἅπαντες.
Ῥεύσει δ' οὐρανόθεν ποταμὸς πυρὸς ἠδὲ θεείου.
Σῆμα δέ τοι τότε πᾶσι βροτοῖς, σφρηγὶς ἐπίσημος

---

[10] J. Collins, *Apocalypse: The Morphology of a Genre* (Missoula, 1979), p. 36.

[11] The acrostic was the common form of many pagan oracles, according to Cicero, *De divinatione*, II.54.112: 'Atque in Sibyllinis ex primo versu cuiusque sententiae primis litteris [illius sententiae] carmen omne praetexitur. Hoc scriptoris est, non furentis, adhibentis dilingentiam, non insani' ('and in the Sibylline (oracles) the entire song is embellished from the first line with the first letters of each phrase. This is proper of the writers and not of madmen, of those applying scrupulous care and not of the insane'); ed. R. Giomini (Leipzig, 1975), p. 130.

[12] In the manuscripts, lines 217–50 are preceded by a rubric, '*ΙΗΣΟΥΣ ΧΡΕΙΣΤΟΣ ΘΕΟΥ ΥΙΟΣ ΣΩΤΗΡ ΣΤΑΥΡΟΣ*'.

Τὸ ξύλον ἐν πιστοῖς, τὸ κέρας τὸ ποθούμενον ἔσται,
Ἀνδρῶν εὐσεβέων ζωή, πρόσκομμα δὲ κόσμου,
Ὕδασι φωτίζον κλητοὺς ἐν δώδεκα πηγαῖς·
Ῥάβδος ποιμαίνουσα σιδηρείη γε κρατήσει.
Οὗτος ὁ νῦν προγραφεὶς ἐν ἀκροστιχίοις θεὸς ἡμῶν.
Σωτὴρ ἀθάνατος βασιλεύς, ὁ παθὼν ἔνεχ' ἡμῶν.    (vv. 217–50)[13]

(Jesus Christ, son of God, saviour, cross.
The earth will sweat when there will be a sign of Judgement.
A king will come from heaven who is to judge
all flesh and the whole world forever when he comes.
Both faithful and faithless men will see God
the Most High with the holy ones at the end of time.
He will judge the souls of flesh-bearing men on the tribunal
when the whole world becomes barren land and thorns.
Men will throw away idols and all wealth.
Fire will burn up land, heaven, and sea,
pursuing the hunt, and will break the gates of the confines of Hades.
Then all the flesh of the dead, of the holy ones, will come
to the free light. The fire will torture the lawless forever.
Whatever one did secretly, he will then say everything,
for God will open dark breasts with lights.
A lament will rise from all and gnashing of teeth.
The light of the sun will be eclipsed and the troupes of stars.
He will roll up heaven. The light of the moon will perish.
He will elevate ravines, and destroy the heights of hills.
No longer will mournful height appear among men.
Mountains will be equal to plains, and all the sea
will no longer bear voyage. For earth will then be parched
with its springs. Bubbling rivers will fail.
A trumpet from heaven will issue a most mournful sound,
wailing for the defilement of limbs and woes of the world.
The gaping earth will then show the abyss of the nether world.
All will come to the tribunal of God the king.
A river of fire and brimstone will flow from heaven.
There will then be a sign for all men, a most clear seal:
the wood among the faithful, the desired horn,
the life of pious men, but the scandal of the world,
illuminating the elect with waters in twelve streams,
An iron shepherd's rod will prevail.
This is our God, now proclaimed in acrostics,
the king, the immortal saviour, who suffered for us.)[14]

These are the lines which were to become famous in the Middle Ages: they were known in Latin translations and contributed to the creation of the rich store of the Sibylline lore.

From the second century, Christian ecclesiastical writers quoted from the surviving books of the *Oracula* as well as from material that is now

---

[13] Ed. Geffcken, *Die Oracula Sibyllina*, pp. 153–7.
[14] Trans. Collins, in Charlesworth, *The Old Testament Pseudoepigrapha*, pp. 423–4.

lost;[15] the Sibyls were mentioned by Athenagoras, Justin, Hippolytus, Clement of Alexandria and Eusebius of Caesarea.[16] Knowledge of the *Oracula* is betrayed, for example, by Tertullian in his *Ad nationes*.[17] The historical and biographical details available in later works, however, as well as the names of the ten Sibyls,[18] all stem from a passage in the *Divinae institutiones* of Lactantius (I.6, 8–17).[19] The quotations from the *Oracula* which occur elsewhere in Lactantius's work are taken from the Greek version of the Sibylline Oracles, but in some early manuscripts of the *Divinae institutiones*, Latin paraphrases and glosses were added to the relevant passages.[20]

The acrostic found a place in the *Oratio ad sanctorum coetum*,[21] a work formerly attributed to the Emperor Constantine, which purports to be a speech of the emperor to an assembly of bishops. The *Oratio*, an apologetic work composed in the 360s against the revival of paganism, quoted the lines from Book VIII of the *Oracula* as a testimony to Christ's divinity.[22]

## Augustine's Version of the Acrostic

The first Latin version of the acrostic in Book VIII of the *Oracula Sibyllina* is found in Augustine, *De civitate Dei* XVIII.23, and proves that, as had already been the case with Lactantius, it was from Africa that the principal impulse for the circulation of the Sibylline prophecies came.[23] The *De civitate Dei* is transmitted in more than 400 manuscripts and the way medieval authors saw the Sibyl and made use of the oracular material was primarily influenced by Augustine.[24] As far as the acrostic is concerned

---

[15] See B. Thompson, 'Patristic Use of the Sibylline Oracles', *Review of Religion* 16 (1952), 118–36 (especially the two appendices). On the patristic attitude toward the *Oracula*, see K. Prümm, 'Das Prophetenamt der Sibyllen in kirchlicher Literatur mit besonderer Rücksicht auf die Deutung der 4. Ekloge Virgils', *Scholastik* 4 (1929), 54–77.

[16] *Praeparatio evangelica* IX.15 and XIII.13: ed. PG XXI, cols. 704 and 1104.

[17] *Ad nationes*, II.12.35: ed. E. Dekkers, CCSL 1 (Turnhout, 1954), p. 64.

[18] Lactantius mentions ten Sibyls: the Persian, Libyan, Delphic, Cimmerian, Erythraean, Samian, Cumaean, Hellespontic, Phrygian and Tiburtine: he drew his list from a lost work of the first century BC, the *Antiquitatum (rerum humanarum et divinarum) Libri XLI* by Varro.

[19] Ed. S. Brandt, CSEL 19 (Prague, Vienna and Leipzig, 1890), pp. 21–5.

[20] See M.-L. Guillaumin, 'L'exploitation des "Oracles Sibyllins" par Lactance et par le Discours à l'assemblée des Saints', in *Lactance et son temps. Recherches actuelles, Actes du IVe Colloque d'Études Historiques et Patristiques, Chantilly 21–23 septembre 1976*, ed. J. Fontaine and M. Perrin (Paris, 1978), pp. 185–200; see also R. M. Ogilvie, *The Library of Lactantius* (Oxford, 1978), pp. 28–36.

[21] See D. De Decker, 'Le "Discours à l'Assemblée des Saints" attribuì à Costantin et l'oeuvre de Lactance', in *Lactance et son temps*, ed. Fontaine and Perrin, pp. 75–87 and R. P. C. Hanson, 'The *Oratio ad Sanctos* attributed to the Emperor Constantine and the Oracle at Daphne', *Journal of Theological Studies* 24 (1973), 505–11.

[22] *Oratio ad Sanctorum coetum*, ch. XVIII: PG XX, cols. 1285–9.

[23] See A. Kurfess, 'Die Sibylle in Augustins Gottesstaat', *Theologische Quartalschrift* 117 (1936), 532–42 and Kurfess, 'Augustinus und die Tiburtinische Sibylle', *Theologische Quartalschrift* 131 (1951), 458–63.

[24] Augustine mentions the Sibyls at several points in *De civitate Dei* and begins chapter XVIII by alluding to the Erythraean Sibyl. This attitude toward the acrostic is remarkable in view of his aversion to forms of apocalyptic prophecy: see Bernard McGinn, *Visions of the End: Apocalyptic Traditions in the Middle Ages* (New York, 1979), pp. 26–7. Augustine betrays a negative attitude

Augustine explains that he became acquainted at first with a scarcely intelligible Latin version of the acrostic, but then an important person named Flaccianus showed him a Greek manuscript containing, among other poems, an acrostic whose initial letters formed a sentence. Augustine was thus able to supply a new and correct translation of the oracular lines:[25]

> Iudicii signum tellus sudore madescet.
> E caelo rex adueniet per saecla futurus,
> Scilicet ut carnem praesens, ut iudicet orbem.
> Unde Deum cernent incredulus atque fidelis
> Celsum cum sanctis aeui iam termino in ipso.
> Sic animae cum carne aderunt, quas iudicat ipse,
> Cum iacet incultus densis in uepribus orbis.
> Reicient simulacra uiri, cunctam quoque gazam,
> Exuret terras ignis pontumque polumque
> Inquirens, taetri portas effringet Auerni.
> Sanctorum, sed enim cunctae lux libera carni
> Tradetur, sontes aeterna flamma cremabit.
> Occultos actus retegens tunc quisque loquetur
> Secreta, atque Deus reserabit pectora luci.
> Tunc erit et luctus, stridebunt dentibus omnes.
> Eripitur solis iubar et chorus interit astris.
> Voluetur caelum, lunaris splendor obibit;
> Deiciet colles, ualles extollet ab imo.
> Non erit in rebus hominum sublime uel altum.
> Iam aequantur campis montes et caerula ponti
> Omnia cessabunt, tellus confracta peribit:
> Sic pariter fontes torrentur fluminaque igni.
> Sed tuba tum sonitum tristem demittet ab alto
> Orbe, gemens facinus miserum uariosque labores,
> Tartareumque chaos monstrabit terra dehiscens.
> Et coram hic Domino reges sistentur ad unum.
> Reccidet e caelo ignisque et sulphuris amnis.[26]

---

toward pagan prophets in *Contra Faustum* (ed. PL 42, col. 290) and in *De civitate Dei* XVIII, 46–7, where he stresses the superiority of the Old Testament prophecies. On all the passages where Augustine mentions the Sibyls, see B. Altaner, 'Augustinus und die Neutestamentlichen Apokryphen, Sibyllen und Sextussprüche', *Analecta Bollandiana* 67 (1949), 244–7.

[25] See G. Bardy, *La cité de Dieu, Livres XV–XVIII: Luttes des deux cités*, Bibliothèque Augustinienne, 5th ser. 36 (Paris, 1960), pp. 755–9; see also U. Pizzani, 'L'acrostico cristologico della Sibilla (Or. Sib. 8, 217–250) e la sua versione latina (August. Civ. Dei 18, 23)', in *Cristianesimo Latino e Cultura Greca sino al sec. IV, XXI Incontro di studiosi dell'antichità cristiana, Roma 7–9 maggio 1992*, Institutum Patristicum Augustinianum (Rome, 1993), pp. 379–90.

[26] Ed. T. Hoffmann, CSEL 40 (Prague, Vienna and Leipzig, 1899–1900), pp. 297–8; Augustine adds this remark to his version of the acrostic: 'In his Latinis uersibus de Graeco utcumque translatis ibi non potuit ille sensus occurrere, qui fit, cum litterae, quae sunt in eorum capitibus, conectuntur, ubi Y littera in Graeco posita est, quia non potuerunt Latina uerba inueniri, quae ab eadem littera inciperent et sententiae conuenirent. Hi autem sunt uersus tres, quintus et octauus decimus et nonus decimus.' ('In these Latin verses, somehow translated from Greek, it was impossible to obtain the legend supplied by linking together the initial letters of the lines, when the Greek has the letter Y, because it was not possible to find Latin words beginning with the same letter which could fit in the lines. This applies to three lines, five, eighteen and nineteen.')

(The earth will sweat at the sign of judgement
from heaven will come the everlasting king
he who shall be present to judge all flesh and the world.
Both faithful and faithless men shall thus behold God,
magnificent with the saints at the very end of time,
thus the souls will come close to the body, that he himself is going
    to judge,
when the whole world becomes barren in thick thorn.
Men will throw away idols and all the wealth,
fire will burn up earth, sea and heaven
pursuing the hunt, and will break the dreadful gates of Hades.
But then all the flesh of the holy ones, to free light
will come. The eternal fire will burn the evils.
Whatever one did in secret, he will tell everything
for God will open the secret breasts with light.
A lament will then rise and gnashing of teeth.
The light of sun and the swarm of stars will be concealed.
The heaven will roll up, the light of the moon will perish;
Hills will be levelled, dales elevated from the bottom.
No longer will there appear among men anything elevated or high.
Mountains will be equal to plains and cerulean sea.
Everything will pass away, earth, all parched, will perish:
in the same way sources and rivers will be burnt with fire.
But then the trumpet will send its mournful sound from high above
to the earth, wailing for the mischiefs of the miserables and the
    several woes of the world.
The earth gaping open shall disclose the abyss of the nether world.
All kings shall stand before the Lord:
a river of fire and brimstone shall fall down from heaven.)

This version lacks the ΣΤΑΥΡΟΣ 'cross' strophe and translates only twenty-seven lines of the Greek; the first letter of each line forms an acrostic which reads 'IESUS CREISTOS TEUDNIOS SOTER'. It must be kept in mind that the acrostic form of these verses that were going to circulate as an independent poem had a significant influence on the text, conditioning both the choice of words and the syntax; it also compelled the translator to introduce several repetitions.

Augustine's version circulated widely in the Middle Ages[27] and stands alone in several manuscripts, for example in Zürich, Zentralbibliothek, C 78, 156r–157v;[28] Munich, Bayerische Staatsbibliothek, lat. 6525, 62v (s.

[27] D. Schaller and E. Könsgen, *Initia Carminum Latinorum Saeculo Undecimo antiquiorum* (Göttingen, 1977) (henceforth S-K), no. 8495 and H. Walther, *Initia Carminum ac Versuum Medii Aevi Posterioris Latinorum* (Göttingen, 1959), no. 9907 (and no. 9911); Walther, *Ergänzungen und Berichtigungen* (Göttingen, 1969); H. Silvestre, 'Revue d'Histoire ecclésiastique' 75 (1980), p. 408 and further additions in 'Mittellateinisches Jahrbuch' 7 (1972), 303; 9 (1974), 330; 12 (1977), 305; 15 (1980), 271; see also B. Stäblein, *Monumenta Monodica Medii Aevi* I (Kassel, 1956), p. 622, 24; U. Chevalier, *Repertorium Hymnologicum*, 6 vols. (Louvain and Brussels, 1892–1920), no. 9876.

[28] In this manuscript, the 'Iudicii signum' occurs together with another passage with prophecies of Christ's passion and resurrection from *De civitate Dei* XVIII, 23, which begins, 'In manus, inquit, infidelium postea ueniet' (from Lactantius, *Divinae institutiones* IV. 8–19, who used the *Oracula*

xii–xiv); Munich, Bayerische Staatsbibliothek, lat. 14498, 14r (s. xi–xii). From the late ninth century the lines of the acrostic are provided with musical notations in several manuscripts,[29] for example in Paris, BN, lat. 1154, 122r (s. ix); Paris, BN, lat. 2832, 123r–v (s. ix)[30] and Paris, BN, lat. 1139 (s. xi).[31]

A pseudo-Augustinian sermon, *Sermo Beati Augustini episcopi de Natale Domini*, known as *Against the Jews, Pagans and Arians*, included the text of the acrostic[32] and contrasted the Old Testament prophets with the Sibyl. Aiming to prove the Jews wrong because they denied the Messiah's birth, the author of the homily calls to witness both the prophets and the Sibyl who sings her prophecy 'Iudicii signum', foretelling the Judgement. The sermon had a large influence on liturgy and the passage which features the Sibyl and her song was introduced in the Christmas office as a separate liturgical lesson:[33] in some churches the *lectio* was abbreviated;[34] elsewhere, as we have remarked above, the *Cantus Sibyllae* was accompanied by musical notation.[35] From the end of the eleventh century, the Latin play of the prophets (*Ordo prophetarum*)[36] drew its material from the sermon and included the Sibyl's song.[37] In the liturgical *lectio*, prophets were summoned to foretell the birth of Christ and the words of Nebuchadnezzar were

Books VI and VIII); the same combination of texts is found in Paris, BN, lat. 2832, 123r–v and in Oxford, Bodleian Library, Add C. 144 (28188), 68v–69r, a manuscript from northern Italy, dated to the tenth century; see N. R. Ker, *Catalogue of Manuscripts Containing Anglo-Saxon* (Oxford, 1957; repr. with appendix, 1990), no. 22A, and, for a description of its content, L. Holtz, *Donat et la tradition de l'enseignement grammatical* (Paris, 1981), pp. 409–12.

[29] See E. De Coussemaker, *Histoire de l'Harmonie au Moyen Age* (Hildesheim, 1966), p. 110 and plates IV, 2, V, VI, XXVI,1 and J. Chailley, *L'école musicale de Saint-Martial de Limoges jusqu'à la fin du XIe Siécle* (Paris, 1960), pp. 130 and 141ff.

[30] In this manuscript the poem 'est écrit sans division par strophes et sans répétition des mots "Judicii signum" qu'on trouve dans les autres manuscrits' ('is written without the strophes' division and without the repetition of the words "Judicii signum" which occur in the other manuscripts'): De Coussemaker, *Histoire*, p. 110.

[31] The manuscript, from St Martial at Limoges, contains the *Troparium Martialense* where the acrostic is part of the Christmas office: see K. Young, *The Drama of the Medieval Church* (Oxford, 1933), II, 126–31.

[32] The sermon is now attributed to Quodvultdeus: ed. R. Braun, CCSL 60 (Turnhout, 1976), pp. 225–58, the acrostic at pp. 248–9.

[33] K. Young, 'Ordo prophetarum', *Transactions of the Wisconsin Academy of Sciences, Arts and Letters* 20 (1922), 1–82 publishes the sermon at 5–12, including the acrostic, in the complete and normal form from the *Lectionarium Arelatense* (Paris, BN, lat. 1018, 129r–132v, s. xii); this version is furnished with musical notation; in Rome, Vatican City, Biblioteca Apostolica Vaticana, Regin. 125, 74r–76v (*Lectionarium Forcalqueriense*), only the first two lines of the acrostic have musical notation.

[34] For example, in Paris, BN, lat. 1255 (*Breviarium gallicanum*) and Paris, BN, lat. 16309 (*Breviarium Santonense*); the *Sermo* also occurs in Paris, BN, lat. 1035 (*Breviarium Carcassonense*); Paris, BN, lat. 16819, 12v–14r (*Lectionarium Compendiense*) and Oxford, Bodleian Library, Canon. Liturg. 391, 11v–14r.

[35] See S. Corbin, 'Le *Cantus Sibyllae*: Origine et premiers textes', *Revue de musicologie* 31 (1952), 1–10.

[36] The version of St Martial at Limoges shows an advance 'toward acted drama' (Young, 'Ordo Prophetarum', p. 39) but lacks rubrics indicating impersonation. In other works, 'impersonation and specific dramatic action are unmistakable', for example in Laon, Bibliothèque de la Ville, 263, 147r–149r; see 'Ordo prophetarum', pp. 39–45.

[37] For the lesson, see Young, *The Drama*, II, 126–31, where the principal *Ordo prophetarum* are printed.

immediately followed by the Sibyl's acrostic. Also, in the *Ordo prophetarum*, the speech of Nebuchadnezzar was accompanied by that of the Sibyl and the acrostic represented the climax of the play.

Isidore of Seville in the *Etymologiae* VIII.8 provided a summary on the Sibyls, and the acrostic found a place in works of varied nature and content: in the Homiliary of Paul the Deacon and in *De universo* of Hrabanus Maurus, which has a chapter (XV.iii) on *De Sibyllis*, with a brief introduction, the names of the Sybils and the acrostic;[38] the poem was also included in *Liber Floridus* of Lambertus of St Omer.[39] The acrostic was also interpolated in the most popular of the new medieval oracles, the Tiburtine Sybil:[40] there are over 130 manuscripts known of the Latin version of the *Sibylla Tiburtina* (the oldest one dates from the middle of the eleventh century)[41] and its presence in this oracle is a significant example of the interpenetration of inherited material and new creation.

Other versions of the acrostic were in circulation,[42] including a prose version of the whole of Book VIII of the *Oracula*,[43] incompletely preserved in Karlsruhe, Badische Landesbibliothek, Aug. CLXXII, 33v–36v (s. ix[in]) and in another manuscript. The poem, which begins with the words 'Mundus origo mea est', is neither a translation nor an adaptation from the Greek *Oracula*, but rather a new creation. This poem is preserved in three manuscripts and is known as the 'Prophetiae Sibillae magae',[44] from the title given by Bischoff who discovered it.[45] According to Ursula Dronke

[38]　See, respectively, PL 95, col. 1474 and PL 111, cols. 420–1.

[39]　P. G. Schmidt, 'Die Mittellateinische Dichtung im Liber Floridus', in *Liber Floridus Colloquium, Gent 1967* (Ghent, 1973), pp. 51–8; the presence of the acrostic in the *Liber Floridus* has a twofold explanation: 'Einmal die Existenz dieser Verse in Hrabans Enzyklopädie, zum andern Lamberts Denken, das so beharrlich um apokalyptische Themen kreist' ('On the one hand the presence of these verses in Hrabanus's Encyclopaedia, on the other hand in Lambert's way of thinking, which so persistently revolved around apocalyptic themes') (p. 54). For further occurrences of the acrostic in the Middle Ages, see the references in note 27.

[40]　As early as the time of Varro, the Latin city of Tibur had laid claim to a Sibyl, as is evident in the list of the Sibyls in *Divinae institutiones* I, 6. For the origin of this new oracle, see P. J. Alexander, *The Oracle of Baalbeck: The Tiburtine Sibyl in Greek Dress*, Dumbarton Oaks Studies 10 (Washington DC, 1967); A. Momigliano, 'From the Pagan to the Christian Sibyl: Prophecy as History of Religion', in *Warburg Institute Surveys and Texts XVI: The Uses of Greek and Latin. Historical Essays*, ed. A. C. Dionisotti, A. Grafton and J. Kraye (London, 1988), pp. 3–18, at p. 15; D. Flusser, 'An Early Jewish-Christian Document of the Tiburtine Sibyl', in *Paganisme, Judaïsme, Christianisme. Mélanges offerts à M. Simon*, ed. A. Benoit and M. Simon (Paris, 1978), pp. 153–83.

[41]　In the Tiburtine Sibyl there are two interpolations, one from Lactantius and one from the acrostic; see E. Sackur, *Sibyllinische Texte und Forschungen: Pseudomethodus, Adso und die Tiburtinische Sibylle* (Halle a.S., 1898), 2nd ed. with introduction by R. Manselli (Tourin, 1963), p. 187. In the edition by Kurfess, *Sibyllinische Weissagungen*, the acrostic is at pp. 278–9.

[42]　See B. Bischoff, 'Die lateinischen Übersetzungen und Bearbeitungen aus den *Oracula Sibyllina*', *Mélanges Joseph de Ghellinck, S. J.*, Museum Lessianum, Section Historique, 13 (Gembloux, 1951) I, 121–47; repr. in his *Mittelalterliche Studien: Ausgewählte Aufsätze zur Schriftkunde und Literaturgeschichte*, 3 vols. (Stuttgart, 1966–81) I.150–71, at 150–4 for the centos 'Dicta Sibyllae magae' and 'Versus Sibyllae'.

[43]　Bischoff, 'Die lateinischen Übersetzungen', repr., pp. 156–63.

[44]　Peter Dronke, 'Medieval Sibyls: Their Character and their "Auctoritas"', *Studi Medievali* 3rd ser. 36 (1995), 581–615, at 582–9.

[45]　Bischoff, 'Die lateinischen Übersetzungen', repr., pp. 164–8 and Peter Dronke, *Hermes and the Sibyls: Continuations and Creations*, Inaugural Lecture of 9 March 1990 (Cambridge, 1990), pp. 16–23 and appendix pp. 30–2 (including lines 1–6, 10–20, 31–2, 84–103 and 133–6 of the poem); repr. in his *Intellectuals and Poets in Medieval Europe* (Rome, 1992), pp. 219–44.

it is 'a well-rounded, radiant and impassioned poem, full of rare ideas and phrasing',[46] and according to Peter Dronke it was composed in seventh-century Spain.[47]

There are descriptions of the performing of the Sibyl's song in different countries. A free translation in ten strophes of the acrostic written in Catalan, beginning 'El jorn del Judici/ parrà qui haur fet servici', was sung in the Cathedral Church of Palma de Maiorca on Christmas Eve;[48] a Provençal version, 'Sebila tot apertamens', is found in Paris, BN, fr. 14973 (s. xv).[49] An important link between the *Versus Sibyllae* and the Legend of the Fifteen Signs before Doomsday is provided by the Anglo-Norman *Jeu d'Adam*, a play of the mid-twelfth century in Tours, Bibliothèque munici-pale, 927, which has a long passage on the Fifteen Signs[50] uttered by the Sibyl[51] and concluding the play.[52] The prophecy of Doomsday is preceded by a comparison between the universe praising the Lord and human misbehaviour: whereas dumb animals, heaven and earth, the sun and the moon, all thank their Creator, men do not (lines 950–6). The play goes on to say that men would rather listen to the story of Roland and Oliver than to Christ's Passion (lines 957–72); the allusion, according to Aebischer,[53] is to an episode of the *Girart de Vienne*.[54] In the following lines the signs are presented with lively and imaginative details. Around the same time, Philippe de Thaon composed his *Livre de Sibile* (*c.* 1140),[55] a verse trans-lation of the Tiburtine Sibyl, a further witness to the enduring interest in this topic in England.

---

[46] Ursula Dronke, '*Voluspá* and Sibylline Traditions', p. 7.

[47] Peter Dronke, 'Medieval Sibyls', p. 615.

[48] P. Aebischer, 'Le "Cant de la Sibilla" de la nuit de noël a Majorque', in his *Neuf études sur le théâtre médiéval*, Université de Lausanne, Publications de la Faculté des Lettres 19 (Genève, 1972), pp. 13–24.

[49] H. Suchier, *Denkmäler provenzalischer Literatur und Sprache* (Halle, 1883).

[50] The lines were included in the editions by V. Luzarche, *Adam, Drame anglo-normand du XIIe siècle* (Tours, 1854) and L. Palustre, *Adam, mystère du XIIe siècle* (Paris, 1877); K. Grass, *Das Adamsspiel, Anglonormannisches Gedicht des XII. Jahrhunderts*, Romanische Bibliothek 6 (Halle a.s., 1891) printed them in his first edition, but excluded the passage from the second and third editions. W. Noomen, *Le Jeu d'Adame* (Paris, 1971) did not include the Sibyl's prophecy.

[51] This version is classified as the Old French Type by W. W. Heist, *The Fifteen Signs before Doomsday* (East Lansing, 1952), pp. 198–199; for the French versions of the Fifteen Signs, see P. Meyer, 'Notice sur un ms. Bourguignon (Musée britannique Addit. 15606)', *Romania* 6 (1877), 23–4; A. Långfors, *Les incipit des poèmes français antérieurs au XVIe siècle*, I (Paris, n.d. [1917]), 243 and 387–8, with addenda in W. W. Heist, 'Four Old French Versions of the Fifteen Signs before the Judgement', *Mediaeval Studies* 15 (1953), 187–9 and 191–3, and Heist, 'The Fifteen Signs before the Judgement: Further Remarks', *Mediaeval Studies* 22 (1960), 192–203.

[52] P. Aebischer, *Le Mystère d'Adam (Ordo representacionis Ade)*, Textes littéraires français 99 (Geneva and Paris, 1963), lines 945–1305. The play contains no rubric indicating that the Sibyl is the speaker. For a discussion of this passage, see Peter Dronke, 'Medieval Sibyls', pp. 589–96.

[53] P. Aebischer, 'Une allusion des *Quinze Signes du Jugement* à l'épisode du Jeu de la quintaine du *Girart de Vienne* primitif', in *Mélanges de linguistique romane et de philologie médiévale offerts à M. Maurice Delbouille*, II *Philologie Médiévale*, ed. J. Renson and M. Tyssens (Gembloux, 1964), pp. 7–19.

[54] *Girart de Vienne. Chanson de geste edited according to MS B XIX (Royal of the British Museum)*, ed. Fr. C. Yeandle (New York, 1930), lines 3061–709.

[55] H. Shields, *Le livre de Sibille de Philippe de Thaon*, Anglo-Norman Text Society 37 (London, 1979).

## The Acrostic in Anglo-Saxon England

The acrostic was the most popular Sibylline text in the Middle Ages. It is likely that more than one version of acrostic was in circulation in the British Isles: the translation of the *De civitate Dei* (XVIII.23),[56] and another version, whose idiosyncrasies have led critics to surmise that one poet tried his hand at a fresh Latin translation from Greek in the seventh or early eighth century.[57]

The 'Iudicii signum' was influential both for its eschatological content and its form:[58] the vogue of acrostic had reached England from Rome and this genre, concentrating on the construction of the lines rather than on the content, was appreciated and practised not only in the first centuries of Anglo-Latin literature, but also in later times.[59] The acrostic attracted the attention of Aldhelm, who might have learned it at Canterbury, and the Latin poem probably served as the model for his own acrostics.[60] Aldhelm quoted it three times in his *De metris*,[61] where he either refers to the acrostic by its title 'Haec . . . versibus Sibillae poetridis continetur' (*De metris*, p. 79, 23) or introduces it with a sentence 'item Sibillinus versus hoc idem declarat' (*De metris*, p. 93, 21) and 'et Sibilla profetissa ait' (*De metris*, p. 93, 32). No further quotations have been discovered in the works of medieval writers,[62] but the acrostic contributed to the impressive list of Doomsday material available in the British Isles.

One eccentric version of the acrostic is found only in Leipzig, Universitätsbibliothek, Rep. I. 74, 24r–25r, a codex which contains Aldhelm's *Enigmata*, as well as other riddles and Latin poems.[63] According to Bulst, this version could have been translated by Aldhelm[64] or by some other

---

[56] The circulation of the acrostic has no connection with that of Augustine's works, for which see J. F. Kelly, 'The Knowledge and Use of Augustine among the Anglo-Saxons', *Studia Patristica* 28 (1993), 211–16.

[57] See Bischoff, 'Die lateinischen Übersetzungen', repr., p. 154 and David Howlett, 'Insular Acrostics, Celtic Latin Colophons', *Cambrian Medieval Celtic Studies* 35 (1998), 27–44, at 44.

[58] See F. Neri, 'Le tradizioni italiane della Sibilla', *Studi medievali* 4 (1912–13), 220–1.

[59] See, for some late examples, Scott Gwara, 'Three Acrostic Poems by Abbo of Fleury', *The Journal of Medieval Latin* 2 (1992), 203–35; Michael Lapidge and Peter S. Baker, 'More Acrostic Verse by Abbo of Fleury', *The Journal of Medieval Latin* 7 (1977), 1–27.

[60] See Michael Lapidge and James Rosier, *Aldhelm: The Poetic Works* (Cambridge, 1985), p. 16 and Andy Orchard, *The Poetic Art of Aldhelm*, CSASE 8 (Cambridge, 1994), pp. 195–200.

[61] 'Vivat ut aeterno bonus ac malus ardeat igne' ('The good will be eternal and the evil will burn in the eternal fire') (line 12) (*De metris*, p. 79, 24); 'Denumerat tacitis tot crimina conscius ultor' ('The conscious avenger lists so many crimes to the silent men') (line 14) (*De metris*, p. 93, 33); and 'Tunc ille, aeterni species pulcherrima regni' ('Then he, the most beautiful shape of the eternal kingdom') (line 28) (*De metris*, p. 93, 22); see also *De virginitate*, line 282, p. 365 for a possible parallel with the Leipzig version. All references are to R. Ehwald, *Aldhelmi Opera*, MGH Auct. Antiq. 15 (Berlin, 1919; repr. 1961).

[62] Lapidge and Rosier, *Aldhelm: The Poetic Works*, p. 22, n. 15.

[63] The manuscript (s. ix$^{2/4}$) probably comes from Orléans; for a description of its content, see E. W. R. Nauman, *Catalogus Librorum manuscriptorum qui in Bibliotheca Senatoria Civitatis Lipsiensis asservantur* (Grimma, 1838), pp. 16–17.

[64] W. Bulst, 'Eine anglo-lateinische Übersetzung aus dem Griechischen um 700', *Zeitschrift für deutsches Altertum* 75 (1938), 105–11; repr. in *Lateinisches Mittelalter: Gesammelte Beiträge*, ed. W. Berschin (Heidelberg, 1984), pp. 57–63, at pp. 57–8.

scholar in the milieu of Theodore of Tarsus.[65] The text of the Leipzig version published by Bulst is defective at several points and has been emended by the editor; there are also many metrical faults and irregularities.[66] The translation is repetitive, as is common with the versions of the acrostic, and extremely free. According to Bischoff, it was directly translated from Greek, but its author knew the 'Iudicii signum': 'Der Übersetzer ist bei seiner Arbeit so frei vorgegangen, dass es im allgemeinen nicht möglich ist zu entscheiden, welche Varianten in seinem griechischen Text standen.'[67]

The Leipzig version is characterized by the choice of rare words, including several loan-words from Greek; the acrostic's bounds are well mastered and the new acrostic formed by the lines is at the same time correct and recherché, IESUS CHRISTUS DEI FILIUS SALVATOR CRUX; suffice to quote its first line: 'Iudicio tellus sudabit maesta propinquo' for 'Ἰδρώσει δὲ χθών, κρίσεως σημεῖον ὅτ' ἔσται.' and lines 9–10 'Ibit in haec cunta glomeratus ignis et astra / soluentur Stygiasque domus rogus unis habebit' for 'Ἐκκαύσει δὲ τὸ πῦρ γῆν οὐρανὸν ἠδὲ θάλασσαν / Ἰχνεῦον, ῥήξει τε πύλας εἱρκτῆς Ἀΐδαο.' instead of 'Exuret terras ignis pontumque polumque / Inquirens, taetri portas effringet Averni'.[68]

Cambridge, Corpus Christi College 173, fols. 57–83[69] includes Augustine's translation of the acrostic (83rb–83ra), followed by yet another version of the poem (83ra–83va). Many of the verses, which are written across the columns of the manuscript, are partly or wholly obliterated and the two versions of the acrostic have never been published or studied. The former is characterized by the presence of several variant readings and the latter should rather be ranked among the independent translations.

There are other versions, unknown and never studied, one of which is found in BL, Royal 15 B. XIX, 125r–125v. Here the poem is preceded by the title 'Versus Sybillae de die iuditii' (*incipit* 'Iuditii signum tellus sudore

---

[65] This translation is considered a product of the Canterbury school by Orchard, *The Poetic Art*, p. 196; Lapidge and Rosier, *Poetic Works*, pp. 16 and 265, n. 8; and B. Bischoff and Michael Lapidge, *Biblical Commentaries from the Canterbury School of Theodore and Hadrian*, CSASE 10 (Cambridge, 1994), pp. 185–6; according to Howlett, however, the composition is Hiberno-Latin: 'Insular Acrostics', pp. 27 and 44.

[66] For an analysis of the Leipzig acrostic, esp. compared with Aldhelm's poetic production, see Orchard, *The Poetic Art*, pp. 197–200.

[67] S-K, no. 8497; Howlett, 'Insular Acrostics', pp. 39–44; Bischoff, 'Die lateinischen Übersetzungen', repr., pp. 154–5.

[68] M. Haupt, 'Über eine Handschrift der Leipziger Stadtbibliothk', in his *Opuscula*, 3 vols. (Leipzig, 1875–76), I.286–302, at 289–90; W. Bulst, 'Eine anglo-lateinische Übersetzung', pp. 57–8. For a translation of the Leipzig version, see Howlett, 'Insular Acrostics', pp. 40–1.

[69] This part of the manuscript was probably written in the eighth century and, according to Lowe, *CLA* II, no. 123, 'in a Kentish centre'; for fols. 57–83, see M. R. James, *A Descriptive Catalogue of Manuscripts in the Library of Corpus Christi College Cambridge*, 2 vols. (Cambridge, 1912), I.400–2; Ker, *Catalogue*, no. 40; Helmut Gneuss, 'A Preliminary List of Manuscripts Written or Owned in England up to 1100', *ASE* 9 (1981), 1–60, no. 53; and Malcolm B. Parkes, 'The Palaeography of the Parker Manuscript of the *Chronicle*, Laws and Sedulius, and Historiography in Winchester in the Late Ninth and Tenth Centuries', *ASE* 5 (1976), 149–71, at 151.

madescet') and is accompanied by a note.[70] The Greek initials of the original acrostic are written in the margin and there are also a few interlinear glosses in Latin. In Cambridge, Corpus Christi College 448, 87r–88r[71] there is a version of the acrostic (*incipit* 'Iudicii signum tellus sudore madescet') which is quite close to the translation of *De civitate Dei*.[72] The twenty-seven lines of the poem are followed by a commentary, which explains how to read the acrostic, and a concluding remark, 'Hos versus sanctus Augustinus ex greco in latinum transtulit'.

The acrostic was also printed in Migne's edition of the works of Bede, with the title 'Versus sibyllini de Christo' as a part of a version of the *Sibylla Tiburtina* (PL 90, col. 1185); the same edition of Bede included the List of the Fifteen Signs before the Judgement, which was to become so popular in the Middle Ages (PL 94, col. 555).[73] As with other works included in this and other volumes of the *Patrologia Latina* we are, at present, unable to determine which manuscript the list was taken from. It purports to be a work by Jerome, as is said at the outset – 'Quindecim signa, quindecim dierum ante diem iudicii, invenit Hieronymus in annalibus Hebraeorum' – but it is neither Jerome's nor Bede's. Rather, it is part of the fondness evident in the Middle Ages and later times for attributing to Bede works on the Last Judgement, not least the poem *De die iudicii*.

The collection of poems gathered by Milred and now known as *Milred's Sylloge*[74] included some Sibylline verses. John Leland, who saw it in the sixteenth century, recorded among the content the 'Versus Sybillini de die iudicii' (item no. 14 in Leland's edition of *Milred's Sylloge*).[75] Leland did

---

[70] The origin of this part of the manuscript is still unknown; see Gneuss, 'A Preliminary List', no. 493; according to F. Carey, 'The Scriptorium of Reims during the Archbishopric of Hincmar (845–882 AD)', in *Classical and Mediæval Studies in Honor of E. K. Rand Presented upon the Completion of his Fortieth Year of Teaching*, ed. L. Webber Jones (New York, 1938), pp. 41–60, at p. 58, fols. 37–102 and 111–196 of the manuscript come from the monastery of St Remi at Rheims.

[71] The manuscript (s. x¹, s. x/xi) comes from Winchester; see Gneuss, 'A Preliminary List', no. 114; James, *A Descriptive Catalogue*, pp. 360–1.

[72] The rubric above the poem reads 'In nomine Domini incipiunt versus de die iudicii Sibille antiqui poetae'; in the Leipzig manuscript, the title is 'Versus Sybille de iudicio Dei'.

[73] The List of the Fifteen Signs before the Judgement was printed in the *Collectanea Pseudo-Bedae*. The *Collectanea* have recently been reprinted by Martha Bayless and Michael Lapidge, *Collectanea Pseudo-Bedae*, Scriptores Latini Hiberniae 14 (Dublin, 1998), nos. 356–71. The volume includes a brilliant reconstruction of the cultural milieu of the first edition of the *Collectanea* (from which the PL edition of the Fifteen Signs before the Judgement was taken), by Peter Jackson, 'Herwagen's Lost Manuscript of the *Collectanea*', pp. 101–20.

[74] On Milred and his Sylloge, see Patrick Sims-Williams, *Religion and Literature in Western England, 600–800*, CSASE 3 (Cambridge, 1990), pp. 328–59; Michael Lapidge, 'Some Remnants of Bede's Lost *Liber epigrammatum*', EHR 90 (1975), 798–820, repr. in his *Anglo-Latin Literature, 600–899* (London and Rio Grande, 1996), pp. 357–79 (with additions at pp. 510–29); Patrick Sims-Williams, 'Milred of Worcester's Collection of Latin Epigrams and its Continental Counterparts', *ASE* 10 (1982), 21–38, at 24, repr. in his *Britain and Early Christian Europe*, Collected Studies Series 514 (Aldershot and Brookfield, 1995), no. 9; Sims-Williams, 'William of Malmesbury and La silloge epigrafica di Cambridge', *Archivum Historiae Pontificiae* 21 (1983), 9–33, at 14, repr. in his *Britain*, no. 10.

[75] Leland included twenty-nine epigrams in his *Collectanea*; in some instances he did not transcribe the poems, but simply recorded their titles. The *Collectanea*, now Oxford, Bodleian, Top. gen. c. 1–4 (*Summary Catalogue*, no. 3118) were published by T. Hearne, *Joannis Lelandi antiquarii De rebus Britannicis collectanea*, 6 vols. (Oxford, 1715; 2nd ed., 1774), III, 114–18, at 115; see Patrizia Lendinara, 'Un'iscrizione di Vercelli nell'Inghilterra anglosassone', in *Vercelli tra Oriente e*

not transcribe them and now it is not possible to establish which work is
meant by that title. We are not in better stead with vol. 297 in Prior Henry
of Eastry's Catalogue, said to contain a 'Prophecia sibille'[76] which was, in
all probability, a Latin poem based upon the *Oracula Sibyllina*.[77]

A penchant for compositions with elaborate form and prophetic content
is also witnessed by Boulogne-sur-Mer, Bibliothèque municipale 189, a
manuscript written *c.* 1000 at Christ Church, Canterbury,[78] containing the
Latin version of the acrostic on 1ra and, on 1rb, a poem formed by the four
main lines of *Carmen* no. 25 of P. Optatianus Porphyrius.[79] It is noteworthy
how the same works occur in more than one Anglo-Saxon manuscript:[80] the
combination of poems of Pope Damasus with the 'Iudicium dei' seems to be
prompted by their form and betrays a predilection for sophisticated
compositions:[81] Cambridge, Corpus Christi College 173, fols. 57–83,
includes Caelius Sedulius's *Carmen Paschale*, Damasus's epigram on St
Paul, and two versions of the *Versus Sibyllae*.

A warning and a 'distinguo' come, as usual, from Ælfric who, in his
*Catholic Homilies* II.1, speaking about prophets, refers to the Sibyl,
remarking that, although she spoke about Christ's birth, passion, resurrection and his coming on the Day of Judgement, she was a heathen.
Interesting is the use of 'leoðcræftes wise' to refer to the Sibylline
prophecies, as well as the additional comment found in Oxford, Bodleian
Library, Hatton 113 and probably drawn from Isidore.[82]

## The Signs of Judgement

The 'Iudicii signum' is one of a number of texts, some of them apocryphal,
which were used as source material for ideas and narrative related to the

---

*Occidente tra tarda Antichità e Medioevo*, ed. V. Dolcetti Corazza, Bibliotheca Germanica, Studi
e Testi 6 (Alessandria, 1998), 183–219.

[76] M. R. James, *The Ancient Libraries of Canterbury and Dover* (Cambridge, 1903), pp. 13–142, at
50; see also Ker, *Catalogue*, p. xlv.

[77] Identification by Helmut Gneuss, 'Origin and Provenance of Anglo-Saxon Manucripts: The Case
of Cotton Tiberius A. III', in *Of the Making of Books: Medieval Manuscripts, their Scribes and
Readers. Essays Presented to M. B. Parkes*, ed. P. R. Robinson and R. Zim (Aldershot, 1997),
pp. 13–48, at p. 21.

[78] Ker, *Catalogue*, no. 7; Gneuss, 'A Preliminary', no. 805.

[79] S-K, no. 1005. P. Optatianus Porphyrius was the author of *carmina figurata* which circulated in
England; see Paul Zumthor, 'Carmina figurata', in his *Langue, texte, énigme* (Paris, 1975), pp. 25–
35; see also W. Levitan, 'Dancing at the End of the Rope: Optatian Porfyry and the Field of
Roman Verse', *Transactions of the American Philological Association* 115 (1985), 245–69 and
G. Polara, 'Optaziano Porfirio tra il calligramma antico e il carme figurato di età medievale',
*Invigilata Lucernis* 9 (1987), pp. 163–73.

[80] Patrizia Lendinara, 'Gregory and Damasus: Two Popes and Anglo-Saxon England', in *Rome and
the North: The Early Reception of Gregory the Great in Germanic Europe*, ed. Rolf H. Bremmer Jr,
Kees Dekker and David F. Johnson, Mediaevalia Groningana (Groningen, 2001) pp. 198–216, at
pp. 210–16.

[81] Five lines of the poem 'De nomine Jesu' attributed to Pope Damasus spell the name of Jesus
(S-K, no. 7913); this and the pseudo-Damasus epigram 'Iure pari regnat communs conditor aevi',
S-K, no. 8563, are both acrostics and telestiches.

[82] *Ælfric's Catholic Homilies: The Second Series*, ed. Malcolm Godden, EETS ss 5 (London, New
York and Toronto, 1979), pp. 9 and 346.

theme of the Last Judgement. The belief in a final destruction of the world was widespread: the Stoics imagined the end of the universe by fire, reshaping an image already in use since Heraclitus. It was the concept of Judgement that was unknown to the Greeks and Jews, and Christians elaborated the picture of a day when God would reveal himself.

The acrostic is of special importance in the shaping of the description of the signs preceding Judgement, a theme which is found in both poetry and prose and in both Old English and Anglo-Latin works. From a close reading of Augustine's version of the acrostic, it is possible to identify the following signs: the earth sweats and becomes barren; fire will ravage earth, heaven and sea; the doors of hell will be opened; the wicked men will be burned by fire; there will be suffering and fright for all men; the sun will no longer shine and stars will dissolve; there will be signs in the sky and the moon will become dark; hills and valleys will sink into the ground, buildings raised by man will fall down; mountains will be levelled, the sea will dry up; springs and rivers will be quenched by fire; a horn will be heard from heaven; the earth will gape open; a rain of fire and brimstone will fall from heaven.

It is noteworthy that the 'Iudicii signum' contains fairly close paraphrases of the Scriptures. The Sibyl prophesied general events such as war and famine, or natural phenomena; she started from the Creation of the World to end with the Last Judgement, a theme developed in the Old Testament in the books of prophets, especially Isaiah and Zephaniah.[83] Universal catastrophe was prophesied in Is. II.18–21, XXIV, XXV.2, XXVI.19–20, XXVII.8–13, XXXIV.4, XL.4; Ez. XXXII.6–8, 13, XXXVIII.9, 19–22; Ioel I.10, 15, 18; Am. VIII.9, 12; Mi. V.10, 12; Za. 12–14, etc. There are general predictions in the Gospels, Revelation, the Epistles and the Acts of the Apostles. Fire is the foremost sign of the Judgement to come (I Pt. 12, see also Ps. XLIX.3); the power of the heavens will be moved (Mt. XXIV.29; Lk. XXI.25; Mk. XIII.25); the moon and the sun will be turned to darkness (Mt. XXIV.29; Mk. XIII.24) or the moon turns to blood (Rev. VI.12); stars fall from heaven (Mt. XXIV.29, Lk. XXI.25, Mk. XIII.25, Rev. VI.13); there is thunder and lightning and earthquakes, voices will be heard (Rev. VIII.5); men will be frightened (Mt. VIII.12, XIII.42); they will cry out (Mt. XXIV.30) and hide themselves (Rev. VI.15–17); heaven will disappear and the elements will be melted by fire, as well as the earth and all its works (II Pt. III.12); the dead will rise again (Acts XVII.32; I Cor. XV.52). The most impressive sign is the advent of the Lord himself (Rev. XX.12–13), coming to judge in great majesty (Mt. XXIV.30, etc.) preceded by the sound of trumpets blown by the angels (Mt. XXIV.31; I Cor. XV.52; I Th. IV.16; 2 Pt. III.12–13; Rev. VII.1).

Many if not all of these biblical signs were reshaped and distributed in the fifteen days preceding the Last Judgement listed in the Latin text preserved

---

[83] References to the wrath of God and his coming as a judge include Sir. XVI.12–13, 16; So. I.2–3,15–18; etc. For the effect on heaven and earth, see Sir. XVI.18: 'ecce caelum et caeli caelorum abyssus et universa terra et quae in eis sunt in conspectu illius commevebuntur 19. montes simul et colles et fundamenta terrae et cum conspexit illa Deus tremore concutientur'; etc.

by the Basel edition of Bede. There was a variety of versions of the list in circulation, which have been grouped into families.[84] The first vernacular version in England dates from the twelfth century and is preserved in BL, Cotton Vespasian, D. xiv, 102r–103v.[85] The date and place of origin of the list that purports to describe the signs preceding the Judgement is unknown and the reference to Jerome is pseudonymous. Jerome could be a mistake for Augustine, who is mentioned in connection with the list and called to witness, for example in the *Jeu d'Adame*, thus providing a further link between the list and the acrostic.

The list shows some overlap with the 'Iudicii signum' in its description of the stars falling from heaven, the moon turning the colour of blood (in the acrostic the moon turns black), and the sea rising and reaching the sky (in the acrostic the sea merges with the earth). The eschatological descriptions based on the list make frequent use of numerological topoi, indulging in the enumeration of the phenomena that announce the Last Judgement; the acrostic, though presenting several signs, is far from being a bare enumeration of portents.

Overlap and differences are also evident when we compare the acrostic with a highly influential apocryphal text, the *Apocalypse of Thomas*. The non-interpolated version provides the following description of the days preceding the Last Judgement. On the first day, a voice is heard from heaven, a bloody cloud is seen and a bloody rain starts to fall; on the second day, a voice comes from heaven and earth is frightened, smoke comes from the gates of heaven now open; on the third day, at the heavenly voice, the ocean cries, heaven bursts open and smoke and stench are everywhere; on the fourth day, the waters melt, idols and buildings fall; on the fifth day, there is thunder and darkness, sun, moon and stars disappear; on the sixth day, heaven is torn out and people run away; on the seventh day, Christ comes and there is war among the angels and people. The influence of the *Apocalypse of Thomas* is evident in several Old English homilies and was quite widespread.[86]

The acrostic had a limited influence on vernacular versions, but occupies an important place in the purely Latin development of the legend.[87] The *De die iudicii*, a poem attributed to Bede,[88] betrays knowledge of the acrostic in

---

[84] See G. Nölle, 'Die Legende von den fünfzehn Zeichen vor dem jüngsten Gerichte', *Beiträge zur Geschichte der deutschen Sprache und Literatur* 6 (1899), 413–76 and Heist, *The Fifteen Signs before Doomsday*.

[85] Ed. R. D.-N. Warner, *Early Homilies from the Twelfth-Century MS. Vespasian D. XIV*, EETS os 152 (London, 1917; repr. 1971), pp. 89–91.

[86] See Max Förster, 'A New Version of the Apocalypse of Thomas in Old English', *Anglia* 73 (1955), 6–35; M. McC. Gatch, 'Two Uses of Apocrypha in Old English Homilies', *Church History* 33 (1964), 379–80; and Mary Swan, 'The *Apocalypse of Thomas* in Old English', *Leeds Studies in English* ns 29 (1998), 333–46.

[87] See Nölle, 'Die Legende', p. 420, who attributes widespread influence to the acrostic in the forming of the legend of the Fifteen Signs; for a different evaluation, see Heist, *The Fifteen Signs before Doomsday*, pp. 24 and 57–9.

[88] See Patrizia Lendinara, 'Alcuino e il *De die Iudicii*', *Pan* 18–19 (2001) (= *Miscellanea di Studi in Memoria di C. Roccaro*), 303–24; the most recent edition of the poem is that of J. Fraipont, *Bedae venerabilis liber hymnorum, rhythmi, variae preces. Bedae opera* IV, CCSL 122 (Turnhout, 1955), 439–44.

its insistence on the role of Christ as judge,[89] the account of his arrival and the signs which precede it, accumulated rather than listed, in a few central lines of the poem (lines 50–7 with a resumption in lines 72–6). The same source must be taken into account for several descriptions of the Last Judgement in Anglo-Latin and Old English literature. The literary legacy of the acrostic is small, but notable for its original – although not apocryphal – motifs. The tumult of Judgement Day and the related themes in Anglo-Saxon literature[90] were shaped through different kinds of sources: scriptural accounts, classical and patristic motifs, and apocryphal references. Writers in England were fascinated by exotic and apocryphal lore such as the Book of Esdra and the *Apocalyse of Thomas*, but also drew liberally on eschatological literature,[91] including the *Oracula Sibyllina*.

### Conclusion

Lactantius in the *Divinae institutiones* (vii, xvi, xix and xx), speaking of Judgement Day, seems to follow not the Bible, but the Sibylline tradition, and more than once calls the Sibyl to witness. Several later authors follow his lead. The acrostic was the best known part of the *Oracula* but, as we have remarked above, it brought along the image of the Sibyl uttering her prophecies and mingled on its way with other eschatological texts. The Sibyl was not mentioned in the acrostic but in the foreword or the rubrics; most importantly, it was she who addressed mortal men reminding them of the Day of Judgement that looms ahead. One proof of the importance and the centrality of the acrostic is provided by one of the earliest portrayals of a Sibyl[92] in the nave of the church of Sant'Angelo in Formis (s. xi), where she holds a cartouche with the inscription 'Iudicii signum, tellus sudore madescit.'

---

[89] Such knowledge is suggested not only by the title given to the poem in several manuscripts and drawn from line 8 ('Iudiciique diem'), but also by lines 9, 36, 38, 44, 49, 61 and 84.

[90] L. Whitbread, 'The Doomsday Theme in Old English Poetry', *Beiträge zur Geschichte der deutschen Sprache und Literatur* 89 (1967), 452–81.

[91] M. McC. Gatch, 'Eschatology in the Anonymous Old English Homilies', *Traditio* 21 (1965), 117–65.

[92] G. Seib, 'Sibyllen', in E. Kirschbaum *et al.*, *Lexikon der christlichen Ikonographie* (Rome, 1968–76), IV, cols. 150–4.

# 5

# Apostolic *Passiones* in
# Early Anglo-Saxon England

AIDEEN M. O'LEARY

T HE apostles' passion-legends in Latin and their deployments in Ireland
and Anglo-Saxon England have been the subject of occasional fascin-
ation among Anglo-Saxonists. However, insufficient consideration of those
Latin *passiones*, and sparse investigations into their Anglo-Latin deployments in particular, have left us with some misleading impressions of the
legends' influence in early Anglo-Saxon England. I have shown in previous
studies of the so-called 'pseudo-Abdias' collection that it is not possible to
define a distinct textual group in medieval Europe.[1] However, Irish
comparanda help to show that a collection of apostles' *passiones* was
known in Insular milieux by about AD 700 – certainly by the late seventh
century in Ireland, and possibly even earlier in Anglo-Saxon England. The
well-documented role(s) of apostles' cults in the Anglo-Saxon world must
be considered along with this specific textual evidence.

Medieval Irish ecclesiastics' enduring interest in apocryphal legends of
the apostles is first evident from St Patrick's earliest hagiographer,
Muirchú, who skilfully portrayed his subject as an Irish equivalent to St
Peter.[2] This, I have argued elsewhere,[3] had profound political implications
in Muirchú's own day, the late seventh century; and there are traces of other
apostolic apocrypha in that work.[4] We have revealing entries too in the

---

[1] Aideen M. O'Leary, *Trials and Translations: The Latin Origins of the Irish Apocryphal Acts of the
Apostles*, Publications of the Journal of Celtic Studies 1 (Turnhout, 2003); A. M. A. O'Leary, 'The
Latin Origins of the Irish Apocryphal Acts of the Apostles' (unpubl. Ph.D. diss., University of
Cambridge, 1997), pp. 219–62; Aideen O'Leary, 'By the Bishop of Babylon? The Alleged Origins
of the Collected Latin Apocryphal Acts of the Apostles', in *The Legacy of M. R. James*, ed. Lynda
Dennison (Donnington, 2001), pp. 128–38. I aim to produce an edited text of apostles' *passiones*,
perhaps even a single-manuscript edition; it has been almost three hundred years since a full
collection was made accessible to those who can use it most. Despite a few good editions of Latin
texts on individual apostles in recent decades, the inaccessibility of the collected *passiones* (so-
called 'pseudo-Abdias') has contributed to the difficulty in identifying apostolic *passiones* as
sources of Latin and vernacular accounts of the apostles, in England and elsewhere, in the Middle
Ages.
[2] *The Patrician Texts in the Book of Armagh*, ed. and trans. Ludwig Bieler and Fergus Kelly
(Dublin, 1979), pp. 88–91.
[3] O'Leary, 'The Latin Origins', pp. 187–94; O'Leary, 'An Irish Apocryphal Apostle: Muirchú's
Portrayal of Saint Patrick', *Harvard Theological Review* 89 (1996), 287–301.
[4] O'Leary, 'The Latin Origins', pp. 194–7.

poetry of Bláthmac, composed about 750 in the Irish language:[5] his particular interest, shared by most Anglo-Latin accounts, was the apostles' deaths. The (probably eighth-century) Gaelic compilation of canon law known as *Collectio canonum hibernensis* drew several of its anecdotes and exempla from apocryphal *acta*.[6] In addition, the pseudo-Isidorian *De ortu et obitu patrum* and the 'Irish Reference-Bible' clearly include elements of apostolic *passiones*[7] – in the case of the 'Reference-Bible' direct quotations – and both are arguably products of eighth- or ninth-century Irish milieux on the European Continent.[8] In the vernacular, a rich knowledge of apostolic apocrypha is almost certainly attested by the 'Martyrology of Oengus' – both its verse text from the same period and the later commentaries;[9] a tenth-century poet clearly adapted an episode from the *passio* of St Thomas;[10] and, by about 1200, there were full Irish translations of at least five apostolic *passiones*.[11] Also in circulation in medieval Ireland was a hymn on the apostles in the Irish *Liber hymnorum*, supposedly by the seventh-century abbot Cumméne Fota,[12] and several listings of apostles' appearances, provenances, deaths, and burial-places (and various combinations thereof).[13]

A broad reassessment of the earliest Anglo-Saxon legends about the apostles is essential, given my findings elsewhere. Here I hope to show when and in what forms apostolic apocrypha reached Anglo-Saxon England, and in which centres of learning they circulated. My findings also have implications for understanding Old English treatments of the apostles.

The question of the form in which such legends arrived in Anglo-Saxon England is perhaps the most straightforward. The collective nature of – and often specific textual references to and borrowings from – apostolic

---

[5] *The Poems of Blathmac, Son of Cú Brettan, together with the Irish Gospel of Thomas and a Poem on the Virgin Mary*, ed. and trans. James Carney (London, 1964), pp. 84–5; O'Leary, 'The Latin Origins', pp. 76–7.

[6] *Die irische Kanonensammlung*, ed. Herrmann Wasserschleben, 2nd ed. (Leipzig, 1885); O'Leary, 'The Latin Origins', p. 288.

[7] *Liber de ortu et obitu patriarcharum*, ed. and trans. José Carracedo Fraga, CCSL 108E (Turnhout, 1996); Munich, Bayerische Staatsbibliothek, MS Clm 14277 (written at the beginning of the ninth century, the earliest manuscript of the unedited 'Reference-Bible'); O'Leary, 'The Latin Origins', pp. 138–54 and 101–19, respectively.

[8] O'Leary, 'The Latin Origins', pp. 138 and 102–3, and the references cited.

[9] *Félire Óengusso Céli Dé. The Martyrology of Oengus the Culdee*, ed. and trans. Whitley Stokes (London, 1905); O'Leary, 'The Latin Origins', pp. 90–100 and 30–44, respectively.

[10] 'Airbertach mac Cosse's Poem on the Psalter', ed. and trans. Pádraig Ó Néill, *Éigse* 17 (1977–79), 19–46, at 39–40; *Die alten lateinischen Thomasakten*, ed. Klaus Zelzer (Berlin, 1977), pp. 7–8; O'Leary, 'The Latin Origins', pp. 78–89.

[11] *The Passions and the Homilies from Leabhar Breac*, ed. and trans. Robert Atkinson (Dublin, 1885–87): Passion of Peter and Paul, pp. 86–95 (text) and 329–39 (translation); Passion of Bartholomew, pp. 95–101 (text) and 339–46 (translation); Passion of James the Greater, pp. 102–6 (text) and 346–51 (translation); Passion of Andrew, pp. 106–10 (text) and 351–6 (translation); Passion of Philip, pp. 110–13 (text) and 356–8 (translation); O'Leary, 'The Latin Origins', pp. 1–29.

[12] *The Irish Liber Hymnorum*, ed. and trans. J. H. Bernard and R. Atkinson, 2 vols. (London, 1898), I.16–21; O'Leary, 'The Latin Origins', pp. 51–9.

[13] O'Leary, 'The Latin Origins', pp. 61–77; Dáibhí Ó Cróinín, 'Cummianus Longus and the Iconography of Christ and the Apostles in Early Irish Literature', in *Sages, Saints and Storytellers*, ed. Donnchadh Ó Corráin *et al.* (Maynooth, 1989), pp. 268–79.

apocrypha in English milieux show that these apocrypha came to England in a collected group,[14] certainly by 731 on Bede's evidence. In his *Retractatio in Actus Apostolorum*, Bede's scathing comments on the author of *passiones apostolorum* not only indicate a probable date, but also clearly show that he was familiar with a collection of apostolic passion-texts in Latin, and that he perceived that collection to be the work of a single author: 'cum ille qui praefatas apostolorum passiones scripsit ipse se certissime incerta et falsa scripsisse prodiderit'[15] ('since he who wrote the aforementioned passions of the apostles himself betrayed that he had written most certainly uncertain and untrue things'). I doubt that he could have based this statement on a reference to any *passiones apostolorum* which he had found elsewhere: he admitted close knowledge of a version of the Matthew-text as part of a collection of apostolic *passiones*, and that is not among the *passiones* widely deployed in the early Middle Ages.[16] Possibly a passional was known even earlier – by about 675 if we take Aldhelm's synod-allusion in his prose *De uirginitate* as referring to the council at Hertford in September 672,[17] though without direct reference to *passiones apostolorum*. In this way he was the first known Anglo-Saxon author to make clear use of apostles' *passiones* in collective fashion.[18]

Bede's knowledge of the existence of a collection may rest partly on his relationship with Acca, bishop of Hexham from 709 to 731, to whom (soon after 709, and perhaps before 716) he had dedicated his earlier *Expositio Actuum Apostolorum*,[19] since Acca's interest in apostles' missions was well known. Bede wrote of Acca that

> Dedit . . . operam . . . ut adquisitis undecumque reliquiis beatorum apostolorum et martyrum Christi in uenerationem illorum poneret altaria . . . sed et historias passionis eorum, una cum ceteris ecclesiasticis uoluminibus, summa industria congregans, amplissimam ibi ac nobilissimam bibliothecam fecit.

> (He took great trouble . . . to gather relics of the blessed apostles and martyrs of Christ from all parts and to put up altars for their

---

[14] Regarding the Twelve, I support the arguments of Alan Thacker, 'In Search of Saints: The English Church and the Cult of Roman Apostles and Martyrs in the Seventh and Eighth Centuries', in *Early Medieval Rome and the Christian West: Essays in Honour of Donald A. Bullough*, ed. Julia M. H. Smith (Leiden, 2000), pp. 247–77, at pp. 267–9. The earliest (Continental) manuscript evidence of assembly of groups of apostles' *passiones* is late eighth century: Guy Philippart, *Les légendiers latins et autres manuscrits hagiographiques* (Turnhout, 1977), pp. 16–18 and 87–93; O'Leary, 'The Latin Origins', pp. 229 and 319–20.

[15] *Retractatio*, I.13: *Bedae Venerabilis Opera, Pars II: Opera Exegetica*, 4, ed. M. L. W. Laistner, CCSL 121 (Turnhout, 1983), p. 107. Cf. C. Jenkins, 'Bede as Exegete and Theologian', in *Bede*, ed. A. H. Thompson (Oxford, 1935), pp. 152–200, at 160–1; Richard A. Lipsius, *Die apokryphen Apostelgeschichten und Apostellegenden*, 2 vols. in 3 and supplement (Braunschweig, 1883–90), I.215. See also pp. 113–14, below.

[16] Interestingly, it was not used by Aldhelm: O'Leary, 'The Latin Origins', p. 175.

[17] This would mean an earlier date for *De uirginitate* (which includes likely elements of apostles' *passiones*) than previously thought: *Aldhelm: The Prose Works*, trans. Michael Lapidge and Michael Herren (Ipswich, 1979), p. 14; cf. pp. 111–12, below.

[18] For discussion see pp. 107–11, below.

[19] *Bedae Venerabilis Expositio Actuum Apostolorum et Retractatio*, ed. M. L. W. Laistner (Cambridge, MA, 1939), pp. xv–xvii.

veneration. . . . He has also built up a very large and most noble
library, assiduously collecting histories of their passions as well as
other ecclesiastical books.)[20]

It follows that Bede might have acquainted himself with apocryphal
*passiones* of the apostles through Acca's library.

On this argument, Monkwearmouth-Jarrow had received a collection by
731 and perhaps by 725, if we follow Laistner's dating of the *Retractatio*.[21]
There is no doubt that they had already had some impact in the south:
Aldhelm deployed several apostolic passion-legends.[22] His fourth so-called
*Carmen ecclesiasticum* may have been a collective dedication of altars to the
apostles,[23] perhaps all in one church.[24] Bede's criticism of, and Aldhelm's
pilfering from, apostolic *passiones*, show that Anglo-Saxon ecclesiastical
scholars – at least those with access to good libraries – treated the apostles
as a group.[25] Certainly the apostles appear together in Anglo-Saxon
litanies,[26] which were probably in wide circulation by the mid-eighth
century.[27] It is not until the eleventh century that we have clear manuscript
evidence for large legendaries (like the 'Cotton-Corpus Legendary') in
England.[28] In parallel with the early development of certain individual
apostolic cults,[29] the Anglo-Saxon ecclesiastical elite seems to have held an
unrealistic perception of the apostles as a happy team, and their early
literature dealt with them as such.

How the collection of *passiones* reached England must be a matter of
speculation, although the obvious possibility of Theodore in the late 660s is
offset by the apparent absence of large-scale Anglo-Saxon devotion to St
Thomas (the major figure in the church of Edessa).[30] It is not impossible

---

[20] *Historia ecclesiastica gentis Anglorum*, V.20: *Bede's Ecclesiastical History of the English People*,
ed. and trans. Bertram Colgrave and R. A. B. Mynors (Oxford, 1969), pp. 530–1.

[21] *Bedae Venerabilis Expositio*, ed. Laistner, p. xvii.

[22] These include direct quotations: cf. pp. 110 and 112, below.

[23] Michael Lapidge, *Anglo-Latin Literature, 600–899* (London, 1996), pp. 8–9 and 49.

[24] Lapidge, *Anglo-Latin Literature*, p. 49; but the poems were not necessarily intended for
inscription in a real church: *Aldhelm: The Prose Works*, trans. Lapidge and Rosier, pp. 36 and
41–5.

[25] An exception is the case of martyrologies. Bede's martyrology, however, has little detail about the
apostles: *Édition pratique des martyrologes de Bède, de l'Anonyme lyonnais et de Florus*, ed.
Jacques Dubois and Geneviève Renaud (Paris, 1976). Cf. pp. 115–16, below, for more discussion
of non-collective uses of apostles' *passiones*.

[26] For instance, *Anglo-Saxon Litanies of the Saints*, ed. Michael Lapidge (London, 1991), pp. 120–1
and 128–9.

[27] Lapidge, *Anglo-Saxon Litanies*, pp. 11–13.

[28] Peter Jackson and Michael Lapidge, 'The Contents of the Cotton-Corpus Legendary', in *Holy
Men and Holy Women: Old English Prose Saints' Lives and their Contexts*, ed. Paul E. Szarmach
(New York, 1996), pp. 131–46. The earliest known Anglo-Saxon passional is Paris, Bibliothèque
nationale, MS lat. 10861 (early ninth century), which includes accounts of Philip and James the
Greater, and has been discussed by Michelle Brown, 'Paris, Bibliothèque Nationale, MS. lat.
10861 and the Scriptorium of Christ Church, Canterbury', *ASE* 15 (1986), 119–37; see also
Jackson and Lapidge, 'The Contents', p. 32.

[29] Cf. pp. 117–18, below.

[30] Cf. David N. Dumville, 'The Importation of Mediterranean Manuscripts into Theodore's
England', in *Archbishop Theodore: Commemorative Studies on his Life and Influence*, ed. Michael
Lapidge (Cambridge, 1995), pp. 96–119, and J. B. Segal, *Edessa: 'The Blessed City'* (Oxford,
1970).

that the texts were imported from Ireland,[31] but there is insufficient textual evidence for this early period. The first identifiable Anglo-Saxon known to have had a particular interest in acquiring apostolic passion-legends and relics was Acca, as reported by Bede,[32] but given the Aldhelmian uses of these texts, he was not the first to do so.[33] At least by Bede's day, the *passiones* were regarded as circulating in a collection. In the later Anglo-Saxon period also, their circulation was demonstrably almost always in collective form.[34]

I look now in more detail at early Anglo-Saxon references to the apostolic collections, beginning with Aldhelm, bishop of Sherborne (d. 709), whose fourth *Carmen ecclesiasticum* is a collective work on the apostles. This *Carmen*, and his two works known as *De uirginitate*, include quotations from, and/or episodes detailed in, several *passiones* of apostles, and these references relate to multiple apostles – both well-known and more obscure. I therefore think it extremely likely that Aldhelm was using a group of apostolic *passiones* which travelled together as a distinct collection.[35]

The principal source for his fourth *Carmen* has been thought to be Isidore's *De ortu et obitu patrum*.[36] This was clearly one major model; however, *passiones* formed an important source regarding at least six apostles.[37] In fact their influence on this *Carmen* has been in some respects overlooked,[38] particularly with regard to some details present in apostolic *passiones* but not in the texts which Aldhelm is thought to have used as a basic framework. The accounts vary considerably in the degrees to which Aldhelm used canonical and apocryphal sources, and none of them seems derived from a single source.[39] Some are largely constructed around apocryphal legends of the apostles, others around material which Aldhelm could have culled directly from the New Testament canon. Also canonical is the sequence of apostles: it corresponds with that in the *Communicantes*-prayer of the Mass.[40] One of the main sources behind Isidore's *De ortu* itself is, of

[31] Cf. Rolf H. Bremmer, Jr, 'The Reception of the Acts of John in Anglo-Saxon England', in *Studies in the Apocryphal Acts of John*, ed. Jan N. Bremmer (Kampen, 1995), pp. 183–96 at pp. 183–4.

[32] Cf. pp.105–6, above.

[33] It is possible that Benedict Biscop had earlier brought apostles' relics to Monkwearmouth-Jarrow: Thacker, 'In Search of Saints', pp. 259–61 (including broader discussion of relics in England); Éamonn Ó Carragáin, *The City of Rome and the World of Bede* (Jarrow, 1995), pp. 3–4.

[34] Cf. pp. 118–19, below.

[35] Here I focus only on the clearest evidence for Aldhelm's deployment of the *passiones*; for fuller source studies of the fourth *Carmen* (following the complete sequence presented by Aldhelm) and the apostolic accounts in both versions of *De uirginitate*, see O'Leary, 'The Latin Origins', pp. 155–84.

[36] O'Leary, 'The Latin Origins', pp. 42–3.

[37] Cf. O'Leary, 'The Latin Origins', pp. 183–4.

[38] For instance, Bremmer, 'The Reception', pp. 184–5, deals with this apostle only, thereby reaching misleading conclusions about Aldhelm's sources.

[39] *Aldhelm: The Poetic Works*, trans. Michael Lapidge and James L. Rosier (Cambridge, 1985), pp. 42–4.

[40] *L'Ordinaire de la Messe*, ed. and trans. B. Botte and C. Mohrmann (Paris, 1953), pp. 76–9; Thacker, 'In Search of Saints', pp. 270–1; *Aldhelm: The Poetic Works*, trans. Lapidge and Rosier, pp. 42–3.

course, apocryphal *acta*, especially in respect of the less prominent apostles, but Aldhelm frequently expanded on, and diverged considerably from, Isidore.[41] In addition to *De ortu*, he occasionally used the apostolic accounts in Isidore's *Etymologiae*,[42] Jerome's *De uiris illustribus*,[43] and Rufinus's translation of the *Historia ecclesiastica* of Eusebius.[44]

The poem on St Peter[45] tells of the apostle's conquest of the evil sorcerer, Simon Magus,[46] the only uncanonical event described here. This account clearly has its main source in apocryphal *acta* – probably the Passion of Peter and Paul by pseudo-Marcellus (*BHL* 6657)[47] if one is to judge by the similar details and vocabulary (although in the Passion, Simon is overcome by the cooperation of the two apostles). Pseudo-Marcellus's description of the scene preceding Simon's defeat is as follows: 'Tunc ascendit Simon in turrim coram omnibus, et extensis manibus coronatus lauro coepit uolare'[48] ('then Simon went up into the tower in front of all, and, with his arms open wide, crowned with laurels, he began to fly'). After a dramatic prayer by Peter (encouraged by Paul), we are told 'continuo dimissus cecidit in locum qui Sacra Via dicitur, et in quattuor partes fractus quattuor silices adunauit'[49] ('immediately he was released [by the demons supporting him], and fell down into the place which is called the Sacred Way, and [his body] broke into four parts and turn into four stones'). Compare Aldhelm's description of Simon:[50]

> Qui praecelsa rudis scandit fastigia turris
> Atque coronatus lauri de fronde uolauit,
> Sed mox aethereas dimittens furcifer auras
> Cernuus ad terram confractis ossibus ambro
> Corruit, et Petro cessit uictoria belli.

[41] Cf. pp. 109–10, below.

[42] 7.ix: *Isidori Hispalensis Episcopi Etymologiarum siue Originum Libri XX*, ed. W. M. Lindsay, 2 vols. (Oxford, 1911), I (no page-numbers); *PL* 82, cols. 287–9.

[43] *Gerolamo. Gli uomini illustri. De uiris illustribus*, ed. and trans. Aldo Ceresa-Gastaldo (Florence, 1988), pp. 72–86 and 92–5; *Hieronymus, Liber de uiris illustribus*, ed. Ernest C. Richardson (Leipzig, 1896), pp. 1–13; §§ 1–5 and 9 on six apostles – Peter, James the Less, Matthew, Jude, Paul and John.

[44] *Eusebius Werke. Die Kirchengeschichte. Die lateinischen Übersetzung des Rufinus*, ed. E. Schwartz and T. Mommsen (Leipzig, 1903–8), II, especially pp. 167–75 and 83–97.

[45] *Aldhelmi Opera*, ed. Rudolf Ehwald (Berlin, 1913–19), pp. 19–20; *Aldhelm: The Poetic Works*, trans. Lapidge and Rosier, p. 50.

[46] *Aldhelmi Opera*, ed. Ehwald, p. 20, lines 25–32; *Aldhelm: The Poetic Works*, trans. Lapidge and Rosier, p. 50. For portrayals of this rivalry in other contexts see H. E. J. Cowdrey, 'Simon Magus in South Italy', *Anglo-Norman Studies* 15 (1992), 77–90, at 79–81; Tamás Adamik, 'The Image of Simon Magus in the Christian Tradition', in *The Apocryphal Acts of Peter: Magic, Miracles and Gnosticism*, ed. Jan N. Bremmer (Leuven, 1998), pp. 52–64.

[47] *Acta apostolorum apocrypha*, ed. Richard A. Lipsius and Maximilian Bonnet, 2 vols. in 3 (Leipzig, 1891–1903), I.119–77.

[48] Lipsius and Bonnet, *Acta*, I.165, lines 11–12 (§ 54).

[49] Lipsius and Bonnet, *Acta*, I.167, lines 9–11 (§ 56). A shorter Passion of Peter and Paul (*BHL* 6667), which also describes this event, is less similar to Aldhelm's account; for instance, it has no reference to Simon's crown of laurels: Lipsius and Bonnet, *Acta*, I.223–34, at 232 (§ 11). The same is true for a similar text known as *Actus Petri cum Simone* (*BHL* 6656): Lipsius and Bonnet, *Acta*, I.45–103, at 83 (§ 32).

[50] *Aldhelmi Opera*, ed. Ehwald, p. 20, lines 28–32; *Aldhelm: The Poetic Works*, trans. Lapidge and Rosier, p. 50.

([Simon] climbed the lofty summits of a new tower and, crowned with a branch of laurel, he set off flying; but the greedy crook fell face-down on the ground, expelling at once his vital breath, with all his bones shattered; and victory in this battle went to St Peter.)

Jerome's *De uiris illustribus* may be behind Aldhelm's description of Peter's martyrdom,[51] but Aldhelm clearly also made use of apocryphal material additional to the *magus*-episode in the work of Isidore, which the latter conveyed in a very concise manner.

The poem concerning Andrew[52] consists of a lengthy account of his calling by Jesus[53] and implicit references to a *passio* of the apostle, probably the 'Letter of Priests and Deacons of Achaia' (*BHL* 428).[54] The question[55]

Quis numerare ualet populosis oppida turbis,
Illius eloquio quae fana profana friabant
Credula pandentes regi praecordia Christo?

(Who would be able to enumerate the many towns with their populous crowds which, as a result of Andrew's teaching, demolished their unholy holies and opened their believing hearts to Christ the King?)

is a rhetorical rendering of the proconsul-executioner Aegeas' accusation, put directly to Andrew, that all the towns were turning away from their pagan gods because of Andrew's preaching, as quoted in the 'Letter of Priests and Deacons': 'Nulla . . . remansit in Achaia ciuitas in qua non templa deorum derelicta sint et deserta'[56] ('no city in Achaia remains in which the temples of the gods have not been forsaken and deserted'). At the beginning and end of his poem, Aldhelm referred in graphic terms to the apostle's crucifixion, which is narrated in the two separate *passiones* of Andrew. Aldhelm stated that the apostle went to his death 'laetus' ('joyful'), an echo either of the 'Letter'[57] or of *Conuersante et docente* (*BHL* 429),[58] a briefer *passio* of Andrew; in both of these, Andrew's delight in and eagerness for martyrdom are obvious. So the poem seems to have much in common with the 'Letter of Priests and Deacons' in particular.

Aldhelm's poem on Bartholomew[59] has a clearer, and even closer,

---

[51] *Aldhelm: The Poetic Works*, trans. Lapidge and Rosier, p. 50 and p. 239, n. 43.
[52] *Aldhelmi Opera*, ed. Ehwald, pp. 22–3; *Aldhelm: The Poetic Works*, trans. Lapidge and Rosier, p. 52.
[53] For example, Matthew IV.18–20.
[54] Lipsius and Bonnet, *Acta*, II.1, pp. 1–37.
[55] *Aldhelmi Opera*, ed. Ehwald, p. 22, lines 10–12; *Aldhelm: The Poetic Works*, trans. Lapidge and Rosier, p. 52.
[56] Lipsius and Bonnet, *Acta*, II.1, p. 20, lines 1–2 (§ 8).
[57] Lipsius and Bonnet, *Acta*, II.1, p. 24, line 6 (§ 10), 'gaudens et exultans ibat' ('he went rejoicing and celebrating'); and p. 25, lines 5–6 (§ 10), 'gaudens uenio ad te' ('I come to you [the cross] rejoicing').
[58] 'Passio sancti Andreae apostoli', ed. Max Bonnet, *Analecta Bollandiana* 13 (1894), 373–8, at 376, line 6 (§ 4): 'laetus pergo ad te' ('I approach you [the cross] joyful').
[59] *Aldhelmi Opera*, ed. Ehwald, p. 28; *Aldhelm: The Poetic Works*, trans. Lapidge and Rosier, p. 55.

connection with the *passio* of the apostle (*BHL* 1002). Even its opening echoes the *passio*:[60]

> Ultima terrarum praepollens India constat,
> Qua⟨s⟩ tres in partes librorum scripta sequestrant.

> (Mighty India stands as the last of the lands of the earth, which the writings in books divide up into three parts.)

There is, of course, no difficulty with this interpretation; however, if one takes the manuscript-reading *Quam* (for Ehwald's *Quas*) into account,[61] Aldhelm's opening would be strikingly similar to that of the *passio*: 'Indiae tres esse ab historiographis adseruntur'[62] ('Historiographies claim that there are three Indias'). Without the emendation Aldhelm's opening in translation reads 'Mighty India, which the writings in books divide up into three parts, stands as the last of the lands of the earth.' There is a strong possibility, therefore, that Ehwald's emendation was unnecessary. The *passio* is certainly reflected in the mention of idolatry among the Indian people,[63] and of Bartholomew destroying the shrines by smashing the idol-gods.[64] Indeed, in this *Carmen*, Aldhelm seems to have enjoyed describing the previous wickedness of the apostles' converts in relation to several mission-fields, particularly those of Thomas, James the Greater, Philip and Jude. The apostle's martyrdom is briefly mentioned – 'martirii mercatur serta cruenta' ('he purchased martyrdom with a bloody garland').[65] The meaning of this is not absolutely clear and does not necessarily follow *De ortu* or the *Breuiarium*, in both of which he was flayed alive,[66] or the *passio*, in which we are also told of his beheading.[67] Clearly, however, the poem draws extensively from apocryphal literature on Bartholomew.

Evidently Isidore's *De ortu* and some apostolic *passiones* were used in varying proportions in the composition of the fourth *Carmen ecclesiasticum*. Aldhelm may also have drawn on select passages of Jerome's *De uiris illustribus* and Rufinus's translation of Eusebius for information on some apostles. However, Aldhelm's impressionistic and homiletic style in drawing

---

[60] *Aldhelmi Opera*, ed. Ehwald, p. 28, lines 1–2; *Aldhelm: The Poetic Works*, trans. Lapidge and Rosier, p. 55. Cf. Louis Duchesne, 'Les anciens recueils de légendes apostoliques', *Compte rendu du troisième Congrès scientifique internationale des catholiques*, V (Bruxelles, 1895), pp. 67–79, at p. 76.

[61] 'Quam *codd.*': *Aldhelmi Opera*, ed. Ehwald, p. 28.

[62] Lipsius and Bonnet, *Acta*, II.1, p. 128, lines 2–3 (§ 1).

[63] *Aldhelmi Opera*, ed. Ehwald, p. 28, line 3; *Aldhelm: The Poetic Works*, trans. Lapidge and Rosier, p. 55; Lipsius and Bonnet, *Acta*, II.1, p. 129, lines 3–10 (§ 1).

[64] *Aldhelmi Opera*, ed. Ehwald, p. 28, lines 4–5; *Aldhelm: The Poetic Works*, trans. Lapidge and Rosier, p. 55; Lipsius and Bonnet, *Acta*, II.1, pp. 143, line 16, 144, lines 1–3 (§ 6), and 149, lines 1–2 (§ 9).

[65] *Aldhelmi Opera*, ed. Ehwald, p. 28, line 12; *Aldhelm: The Poetic Works*, trans. Lapidge and Rosier, p. 55.

[66] *De ortu*: *Isidoro de Sevilla, De ortu et obitu patrum*, ed. and trans. César Chaparro Gómez (Paris, 1985), pp. 210–11 (§ 74); *PL* 83, cols. 152–3 (§ lxxv, 133). *Breuiarium*: 'Martyrologium hieronymianum e codice Treuirensi nunc primum editum', ed. Socii Bollandiani, *Analecta Bollandiana* 2 (1883), 7–34, at 10 (there is a reference in the latter to his beheading also).

[67] Lipsius and Bonnet, *Acta*, II.1, p. 149, lines 4–5 (§ 9).

out his comparatively terse sources – I assume that the expansions are his own – make it difficult to identify the precise sources which he used. In sum, there is a strong case for his use of *passiones* of Peter and Paul, Andrew, and Bartholomew, and much of this evidence is consolidated and expanded by Aldhelm's accounts in both the prose and verse *De uirginitate*.

The prose version of *De uirginitate* highlights just three of the apostles, either because only these three among the Twelve were virgins or because these were the only apostles whose virginity was sufficiently well documented for inclusion in such a treatise. In the passage on John,[68] Aldhelm's account of John's miracles was clearly influenced by apocryphal legends, in particular the *uita* known as *Virtutes Iohannis* (*BHL* 4316)[69] and the pseudo-Mellitus *passio* (*BHL* 4320).[70] The best examples are the apostle's reassembly of jewels which had been dropped on the ground by two brothers following the advice of a supposed wise man;[71] the raising to life of a woman (Drusiana);[72] and, most famously, his drinking of a poisoned draught without suffering any harm, as well as raising two people from the dead.[73] All these episodes are included in the two major Latin apocryphal texts on John; but the background to the Drusiana-episode is told in briefer fashion in the pseudo-Mellitus text. However, part of the poison-episode was lost from Aldhelm's account, since he did not state – as did Isidore – that the people raised by John had in fact been killed by the same poison or that they had been put to death as condemned criminals. Aldhelm's expansion of events (if we take *De ortu* as his source) included a wonderfully detailed list of ingredients of the poison and a more substantial description of the apostle's courage in facing this test, as well as a fuller account of John's miracles in relation to the natural world, including changing branches into gold and pebbles into jewels.[74] Much of this passage almost certainly derives from Isidore's *De ortu*, but that was not the only source since, although Isidore described the miracle of the jewels, the raising of Drusiana, and the poisoned cup, *De ortu* does not offer enough detail to have provided the sole exemplar.

The account of Thomas – whom Aldhelm included only in the prose *De uirginitate*[75] – gives us the strongest evidence of all for Aldhelm's use of

---

[68] *Aldhelmi Opera*, ed. Ehwald, pp. 254–5; *Aldhelm: The Prose Works*, trans. Lapidge and Herren, pp. 80–1.

[69] *Acta Iohannis*, ed. and trans. Eric Junod and Jean-Daniel Kaestli, 2 vols., CCSA 1–2 (Turnhout, 1983), II.799–834.

[70] *Codex Apocryphus Novi Testamenti*, ed. I. A. Fabricius, 2nd ed., 3 vols. (Hamburg 1719), III.604–24.

[71] Both Aldhelm and Isidore mention the *gemmarum fragmina*, 'fragments of jewels', though only Aldhelm gives the background of their being dropped on the ground at the advice of a wise man; see *Aldhelmi Opera*, ed. Ehwald, p. 254, lines 15–17; *Aldhelm: The Prose Works*, trans. Lapidge and Herren, p. 80.

[72] *Aldhelmi Opera*, ed. Ehwald, pp. 254, line 17, and 255, lines 1–3; *Aldhelm: The Prose Works*, trans. Lapidge and Herren, p. 80.

[73] John's raising two people from the dead is not mentioned by Isidore; see *Aldhelmi Opera*, ed. Ehwald, p. 255, lines 3–10; *Aldhelm: The Prose Works*, trans. Lapidge and Herren, p. 80.

[74] Isidore, *De ortu: Isidoro*, ed. and trans. Chaparro Gómez, pp. 206–7 (§ 71,3); *PL* 83, col. 151 (§ lxxii, 128).

[75] *Aldhelmi Opera*, ed. Ehwald, p. 255; *Aldhelm: The Prose Works*, trans. Lapidge and Herren, p. 81.

apostolic *passiones*, for it includes a direct quotation from the *passio* of Thomas (*BHL* 8136).[76] We are told that Thomas annulled pagan practices by instructing that marriage-partners be taught the praises of virginity. There follows this quotation of Thomas's words:[77]

> 'Habetis', inquit, 'integritatem, quae est omnium regina uirtutum et fructus perpetuae uirginitatis. Virginitas soror est angelorum et omnium bonorum possessio, uirginitas uictoria libidinum, tropeum fidei, uictoria de inimicis et uitae aeternae securitas.'

> (He said: 'You have innocence, which is the queen of all virtues and the reward of perpetual virginity. Virginity is the sister of the angels and the possession of all good things, virginity is victory over desires, the trophy of faith, a triumph over enemies and the surety of eternal life.')

The apostle's words, extracted from a longer exhortation, were relayed verbatim by Aldhelm. Thomas had blessed the young betrothed couple, Dionysius and Pelagia (the king's daughter), but later reappeared to them to extol in this way the beauty of virginity. Aldhelm concluded the passage with a brief eulogy of Thomas.

It is very likely, from the evidence of apocryphal information in Aldhelm's works, that he used apocryphal *passiones* in his apostolic accounts, though less systematically than did Isidore in *De ortu*. Occasionally he even quoted directly, as from the *passiones* of Bartholomew (*BHL* 1002) and Thomas (*BHL* 8136). It is remarkable, in my view, that he chose to stick so closely to his sources, even despite his presumed lack of information on apostles who were relatively minor in the Insular context.

When we combine all this evidence, there is strong testimony to his deployment of apocryphal *passiones* concerning six apostles: Peter and Paul (together), Andrew, Bartholomew, John, and Thomas. For these five *passiones* the evidence is strong; others among Aldhelm's apostolic passages were possibly drawn from *passiones* also.[78] I think it extremely likely, therefore, that he had access to a full collection of apostolic *passiones*. From these he selected particular events or images, combining them with a number of other sources to create a new account of the apostle in question. He expanded considerably the material in his sources, often using Isidore's *De ortu* as his starting point but omitting a large proportion of that source's information. Most of this expansion was of a rhetorical, not informative, nature: the descriptions portray an intense devotion to these saints. Much of the information was imparted by implication rather than by straightforward utterance and, on the subject of the apostles' deaths, Aldhelm was often unusually concise or circumspect. In sum, the

---

[76] *Die alten lateinischen Thomasakten*, ed. Zelzer, p. 10, lines 3–6 (§ 12). Cf. *Aldhelmi Opera*, ed. Ehwald, p. 255, n. 3, and *Aldhelm: The Prose Works*, trans. Lapidge and Herren, pp. 81 and 194–5, n. 12, who all confessed to being unsuccessful in identifying the source.

[77] *Aldhelmi Opera*, ed. Ehwald, p. 255, lines 20–3; *Aldhelm: The Prose Works*, trans. Lapidge and Herren, p. 81.

[78] O'Leary, 'The Latin Origins', pp. 165–76.

events narrated in earlier sources were transformed by Aldhelm's elo-
quence.

Circulation of this collection possibly moved northwards in the early
eighth century. Bede's awareness of apostles' *passiones* is especially evident
in his *Retractatio in Actus Apostolorum*, written about 725,[79] in which a brief
passage on Simon and Jude includes reference to – and a short quotation
from – the *passio* of those two apostles: 'Hos referunt historiae, in quibus
passiones apostolorum continentur et a plurimis deputantur apocryfae,
praedicasse in Perside ibique *a templorum pontificibus in ciuitate Suanir
occisos* gloriosum subisse martyrium'[80] ('the narratives in which the passions of the apostles are contained and which are condemned by most as
apocryphal, say that these men [Simon and Jude] preached in Persia, and
there were killed by the priests of the temples in the city of Suanir, [and] to
have suffered a glorious martyrdom'). He referred later in the same work to
such texts in terms of a block of material by a single author.[81]

In his *Retractatio*, Bede set out to provide revision and clarification of
parts of the *Expositio*, including additional explanatory material and
correction of passages where he felt that he had been misled.[82] Such a
process may have been behind his denial of the authenticity of the passions
of the apostles. For, while clarifying some of his previous statements in
which he had trustingly followed information provided by Jerome and by
Rufinus' translation of Eusebius' *Historia ecclesiastica*,[83] he took the
opportunity to criticise the author of the *passiones*, which he had by that
time found to be the basis of Isidore's and others' accounts and which he
did not regard as authoritative or trustworthy.[84] His comment was illustrated by a single example, from the Passion of St Matthew. Bede's own
research and comparison with works of great authority showed that the
name 'Candacis' – given in the passion-text to a eunuch associated with
Matthew and Ethiopia[85] – was in fact the woman's name Candace, referring
to the queen of Ethiopia.[86] This very passage was presumably the source of
the author's mistake.[87] It is interesting that such a misreading apparently

---

[79] Cf. p. 105, above.
[80] *Retractatio*, I.13: *Bedae Venerabilis Opera, Pars II: Opera Exegetica*, 4, ed. Laistner, p. 106. The
text highlighted by Laistner is the quotation from the *passio*. Cf. Charles D. Wright, 'Apocryphal
Acts', in *Sources of Anglo-Saxon Literary Culture: A Trial Version*, ed. Frederick M. Biggs *et al.*
(Binghamton, NY, 1990), pp. 48–63, at p. 48.
[81] Cf. p. 105, above.
[82] George Hardin Brown, *Bede the Venerable* (Boston, MA, 1987), p. 58.
[83] *Retractatio*, I.13: *Bedae Venerabilis Opera, Pars II: Opera Exegetica*, 4, ed. Laistner, p. 107.
[84] Cf. p. 105, above.
[85] *Codex*, ed. Fabricius, II.640–3 (Book 7, §§ 3–4) and 649–50 (Book 7, § 7).
[86] *Retractatio* I.13: *Bedae Venerabilis Opera, Pars II: Opera Exegetica*, 4, ed. Laistner, p. 107. A
canonical anecdote (Acts VIII.27–39) about the conversion of a eunuch-official of Candace by
Philip the Deacon, begins as follows: 'And behold an Ethiopian man, a eunuch, of great
authority under Candace the queen of the Ethiopians, who had charge over all her treasury, had
come to Jerusalem to adore.'
[87] Cf. also Bede's *Expositio* on Acts VIII.27: *Bedae Venerabilis Opera, Pars II: Opera Exegetica*, 4,
ed. Laistner, pp. 41–2, where it is said that rule by women was customary in Ethiopia: 'Moris
quippe fuit illi nationi semper a feminis regi easque candaces appellare' ('indeed it was the custom
for that people to be permanently ruled by women and to call them Candace') (p. 41, lines 74–5).

persisted from the time of composition of the Passion of Matthew (possibly the sixth century) without known criticism or correction until the eighth century.

Though few in number, Bede's references to apocryphal *passiones* in his apostolic commentaries shed much light on which texts he knew and his opinions thereof. His acquaintance with these texts is also evident from his poetry.[88] Some of his hymns, notably those composed for the feasts of SS Peter and Paul, Andrew, and John the Baptist, refer to the deaths of holy figures.[89] The most outstanding example is the second of the two hymns for the feast of St Andrew,[90] in which the apostle's speech to the cross is extensively 'quoted' in the first seven stanzas, followed by a fairly detailed account of his crucifixion and a final prayer. Episodes which most vividly recall the passion-texts are Andrew's joyful procession to the cross[91] – particularly his prayer that he not descend alive[92] – and the scene of his death, when a bright light envelops him so that he is rendered invisible and his soul is carried into heaven.[93] Here are the two latter stanzas:

> 'Iesu, precor,' dixit, 'bone
> Magister, ista de cruce
> Me nemo uiuum in corpore
> Vinclis solutis auferat.'

> Haec dixit, et caelestibus
> Emissa lux e edibus
> Circumdederit fortissimum
> Christi corusca martyrem.

('Jesus, I pray,' he said, 'good Master, let no-one carry me away from this cross alive in body with chains loosed.' He said this, and a light was sent out from the heavenly dwellings and surrounded Christ's bravest martyr with a flash.)

This hymn closely resembles both extant Latin passion-texts of Andrew in terms of events, emotions, and vocabulary, but these details are especially similar to the longer version in the 'Letter of Priests and Deacons of Achaia' (*BHL* 428):[94]

> Tunc uoce magna sanctus Andreas dixit, 'Domine Iesu Christe, magister bone, iube me de ista cruce non deponi nisi ante spiritum meum susceperis.' Et cum haec dixisset, uidentibus cunctis splendor

[88] Cf. Josef Szövérffy, *Die Annalen der lateinischen Hymnendichtung: Ein Handbuch*, 2 vols. (Berlin, 1964/5), I.168–70 and 174–6, and Michael Lapidge, *Bede the Poet* (Jarrow, 1994), p. 1.

[89] *Bedae Venerabilis Opera, Pars IV: Opera Rhythmica*, ed. J. Fraipont, CCSL 122 (Turnhout, 1955), pp. 405–70. A list of the hymns which refer to the apostles has been provided by Lapidge, *Bede the Poet*, pp. 8–9.

[90] *Bedae Venerabilis Opera, Pars IV: Opera Rhythmica*, ed. Fraipont, pp. 437–8.

[91] Stanza 8: Fraipont, *Opera Rhythmica*, p. 437.

[92] Stanza 12: Fraipont, *Opera Rhythmica*, p. 438.

[93] Stanza 14: Fraipont, *Opera Rhythmica*, p. 438.

[94] Lipsius and Bonnet, *Acta*, II.1, pp. 32, lines 3–4, 33, lines 1–4, and 34, lines 1–2 (§ 14).

nimius sicut fulgor de caelo ueniens ita circumdedit eum ut penitus
prae ipso splendore oculi eum non possent eum aspicere.

(Then holy Andrew said in a loud voice, 'Lord Jesus Christ, great
Master, command that I not be taken down from this cross unless
you have already received my spirit.' When he had said this, a great
brightness just like lightning came from heaven in sight of all, and
surrounded him in such a way that human eyes could not see him
because of that brightness.)

Bede clearly intended his hymn not only to retell the legend of this apostle's
martyrdom, but to illustrate his courage and humanity.

We may deduce, then, that apostolic *passiones* circulated in a distinct
group which reached England (perhaps before arriving in Ireland) by about
AD 700. With regard to Insular transmission, Bede's perception of a
collection of these *passiones* was supported – though without reference to
a single author – in *Collectio canonum hibernensis*.[95] The passage at issue
may also have implications for the question of which recension (A or B) has
priority.[96]

Dramatic excerpts from apostles' *passiones* sometimes made their way
into other forms. One important Anglo-Saxon private prayer-book is the
Book of Cerne[97] (whose contents are partly of Irish textual origin), dated to
the earlier ninth century.[98] The Book includes three prayers also present in
apostolic *passiones*.[99] The first is the address by Andrew to his cross when
he first saw the instrument of his execution,[100] found in the aforementioned
Andrew-passion known as the 'Letter of Priests and Deacons of Achaia';[101]
Andrew's invocation of his cross evokes the larger legend around that
prayer. Another is the prayer of John the Evangelist prior to his drinking a
cup of poison,[102] as in the apocryphal texts on his death, the so-called
*Virtutes Iohannis* (*BHL* 4316) and the *passio* by pseudo-Mellitus (*BHL*
4320); it is a very good example of a *lorica*, or an appeal for protection

---

[95] *Die irische Kanonensammlung*, ed. Wasserschleben, p. 166.

[96] O'Leary, 'The Latin Origins', p. 288.

[97] Cambridge, University Library, MS Ll.i.10 (2139): *The Prayer Book of Aedeluald the Bishop commonly called the Book of Cerne*, ed. A. B. Kuypers (Cambridge, 1902); James F. Kenney, *The Sources for the Early History of Ireland: Ecclesiastical* (New York, 1929; rev. imp., by L. Bieler, 1966), pp. 720–2 (no. 578); cf. D. N. Dumville, 'Biblical Apocrypha and the Early Irish: A Preliminary Investigation', *Proceedings of the Royal Irish Academy* 73C (1973), 299–338, at 320–1, and O'Leary, 'The Latin Origins', pp. 199–218.

[98] Neil R. Ker, *Catalogue of Manuscripts Containing Anglo-Saxon* (Oxford, 1957), pp. 39–40 (no. 27), and David N. Dumville, 'Liturgical Drama and Panegyric Responsory from the Eighth Century? A Re-examination of the Origin and Contents of the Ninth-Century Section of the Book of Cerne', *Journal of Theological Studies* ns 23 (1972), 374–406, at 395. Cf. Patrick Sims-Williams, *Religion and Literature in Western England, 600–800*, CSASE 3 (Cambridge, 1990), pp. 275–327.

[99] Prayers and hymns (in an Irish context) were termed 'extraliturgical and private devotional exercises' by Kenney, *The Sources*, p. 687.

[100] Fol. 81r: *The Prayer Book*, ed. Kuypers, p. 161, lines 4–15; Martin McNamara, *The Apocrypha in the Irish Church* (Dublin, 1975), pp. 92–3 (no. 80B).

[101] Lipsius and Bonnet, *Acta*, II.1, pp. 24, line 8, 25, lines 1–11, and 26, line 1 (§ 10).

[102] Fol. 79r: *The Prayer Book*, ed. Kuypers, p. 157, lines 7–19; and McNamara, *The Apocrypha*, pp. 98–9 (no. 84).

against evil,[103] and was probably selected for inclusion on this basis alone. The prayer is introduced by the same passage, written in red, which precedes it in both John-apocrypha: 'Tunc beatus Iohannes iacentibus mortuis qui uenenum biberunt intrepidus et constans accipit calicem et signaculum crucis facians in eo et dixit . . .' ('then, as those who had drunk the poison lay dead, holy John, fearless and persevering, took the chalice and, making the sign of the cross over it, said . . .').[104] We find a third apocryphal prayer, uttered by St Peter, in which he asks the Lord to protect him and his followers as he goes to his crucifixion.[105] The source for (at least the second part of) this was pseudo-Marcellus's Passion of Peter and Paul (*BHL* 6657).[106] With the exception of the John-passage, the apostolic prayers are presented in the manuscript as free-standing pieces with no explicit indication of the narratives in which they are known to have played a part. However, these climactic episodes were clearly extracted from *passiones* and disseminated for private study. Readers of such books were probably very familiar with the apostles' prayers in their narrative contexts and therefore all the more receptive to their immediate practical applications.

The issue of which collection of *passiones* might have circulated in early Anglo-Saxon England is a difficult one. The collected texts are sometimes known as 'pseudo-Abdias' since in one *passio* a collection is attributed to Abdias, supposedly ordained bishop of Babylon by Simon and Jude.[107] This origin is unlikely. I have formed some idea of what constituted the original collection based on manuscript evidence – there are at least seventy-three manuscripts including groups dating from the late eighth and early ninth centuries onwards.[108] The issue is complex because there are 'alternative' texts for six apostles,[109] and all manuscript collections consist of combinations and permutations of those alternatives. The theory, promulgated by Richard Lipsius and followed by others,[110] that there were two distinct groups, *passiones* and *uirtutes*, cannot be proved from the manuscript evidence.[111] The date of the original collection may be the late sixth century, as Gregory of Tours's book on the miracles of St Andrew may have been a component.[112] At any rate, there must have been more than one author. For early Anglo-Saxon England, we have strong evidence for at least the following *passiones* travelling in an apostolic collection: pseudo-Marcellus

---

[103] Cf. Sims-Williams, *Religion*, pp. 278–9.

[104] Fol. 79r: *The Prayer Book*, ed. Kuypers, p. 157, lines 4–6. *Virtutes Iohannis: Acta Iohannis*, ed. Junod and Kaestli, II.825, lines 43–6 (§8); *passio: Codex*, ed. Fabricius, III.618.

[105] *The Prayer Book*, ed. Kuypers, pp. 157, lines 21–2, and 158, lines 1–15; McNamara, *The Apocrypha*, pp. 101–2 (no. 86B).

[106] Lipsius and Bonnet, *Acta*, I.173, lines 4–8 (§62); *The Prayer Book*, ed. Kuypers, p. 158, lines 10–15.

[107] *Sanctuarium seu Vitae Sanctorum*, ed. Boninus Mombritius, 2nd ed., 2 vols. (Paris 1910), II.539. Cf. Wright, 'Apocryphal Acts', pp. 50–63.

[108] O'Leary, 'The Latin Origins', pp. 219–20 and 319–20 (table of manuscripts).

[109] O'Leary, 'The Latin Origins', pp. 230–50.

[110] Lipsius, *Die apokryphen Apostelgeschichten*, I.150–78; *Acta Iohannis*, ed. and trans. Junod and Kaestli, II.754.

[111] O'Leary, 'The Latin Origins', pp. 238–45.

[112] O'Leary, 'The Latin Origins', pp. 246–9 and 288–94.

on Peter and Paul (*BHL* 6657), 'Letter of Priests and Deacons of Achaia' on Andrew (*BHL* 428), pseudo-Mellitus on John (*BHL* 4320), and the *passiones* of Thomas (*BHL* 8136), Bartholomew (*BHL* 1002), Matthew (*BHL* 5690), and Simon and Jude (*BHL* 7749 or 7750).

The considerable textual evidence for these *passiones* is mirrored by practical veneration of the apostles in Anglo-Saxon England, at least among the ecclesiastical elite, in the seventh and eighth centuries. On the latter, we have a more substantial body of scholarship.[113] Only by considering both textual and tangible devotion can we arrive at the full extent and significance of Anglo-Saxon apostolic legend.

We know that apostles were frequently chosen as patrons for churches in the first century of Roman Christianity in England.[114] Not surprisingly, St Peter carries the highest distribution – in his archaeological survey, Richard Morris has counted fifteen church-dedications to Peter (out of his list of ninety-nine churches built in the seventh century); two to Paul; and another three to Peter and Paul together.[115] St Andrew has three also.[116] Of these twenty-three churches, nine were episcopal sees.[117] Patrons are identified for thirty-four churches in all; so apostolic dedications, perhaps easier to identify from literary sources, form the majority of these. We cannot be certain why, how, or admittedly when such dedications to particular saints were made,[118] even though the connection between St Peter and Rome is obvious as background. In addition, as circumstances changed, so could one's patron saint, as in the rededication of the abbey of SS Peter and Paul at Canterbury to St Augustine.[119] Probably each church possessed some relics of its patron, though not necessarily at the time of its dedication in the seventh century.[120] The ceremony involved was described by Stephen of Ripon with respect to Wilfrid's dedication of that church to St Peter;[121] and Aldhelm's fourth *Carmen ecclesiasticum* dedicated altars to all twelve apostles.[122] As I have remarked, however, Bede's account of Acca demonstrated the first explicit link made by an Anglo-Saxon ecclesiastic (i.e. Acca) between apostles' roles as Anglo-Saxon church-patrons and their *passiones*.[123]

Finally, let us consider early Anglo-Saxon attitudes to apostles and their resulting significance in English Christianity. The evidence ranges from the

---

[113] See especially Thacker, 'In Search of Saints', and Ó Carragáin, *The City of Rome*.

[114] Wilhelm Levison, *England and the Continent in the Eighth Century* (Oxford, 1946), pp. 35–6 and 259–63.

[115] Richard Morris, *The Church in British Archaeology* (London, 1983), pp. 36–8. For the cult of St Peter in Ireland, cf. *Corpus Inscriptionum Insularum Celticarum*, ed. R. A. S. Macalister, 2 vols. (Dublin, 1945/9), II.114–15.

[116] Morris, *The Church*, pp. 36–8.

[117] Morris, *The Church*, pp. 36–8.

[118] David Rollason, *Saints and Relics in Anglo-Saxon England* (Oxford, 1989), p. 25.

[119] Rollason, *Saints and Relics*, p. 14.

[120] Rollason, *Saints and Relics*, p. 25.

[121] *The Life of Bishop Wilfrid by Eddius Stephanus*, ed. and trans. Bertram Colgrave (Cambridge, 1927), pp. 34–7.

[122] Cf. p. 107, above.

[123] Cf. pp. 105–6, and n. 24, above.

practical to the purely emblematic. In the first third of the seventh century, Edwin, king of Northumbria, had become Christian – with many of his people – when he was killed in battle in October 633 by the forces of Cadwallon, (Christian) king of Gwynedd.[124] Edwin had been in the process of erecting a church to St Peter in York, and it was there that his head was later buried. His death has been seen by N. J. Higham as a major setback to the Christianity of St Peter;[125] it seems that some early political overtones may thereby be associated with Peter's cult.[126] Bishop Wilfrid was clearly attached to both SS Peter and Andrew, perhaps especially the latter; he dedicated his churches at Ripon and Hexham to Peter and Andrew respectively.[127] As is well known, his invocation of Peter's authority won the day at the Council of Whitby in 664 – St Columba had no chance.[128] This has been thought another step in the process by which Scotland eventually adopted St Andrew as its patron-saint, probably as a suitable political rival to his brother Peter.[129]

The more refined or symbolic reflections of devotion to apostles include the similarity in landscape between the churches of Peter and Paul at Rome and at Monkwearmouth-Jarrow,[130] and Ceolfrith's processional visits to the churches of Peter, Mary, and Lawrence on the eve of a pilgrimage to Rome.[131] Wilfrid's church of St Andrew may have been modelled on Andrew's church at Rome.[132] This concept of *romanitas* can, on current evidence, be attributed most easily to Northumbria and to a few apostles.[133] Both practical and symbolic devotion to at least some apostles may have influenced the daily activities of ordinary ecclesiastics (in a wider geographical context), as well as those of important individuals.

With regard to later vernacular evidence, apostles are of course included in the Old English *Martyrology*, probably of the early ninth century.[134] The clearest evidence is for *passiones* of Bartholomew, Matthew, Simon and

[124] Cadwallon is condemned by Bede as Christian in name only and a very nasty character. On Cadwallon and Edwin, see Bede, *Historia ecclesiastica gentis Anglorum*, II.20: *Bede's Ecclesiastical History*, ed. and trans. Colgrave and Mynors, pp. 202–5.

[125] Nicholas J. Higham, *The Convert Kings: Power and Religious Affiliation in Early Anglo-Saxon England* (Manchester, 1997), pp. 201–2.

[126] Cf. Henry Mayr-Harting, *The Coming of Christianity to Anglo-Saxon England*, 3rd ed. (London, 1991), pp. 66–8.

[127] *The Life of Bishop Wilfrid*, ed. and trans. Colgrave, pp. 36–7 and 44–7.

[128] Bede, *Historia ecclesiastica gentis Anglorum*, III.26: *Bede's Ecclesiastical History*, ed. and trans. Colgrave and Mynors, pp. 306–9; *The Life of Bishop Wilfrid*, ed. and trans. Colgrave, pp. 20–3.

[129] Cf. Ursula Hall, *St Andrew and Scotland* (St Andrews, 1994), pp. 46–80.

[130] Ó Carragáin, *The City of Rome*, p. 10.

[131] Ó Carragáin, *The City of Rome*, p. 13. For Lawrence's cult in Ireland, cf. Maurice P. Sheehy, 'The Relics of the Apostles and Early Martyrs in the Mission of St. Patrick', *Irish Ecclesiastical Record* 5th series 95 (1961), 372–6; and Richard Sharpe, 'Armagh and Rome in the Seventh Century', *Ireland and Europe*, ed. Próinséas Ní Chatháin and Michael Richter (Stuttgart, 1984), pp. 58–72.

[132] *The Life of Bishop Wilfrid*, ed. and trans. Colgrave, pp. 44–7.

[133] Cf. Thacker, 'In Search of Saints', pp. 270–4.

[134] *Das altenglische Martyrologium*, ed. G. Kotzor, 2 vols. (Munich, 1981); cf. James E. Cross, 'The Apostles in the *Old English Martyrology*', *Mediaevalia* 5 (1979), 15–59.

Jude, and Thomas.[135] Although it is difficult to demonstrate that a distinct group of *passiones* lies behind the *Martyrology*'s apostolic accounts,[136] the sources for these passages may have been acquired in collective form and then interwoven with other material.[137] Cynewulf's *Fates of the Apostles* (also probably from the early ninth century) provides surprisingly meaty apocryphal narratives on the apostles. James Cross argued convincingly that full narratives and not a so-called 'catalogue' like *Breuiarium apostolorum* lay behind the poem.[138] I have suggested elsewhere that Ælfric's late tenth-century homilies on the apostles were based on his relatively straightforward treatment of an apostolic passion-collection[139] – at least relative to the transformation of the *passio* of Thomas by the Irish poet Airbertach mac Coisse in precisely the same period.[140] Airbertach adapted the setting considerably to suit Irish heroic norms and *mores*.[141] Indeed, his poem is based on precisely the same episode which seemed so suspect to Ælfric.[142]

I do not wish to engage in generalized comparison between Anglo-Saxon and Irish treatments of the Twelve; having said that, I think that the political overtones to apostolic legend (especially on St Peter) were fuelled in England by historical matters like church-dedication, and in Ireland by more purely literary attributes. The type of 'appearance-texts' clearly popular in Ireland are not so evident in the Anglo-Saxon context. The collective biographies of apostles found in the works of Aldhelm, Cynewulf, and Ælfric are paralleled in Ireland by the five Irish translations made around the eleventh century, and by the earlier pseudo-Isidorian *De ortu* and the 'Irish Reference-Bible', both likely products of Irish milieux on the Continent. As in Ireland, the Anglo-Saxon traditions of the apostles as a group existed in significant measure before their reworking into the vernacular. In this way, they can provide us with a clearer understanding of Old English versions of the apostles' busy lives and gory deaths.[143]

---

[135] *Das altenglische Martyrologium*, ed. Kotzor, II.186–8 (Bartholomew), 212–14 (Matthew), 240 (Simon and Jude), and 264–6 (Thomas).

[136] Cross, 'The Apostles'.

[137] Christine Rauer, 'The Sources of the Old English Martyrology', 2000, *Fontes Anglo-Saxonici: World Wide Web Register*, http://fontes.english.ox.ac.uk/, accessed February 2002.

[138] James E. Cross, 'Cynewulf's Traditions about the Apostles in *Fates of the Apostles*', *ASE* 8 (1979), 163–75. Cf. Michael Lapidge, 'The Saintly Life in Anglo-Saxon England', in *The Cambridge Companion to Old English Literature*, ed. Malcolm Godden and Michael Lapidge (Cambridge, 1991), pp. 243–63, at p. 259; and John M. McCulloh, 'Did Cynewulf use a Martyrology? Reconsidering the Sources of *The Fates of the Apostles*', *ASE* 29 (2000), 67–83. I am currently completing a study of the *Fates* to determine more precisely Cynewulf's most likely source and its origin (I think that his main source was a group of *passiones*).

[139] Aideen O'Leary, 'An Orthodox Old English Homiliary? Ælfric's Views on the Apocryphal Acts of the Apostles', *NM* 100 (1999), 15–26.

[140] 'Airbertach mac Cosse's Poem', ed. and trans. Ó Néill, pp. 39–40.

[141] O'Leary, 'The Latin Origins', pp. 85–9; Aideen O'Leary, 'The Identities of the Poet(s) mac Coisi: A Reinvestigation', *Cambrian Medieval Celtic Studies* 38 (1999), 53–71.

[142] O'Leary, 'An Orthodox Old English Homiliary?', pp. 17–19.

[143] I wish to thank Professors David Dumville and Michael Lapidge for reading earlier drafts of this paper and for providing much valuable comment.

# 6

# The Fall of the Angels in *Solomon and Saturn II*

## DANIEL ANLEZARK

ACCOUNTS of the fall of the angels are a recurrent motif across the Old English poetic corpus. Versions of Lucifer's sin and its consequences vary greatly in length and detail, occurring in biblical poetry, saints' lives and wisdom literature. All descriptions of the fall of the angels are necessarily apocryphal, as the Bible provides only the slightest hints concerning the fall of Lucifer and his followers at the beginning of creation. Legends of the fall represent in their variety of detail the product of a Christian tradition which regarded the fall of the angels as a foundational event in cosmic history – the event which introduced evil into creation – but at the same time they offered no authoritatively sanctioned version of this event.[1] The tradition was enriched (and complicated) by the fact that interest in the fall of the angels was shared by early Christian apocryphal authors and their Jewish contemporaries. One work which emerged from the early Christian centuries with a degree of popular authority concerning Satan's fall was the Book of Enoch. That this work may have been known in Anglo-Saxon England is suggested by Bede's comments in his *Commentary on the Seven Catholic Epistles*,[2] but familiarity with Enoch is more clearly suggested by the ninth-century BL, Royal 5.E.XIII, 79v–80r, a manuscript fragment of Breton origin which was in England in the ninth century.[3] It has also been suggested by a number of critics that knowledge of the book and its fallen angelic watchers lies somewhere in the background of the *Beowulf* poet's conception of the race of Grendel.[4] A more orthodox channel by which the story of the Satanic fall and associated demonology

---

[1] The fall is suggested, rather than described in biblical passages; compare Gen. VI.2–4, Isa. XIV.12–15, Rev. XII.1, Tim. III.6, Luke X.18, and Jude 6; all biblical quotes are from *Biblia sacra iuxta Vulgatam versionem*, ed. R. Weber (Stuttgart, 1975).

[2] See Bede, *Commentarius in epistolas VII catholicas*, ed. D. Hurst, CCSL 121 (Turnhout, 1983), 340, at lines 220 and 226–7, who may simply be borrowing the reference from Augustine; see Andy Orchard, *Pride and Prodigies: Studies in the Monsters of the Beowulf Manuscript* (Cambridge, 1995), p. 65; David N. Dumville, 'Biblical Apocrypha and the Early Irish: A Preliminary Investigation', *Proceedings of the Royal Irish Academy* 73C (1973), 299–338, at 330–1. Also see Frederick R. Biggs, 'I Enoch', in *Sources of Anglo-Saxon Literary Culture: A Trial Version*, ed. Frederick R. Biggs, Thomas D. Hill and Paul E. Szarmach, MRTS 74 (Binghamton, NY, 1986), pp. 25–7. Helmut Gneuss, *Handlist of Anglo-Saxon Manuscripts: A List of Manuscripts and Manuscript Fragments Written or Owned in England up to 1100* (Tempe, AZ, 2001), no. 459.

[3] See M. R. James, ed., *Apocrypha Anecdota*, Texts and Studies II.3 (Cambridge, 1893), pp. 140–50.

[4] R. E. Kaske, '*Beowulf* and the Book of Enoch', *Speculum* 46 (1971), 421–31.

came to England was the works of Gregory the Great. While many of his works refer to various aspects of the role of Satan in the doctrine of sin, most important among them are his homily 34 on the Gospels and his *Moralia in Iob*.[5] Gregory, following scripture, taught that the devil had sinned through pride, and persuaded half of all the higher spirits to follow him in his rebellion.[6] According to Gregory these angels cannot be forgiven because as pure spirits they had not been tempted to sin in the flesh, but had sinned anyway,[7] an idea which is also found in the Book of Enoch XV. In Gregory's teaching the void created by the expulsion of the rebels is to be filled by a number of redeemed humanity equal to those angels which did not fall.[8]

The best known account of the fall of the angels in Anglo-Saxon literature is found in *Genesis B*. Full accounts are also to be found in *Genesis A* and *Christ and Satan*, while succinct narratives of the angelic fall are also found in *Juliana*, *Elene*, *Andreas* and *Vainglory*.[9] One version of the fall of the angels which has received very little critical attention is that found in *Solomon and Saturn II*.[10] The description of the fall by Solomon comes in response to a question by Saturn about fate and suffering:

Salomon cwæð:
Nolde gæd geador   in Godes rice
eadiges engles   and ðæs ofermodan;
oðer his dryhtne hierde,   oðer him ongan wyrcan ðurh dierne
    cræftas
segn and side byrnan,   cwæð ðæt he mid his gesiðum wolde
hiðan eall heofona rice   and him ðonne on healfum sittan,
tydran him mid ðy teoðan dæle,   oððæt he his tornes geuðe

---

[5] See Charles Abbetmeyer, *Old English Poetical Motives Derived from the Doctrine of Sin* (Minneapolis, 1903), pp. 9–21.

[6] *Homiliae in Euangelia*, ed. Raymond Étaix, CCSL 141 (Turnhout, 1999), Abbetmeyer, *Old English Poetical Motives*, p. 9.

[7] See, for example, *Moralia in Iob*, ed. Marcus Adriaen, CCSL 143–143B (Turnhout, 1979–85), 4.3, 9.50, pp. 168–9 and 510; see also Bede, *In Genesin*, ed. Charles W. Jones, CCSL 118A (Turnhout, 1967), p. 61; and see Judith N. Garde, *Old English Poetry in Christian Perspective: A Doctrinal Approach* (Cambridge, 1991), p. 34.

[8] *Moralia* 30.49, CCSL 143B, 1618–19; *Homiliae in Euangelia*, ed. Raymond Étaix, CCSL 141 (Turnhout, 1999), 34, 309, lines 267–73.

[9] *Vainglory* 57–67 and *Juliana* 418–29; see *The Exeter Book*, ed. George Philip Krapp and Elliott van Kirk Dobbie, ASPR 3 (New York, 1936); *Andreas* 1185–94, 1376–85 and *Elene* 759–71, 939–52; see *The Vercelli Book*, ed. George Philip Krapp, ASPR 2 (New York, 1932). There are also numerous passing mentions of the fall in Old English poetry and prose which provide little or no detail of the circumstances.

[10] The two Old English dialogue poems involving Solomon and Saturn are found in two manuscripts, Cambridge, Corpus Christi College 41 (in the margins of pp. 196–8), and Cambridge, Corpus Christi College 422 (pp. 1–26, where the poetic text is interrupted by a prose dialogue, pp. 6–12); see N. R. Ker, *Catalogue of Manuscripts Containing Anglo-Saxon* (Oxford, 1957), items 32 and 70A. Daniel Donoghue, in *Style in Old English Poetry: The Test of the Auxiliary* (New Haven, CT, 1987), p. 105, suggests both poems are by the same author, while Charles D. Wright, *The Irish Tradition in Old English Literature*, CSASE 6 (Cambridge, 1993), p. 233, whose book offers the most recent comprehensive discussion of both poems and their possible sources, treats the question of authorship as an open one. Patrick P. O'Neill, 'On the Date, Provenance and Relationship of the "Solomon and Saturn" Dialogues', *ASE* 26 (1997), 139–68, at 165, suggests that they are Alfredian or post-Alfredian.

ende ðurh insceafte    Ða wearð se æðelra ðeoden
gedrefed ðurh ðæs deofles gehygdo;    forlet hine ða ofdune
    gehreosan,
afielde hine ða under foldan sceatas,    heht hine ðær fæste gebindan.
ðæt sindon ða usic feohtað on.
Forðon is witena gehwam    wopes eaca.
Ða ðæt eadig onfand    engla dryhten,
ðæt heo leng mid hine    lare ne namon,
aweorp hine ða of ðam wuldre    and wide todraf,
and him bebead    bearn heofonwara
ðæt hie ec scoldon    a ðenden hie lifdon
wunian in wylme,    wop ðrowian,
heaf under hefonum,    and him helle gescop,
wælcealde wic    wintre beðeahte,
wæter in sende    and wyrmgeardas,
atol deor monig    irenum hornum,
blodige earnas    and blace nædran,
ðurst and hungor    and ðearle gewin,
egna egesan,    unrotnesse;
and æghwylc him ðissa earfeða    ece stondeð
butan edwende    a ðenden hie lifigað.    (441–66)[11]

Traditions concerning the fall of the angels in Anglo-Saxon England are complex and overlapping ones. This idiosyncratic account shares certain features with most Anglo-Saxon versions of the fall, but its unusual formulation of these ideas points to a closer relationship to *Christ and Satan* than to any other account. Other elements of *Solomon and Saturn II* which are not shared by any other poetic account of the fall of the angels suggest a connection to an alternative apocryphal tradition in Anglo-Saxon England, one derived from the *Visio Pauli*.[12]

---

[11] 'In God's kingdom he did not wish for society together of the blessed angel and of the proud one. One obeyed his Lord, and the other began to make for himself a standard and broad armour through secret crafts. He said that with his companions he wished to completely ravage the kingdom of the heavens and to occupy half himself, and procreate himself with the tenth part, until through this internal propagation he could give his anger an end. Then the chief of princes was disturbed by the devil's thought, caused him to fall down, brought him then under the surfaces of the earth, ordered him to be bound fast there. That is what fights against us, therefore there is an increase of woe for each of the wise. When the blessed lord of the angels discovered that they would not take instruction from him any longer, then he threw him from that glory and drove him far away, and commanded them, the children of the heaven-dwellers, that they also, forever while they lived, must dwell in the surge, suffer sorrow, lamentation under the heavens; and he made hell for them, a place of deadly cold covered in winter, sent water in there, and snake-pits, and many terrible beasts with iron horns, bloody eagles and black adders, thirst and hunger and severe fighting, sorrowful things, terrible for the eyes; and for each of them these torments remain forever, without alteration, forever while they live.' Robert J. Menner, ed., *The Poetical Dialogues of Solomon and Saturn* (New York, 1941); I have incorporated R. I. Page's results of a reading of the manuscript text using ultraviolet light, which does not change Menner's lineation: see Page, 'A Note on the Text of MS. CCCC 422 (*Solomon and Saturn*)', *MÆ* 34 (1965), 36–9. See also *Poems of Wisdom and Learning in Old English*, ed. T. A. Shippey (Cambridge, 1976), pp. 98–100, 146.

[12] See *Visio Sancti Pauli: The History of the Apocalypse in Latin together with Nine Texts*, ed. T. Silverstein, Studies and Documents 4 (London, 1935), for an overview of the tradition and variant texts.

*Solomon and Saturn II* alludes to the universally accepted reason for the fall, the sin of pride (441–2): 'Salomon cwæð:/ Nolde gæd geador in godes rice/ eadiges engles and ðæs ofermodan' ('In God's kingdom he did not wish for society together of the blessed angel and of the proud one'). That Lucifer, 'the proud one', fell because of this pride is one of the few elements of fall narratives which is authentically biblical. This is clearly outlined in I Tim. III.6, where Paul advocates humility for members of the Church: 'ne in superbia elatus in iudicium incidat diaboli'.[13] However, pride is not the only reason for the fall in the poem but is coupled here with disobedience. Also a 'blessed angel' is mentioned as well as 'the proud one', whose disobedience is manifested in war preparations, and contrasted with the obedience of this 'blessed angel' (443). In other Old English versions the sin of envy is also associated with Satan's pride (*Genesis A*, lines 29 and 32) and/or greed (*Christ and Satan*, lines 32 and 192). In *Solomon and Saturn II* neither angel is named, though the 'proud one' is clearly Lucifer/Satan.[14]

The military nature of this rebellion is a common feature of Old English poetic accounts of the fall, but the nature of the kingdom which the proud angel intends to establish in *Solomon and Saturn II* is not exactly paralleled by other versions which among themselves exhibit a degree of uniformity (443b–447). The rebellion here is twofold: against fellowship with the obedient angel (who perhaps might be identified with Michael), and against the Lord whom the proud one does not wish to obey. In *Genesis A* (lines 20–33 and 47), the proud rejection of God's friendship is accompanied by the boast that the rebellious angels could partition the place with God; this is signalled by the plan to set up a throne in northern part of kingdom. This last element, scriptural in origin and discussed by Gregory the Great in his homily 34,[15] is not found in *Solomon and Saturn II*. As has been noted by a number of critics, not least the poem's most recent editor, the whole episode in *Genesis A* is couched in familiar heroic language.[16] This is also true of *Genesis B*, which provides a much more detailed account of the character of Satan before and after fall: we are told of his intellect and splendour (246–60), his boasting, his malicious talk, and his vanity about his bright body. These qualities lead him to reject subservience, and as in *Genesis A*, he will start building in the west and north (261–77). The language used to describe

---

[13] 'in case pride turn his head and he be condemned as the devil was'.

[14] Abbetmeyer, *Old English Poetical Motives*, pp. 29–35. These ideas are found across Gregory's works: Lucifer was the first created, most eminent angel (*Homiliae* 34, 305–6, lines 165–77; *Moralia* 32.23, CCSL 143B, 1665–68). Through pride he lost reverent fear, and sought dominion and independence for himself, so losing all his former dignity (*Moralia* 21.2, CCSL 143A, 1065–68; 34.21, CCSL 143B, 1761–62). He cannot rise from darkness or hope for forgiveness (*Moralia* 4.5, CCSL 143, 169–70; 32.23, CCSL 143B, 1665–68). His angelic nature towers above that of men, but he has lost the blessedness of his nature, not its greatness (*Moralia* 24.20, CCSL 143B, 1222; 32.12, 15, CCSL 143B, 1640–42, 1646–51). He takes pleasure in tempting men by lying promises (*Moralia* 4.9, CCSL 143, 172–4). He is the murderer from the beginning (*Homiliae* 25.8, CCSL 141, 213–15). Only the elect, since the death of Christ, can resist him (*Moralia* 4.5, CCSL 143, 169–70), and he exercises power only by God's permission (*Moralia* 32.24, CCSL 143B, 1668–69; 14.38, CCSL 143A, 725–7).

[15] Isa. XIV.13–14, *Homiliae* 34, 307, lines 199–212; as noted by Wright, *The Irish Tradition*, p. 129, the location of hell itself in the north becomes a commonplace.

[16] See *Genesis A: A New Edition*, ed. A. N. Doane (Madison, WI, 1978), pp. 40–1.

the rebellion is martial (278–91), though there is no direct mention made, either here or in *Genesis A*, of the devil's weapons. In *Christ and Satan* the fall is brought about by pride (19–24), though in contrast to *Genesis A* and *B*, the aim of the rebellion is to take over 'the entire government of the strongholds' (81–88, 245–53), rather than part of the heavenly kingdom. Also in contrast to the *Genesis* poems, the rebellion in *Christ and Satan* is directed against Christ, rather than God in general. This idea that the revolt was directed against Christ is also found in *Guthlac A* (line 570) and *Juliana* (line 421), and is suggested by two scriptural verses. In Luke X.18 Jesus states 'videbam Satanan sicut fulgur de caelo cadentem',[17] and Jude 6 tells of 'angelos vero qui non servaverunt suum principatum, sed dereliquerunt suum domicilium, in iudicium magni diei vinculis aeternis sub caligine reservavit',[18] in the context of a discussion of Christ's victorious role in salvation history. This allusion is developed by Bede, who states clearly in his *Commentary on the Seven Catholic Epistles* that the conflict was between Christ and Lucifer.[19]

These analogues may suggest that the 'blessed angel' of *Solomon and Saturn II* should be identified with Christ, obedient to the Godhead. However, such an understanding implies a subordination of Christ's divinity, as in context he would be of equal status with the highest angel; such a reading would be more heretical than apocryphal. It is distantly possible that the 'blessed angel' may be an obedient pre-lapserian Adam.[20] Such a reading is at least credible in the light of the tradition found in the apocryphal book, the *Vita Adae et Evae*, where Adam and Eve are created before the fall of angels, with Satan's rebellion characterized by his disobedience in refusing to worship Adam, created in God's image and likeness. Charles Wright has shown that the *Vita Adae et Evae* was known in Ireland, and probably in Anglo-Saxon England as well.[21] The focus on the proud one's disobedience, rather than simply on his pride itself, and the contrast to the obedience of the 'blessed one' may suggest this tradition lies in the background of the poem, though with such scant detail it is difficult to draw conclusions. And if ideas found in the *Vita Adae et Evae* are to be considered to lie somewhere behind the portrayal of the rebellion, it is more likely that the blessed angel is Michael, who in contrast to Satan, obeys God's command to worship Adam.[22]

[17] 'I watched Satan fall like lightning from heaven.'

[18] ' . . . the angels who kept not their principality but forsook their own habitation, he has reserved under darkness in everlasting chains, unto the judgement of the great day'.

[19] CCSL 121, 336; see Robert Emmett Finnegan, *Christ and Satan: A Critical Edition* (Waterloo, Ont., 1977), p. 40. The idea is widely attested; see, for example, Augustine, *Tractatus in Euangelium Iohannis*, ed. R. Willems, CCSL 36 (Turnhout, 1954), 42.11, 370; Thomas D. Hill, 'The Fall of Satan in the Old English *Christ and Satan*', *Journal of English and Germanic Philology* 76 (1977), 315–25, at 318–20.

[20] Compare *Christ and Satan* 19–20; the priority of the creation of the angels was the normally accepted tradition; see Merrel Dare Clubb, *Christ and Satan: An Old English Poem*, Yale Studies in English 70 (New Haven, CT, 1925), 50–1.

[21] Charles D. Wright, 'Apocryphal Lore and Insular Tradition in St Gall, Stiftsbibliothek MS 908', in *Irland und die Christenheit: die Kirche im Frühmittelalter*, ed. P. Ní Chatháin and M. Richter (Stuttgart, 1984), pp. 124–45, at p. 130; Wright, *The Irish Tradition*, p. 23.

[22] See Wright, 'Apocryphal Lore', p. 131.

Another feature the *Solomon and Saturn II* account shares with many others is the enumeration of ten angelic orders before the fall, one of which the proud one leads in his rebellion (446a, 'mid ðy teoðan dæle', ['with the tenth part']). Two notions circulated in the Middle Ages about the number of angelic orders: there were either ten orders or nine. The idea that there were ten orders before the fall of Lucifer is not found in Gregory, who argues rather that there were nine angelic orders, and that saved humanity will make up a tenth: 'nouem sunt ordines angelorum. Sed ut completeretur electorum numerus, homo decimus est creatus.'[23] Gregory's point of view was influential, especially as this sermon made its way into the homiliary of Paul the Deacon as the sermon for the third or fourth Sunday after Pentecost. The implication in Gregory may well be that a displaced tenth order was formed around the rebel leader, but this is not spelled out.[24] Haymo of Auxerre, in his homily 114, certainly interpreted Gregory in this way, altering his source and making the relationship clear: 'Novem enim sunt ordines angelorum . . . Decimus enim per superbiam cecidit. Sed electorum numerous compleretur, ad illius restaurationem homo decimus creatus est.'[25] Ten orders existing before the fall are found in both *Christ and Satan* (365a),[26] and *Genesis B* (246–48), where God creates ten *engelcynna* ('races of angels'). The number is also found in Ælfric's *Sermo de initio creaturae*,[27] and in his treatise *On the Old and New Testaments*, with 'tyn engla werod' ('ten angel troops') being created by God on the first day.[28] It is of course impossible to source such a widely shared tradition, but the ultimate origin for this notion may be the Book of Enoch VI, which refers to ten orders of angels.[29] The 'dierne cræftas' ('secret crafts', 443b) which are

---

[23] *Homiliae* 34, 304, lines 143–5 (' . . . the number of the orders of angels is nine. But man was created so that the number of the elect might be complete'). Gregory's homily is on the lost ten drachmas of Luke XV.8–10.

[24] *The Saxon Genesis*, ed. A. N. Doane (Madison, WI, 1991), p. 98.

[25] PL 118, 613 ('there are nine orders of angels . . . The tenth fell because of pride. But man was created the tenth to restore this, so that the number of the elect might be complete'); cited Doane, *ibid.*, p. 98.

[26] Here the word *engelcyn*, 'angel-race', enigmatically refers to Satan himself.

[27] *Ælfrics's Catholic Homilies: The First Series: Text*, ed. Peter Clemoes, EETS ss 17 (Oxford, 1997), p. 179, line 22.

[28] Doane, *The Saxon Genesis*, p. 98. *The Old English Version of the Heptateuch, Ælfric's Treatise on the Old and New Testament and his Preface to Genesis*, ed. S. J. Crawford, EETS os 160 (Oxford, 1922), p. 18, line 53.

[29] Clubb, *Christ and Satan*, p. 96, notes a less likely source in the Book of the Secrets of Enoch 29.3–4 (also known as the Slavonic Enoch), but in which the events of the fall match *Solomon and Saturn II* more closely: 'And from the rock I cut off a great fire; and from the fire I created the orders of the incorporeal ten troops of angels, and their weapons are fiery and their raiment a burning flame, and I commanded each one should stand in his order. Here Satanail with his angels was thrown down from the height. And one from out the order of angels, having turned away from the order that was under him, conceived an impossible thought, to place his throne higher than the clouds above the earth, that he might become equal in rank to my power.' This work may lie behind the description of the fall of the angels in the *Cosmographia* of Aethicus Ister: 'Paradisus de ea massa, quae meliora fuit indiscretus credatur fuisse cum novem ordinibus angelorum. Sursum primam elevatam ordinem decimam ignis spirans flatum in ordinem refulgentem conditam factore signaculo, quae ruinam fecit' (O. Prinz, ed., *Die Kosmographie des Aethicus*, MGH Quellen zur Geistesgeschichte des Mittelalters Band 14 (Munich, 1993), p. 90, lines 4–8) ('It is believed paradise, which is better, was made unseparated from this substance, with nine orders of angels. At first on high the tenth order was lifted up, breathing a fiery blast, a

employed in the making of war equipment by the rebellious angel probably originate in the legend in the Book of Enoch VIII, where the discovery by the evil angels under Azazel of metals and magic arts leads to the manufacture of weapons.[30] It should be noted however, that if Book of Enoch VIII is the ultimate or direct source for *Solomon and Saturn II*, either the poet or the tradition to which he is heir has transferred the acquisition of this skill to the time before the fall: here the standard raised is a sign of his rebellion in heaven, and the armour is to be used in it.

No source has yet been suggested for the enigmatic detail that Lucifer/ Satan 'wolde . . ./ tydran him mid ðy teoðan dæle, oððæt he his tornes geuðe/ ende ðurh insceafte'.[31] The text is not only obscure, but damaged at this point, but the desire to *tydran* by *insceafte* (446–7a, a *hapax legomenon*) is quite clear.[32] The Book of Enoch VI, in a well known passage, tells of the fallen angelic watchers having sexual intercourse with the daughters of men and so producing a monstrous race. Given the motifs shared by *Solomon and Saturn II* and the Book of Enoch, it is possible that there is a link between this miscegeny, after the fall, and the idea that Lucifer propagated before the fall. In an obscure passage in *Christ and Satan*, Satan's companions in hell complain of one of his lies (63–64): 'Segdest us to soðe ðæt ðin sunu wære/ meotod mancynnes: hafustu nu mare susl.'[33] James Morey has recently suggested that this verse, previously considered to be a confused reference to the future Antichrist,[34] reflects another apocryphal tradition concerning the fall of the angels. The problem of chronology is not easily avoided: this son of Satan appears at the beginning of the world, the Antichrist at its end. The *Questions of Bartholomew*, an apocryphon available in at least one known Latin translation from the sixth or seventh century, describes the fall and includes details not found in other works. Morey points to the link between the Greek text's mention (one not found in the Latin) of Satan's son, Salpsan, and these lines in *Christ and Satan*, which seem to refer to an unnamed son of Satan: 'I looked about and saw the six hundred who were under me senseless. And I awakened my son Salpsan and took him to counsel how I might deceive the man on whose account I was cast out of

---

sign created in the shining order, which was ruined'). This work was available in England, at least from the second half of the tenth century, see Gneuss, *Handlist of Anglo-Saxon Manuscripts*, nos. 386, 439 and 839.

[30] Menner, *Solomon and Saturn*, p. 140. See further Louis Ginzberg, *The Legends of the Jews* (Philadelphia, 1909–38), I.125; V.153–6.

[31] 'intended to procreate himself with the tenth part, until through this internal propagation he could give his anger an end'.

[32] See Page, 'A Note on the Text', 36–9. Menner, *Solomon and Saturn*, p. 140, discusses some of the editing difficulties of this page, and notes the unique occurrence of the word *insceafte*, but offers no source.

[33] 'Truly you told us that your son was the Lord of mankind; now you have greater punishment.'

[34] James H. Morey, 'Adam and Judas in the Old English *Christ and Satan*', *Studies in Philology* 87 (1990), 397–409. Clubb, *Christ and Satan*, pp. 62–3, discussing the passage comments: 'It seems possible that these lines contain a reference (anachronistic, of course, in the context) to a common mediaeval conception of the Antichrist.' Hilary uses the phrase 'Antichristus . . . diaboli filius', *Commentarius in Mattheum*, PL 9, 1056D; the idea is developed by Adso in his *Libellus de Antichristo* (c. 954), see PL 101, 1293.

the heavens.'[35] Wright has argued convincingly that this apocryphon was known in early medieval Ireland and that some ideas it contains, if not the work itself, may have been known in Anglo-Saxon England.[36] The text of *Solomon and Saturn II* not only suggests that the proud one wished to propagate by *insceafte*, but implies that Lucifer did propagate before the fall, and that the offspring of this propagation fell with him into hell. The poem clearly refers to a son, or sons, of the heaven-dwellers, who share Satan's fate (454–58a): 'aweorp hine/ ða of ðam wuldre and wide todraf,/ and him bebead bearn heofonwara/ ðæt hie ec scoldon/ a ðenden hie lifdon/ wunian in wylme, wop ðrowian,/ heaf under hefonum'.[37]

Once hell has been reached, the devil's punishment for his pride is conventional enough (447b–449): 'se æðela ðeoden/ gedrefed ðurh ðæs deofles gehygd, forlet hine ða ofdune gehreosan/ afielde hine ða under foldan sceatas, heht hine ðær fæste gebindan.'[38] Chains binding the devil are a common motif, and are described in Jude 6 ('vinculis aeternis' ['ever-lasting chains']).[39] God is certainly casting down the devil, but *Solomon and Saturn II* does not spell out who binds him. The fact that the binding is 'ordered' (*heht*, 449b) suggests a role for Michael, probably anticipating the archangel's future role in binding the dragon at God's command (Rev. XX.1–2). Given this allusion, Michael is clearly the preferred candidate for the character of the blessed angel first mentioned at line 442a.[40]

The poet's description of hell (459–66) presents a curious mixture of commonplace and unusual detail. The 'wælcealde wic wintre beðeahte' ('a place of deadly cold covered in winter'), the 'wyrmgeardas' ('snake pits'), the 'blace nædran' ('black adders') and finally the 'ðurst and hungor and ðearle gewin,/ egna egesan, unrotnesse' ('thirst and hunger and severe fighting, sorrowful things, terrible for the eyes'), are all elsewhere attested in Anglo-Saxon hells, and these punishments will continue forever ('ece

---

[35] See *The Apocryphal New Testament*, trans. M. R. James (Oxford, 1924), p. 178. This attribution follows up a suggestion by Israel Gollancz that *Christ and Satan* was influenced by *The Questions of Bartholomew*; see *The Cædmon Manuscript of Anglo-Saxon Biblical Poetry: Junius XI in the Bodleian Library*, ed. Israel Gollancz (London, 1927), p. civ. Morey ('Adam and Judas', p. 401) notes another point where *The Questions of Bartholomew* provide an analogue for *Christ and Satan,* on the prior creation of Adam: 'Adam ærest' ('Adam first', 20a); see Umberto Moricca, ed., 'Un nuovo testo dell' "Evangalio di Bartolomeo"', *Revue Biblique* 30 (1921), p. 512; this is a sixth- or seventh-century translation of the Greek version (of the third- or fourth-century), in an eleventh-century manuscript. See F. Stegmüller, *Repertorium Biblicum Medii Aevii* (Madrid, 1940), I.109, no. 135,3.

[36] Charles D. Wright, 'Questions of Bartholomew', *Sources of Anglo-Saxon Literary Culture*, ed. Biggs, Hill and Szarmach, pp. 35–6.

[37] 'then he threw him from that glory and drove him far away, and commanded them, the children of the heaven-dwellers, that they also, forever while they lived, must dwell in the surge, suffer sorrow, lamentation under the heavens'. There is no need to read *bearn heofonwara* as 'a slightly improper description of Christ', as does Shippey (*Poems of Wisdom and Learning*, p. 138, n. 22), as a way of resolving the difficulties raised by Menner (*Solomon and Saturn*, p. 141).

[38] 'The noble chieftain aroused by the devil's pride, let him fall down, brought him then under the surfaces of the earth, ordered him to be bound fast there.'

[39] Compare *Christ and Satan* 49a.

[40] The anonymous homily *In laudem S. Michaelis* looks forward to Michael's role in fighting the dragon, and in this context briefly recounts the fall of Satan; see H. C. L. Tristram, *Vier altenglischen Predigten aus der heterodoxen Tradition* (Freiburg-im-Breisgau, 1970), p. 160; see also Wright, *The Irish Tradition*, p. 262.

stondeð/ butan edwende a ðenden hie lifigað' ['these remain forever, without alteration, forever while they live']).[41] However, extra elements make this description of hell unique, and one of these elements, water ('wæter in sende'), seems incompatible with the poet's earlier mention of hell's fires with the 'wylm' ('surge') of flame (457a). There can be no doubt that water is a strange element to co-exist with fire. I have so far been unable to find any other reference to God pouring waters into hell as a form of punishment for the fallen angels. The idea that the underworld might be full of water is certainly implied in the accounts of creation and the universal deluge of Noah's day, but the waters under the earth are not associated with hell.[42] Classical versions of the underworld tend to be more watery than their Jewish or Christian counterparts; Hades is surrounded by and reached by crossing water: 'fas obstat, tristisque palus inamabilis undae/ alligat et novies Styx interfusa coercet'.[43] In early medieval cosmography, the waters surrounding the earth are also understood as the great world-ocean. This ocean or stream, which is referred to at the opening of *Christ and Satan*,[44] is described in the *Visio Pauli* as a division between this world and the next, and in at least one redaction of the vision this body of water merges with the

---

[41] Compare *Christ and Satan* 27–8, 30 and 39; the tradition of surging flame is widespread, but see Rev. XIX.20, 'stagnum ignis', Clubb, *Christ and Satan*, p. 53. The cold of hell is also widely attested; see *Christ and Satan* 131a, 'Hwaet! Her hat and ceald'; in the Book of Enoch XIV.13, hell is described as being 'as hot as fire and cold as ice: there were no delights of life therein'. In the Book of the Secrets of Enoch (Version A) X.2, hell is both hot and cold as well as dark, and also a place of thirst (Clubb, *Christ and Satan*, 70); the element of thirst recalls the thirst of Dives in hell, Luke XVI.24. The vision of Dryhthelm, with souls leaping from one place 'flammis ferventibus nimium terribile' ('exceedingly terrble with raging flame') to another 'furenti grandine ac frigore nivium omnia perflante atque verrente non minus intolerabile praeferebat' ('no less intolerable on account of the violent hail and icy snow which was drifting and blowing about everywhere') presents some similarities; see Bede, *Ecclesiastical History of the English People*, ed. Bertram Colgrave and R. A. B. Mynors (Oxford, 1969), 5.12, pp. 488–91. Serpents are another widely attested feature; compare *Christ and Satan* 134b–135a, 'hwilum nacode men windað ymb wyrmas', and the *Apocalypse of Peter* 10: 'And I saw the murderers . . . cast into a certain narrow place full of evil reptiles, and being smitten by those beasts.' See Clubb, *Christ and Satan*, p. 71.

[42] See Gen. I.6–7 and 9; VII.11: 'omnes fontes abyssi magnae' ('all the fountains of the great deep'). The Anglo-Saxons were familiar with the concept of waters under the earth and tried to explain it; see, for example, *The Old English Metres of Boethius*, Metre 20, lines 166–75, in *The Paris Psalter and the Meters of Boethius*, ed. George P. Krapp, ASPR 5 (New York, 1932), and The *Old English Martyrology* for the second day of creation in *Das altenglische Martyrologium*, ed. Günter Kotzor, 2 vols. (Munich, 1981), II, p. 34, both of which use the example of an egg to explain how the earth is surrounded by waters. J. E. Cross, '*De Ordine Creaturarum Liber* in Old English Prose', *Anglia* 90 (1972), 132–140, at 133, notes that the martyrologist's source is almost certainly this seventh-century Irish work (*Liber de Ordine Creaturarum: Un anónimo irlandés del siglo VII*, ed. Manuel C. Díaz y Díaz (Santiago de Compostela, 1972), 4.1, and that the image also appears in an Irish vernacular work *Saltair na Rann*, ed. Whitely Stokes, Anecdota Oxoniensia, Medieval and Modern Series, I, iii (Oxford, 1883), lines 165–9.

[43] R. A. B. Mynors, ed., *Virgilii Maronis Opera* (Oxford, 1969, repr. 1990), p. 240, Book 6, lines 438–39 ('Fate withstands; the unlovely mere with its dreary water enchains them and Styx imprisons with his ninefold circles'). Translated H. R. Fairclough, *Virgil: Volume I: Eclogues, Georgics, Aeneid I–VI* (Cambridge, MA, 1953). See Andy Orchard, *Pride and Prodigies*, pp. 44–5 for a full discussion of classical analogues of Grendel's mere.

[44] See *Christ and Satan* 5b, 'stream ut on sae'; Thomas D. Hill, 'Apocryphal Cosmography and the Stream *ut on sæ*: A Note on *Christ and Satan*, lines 4–12', *PQ* 48 (1969), 550–4, sees this as a reference to the *oceanus* of classical mythology, which was often identified with the cosmic Jordan of apocryphal cosmography, and discusses the relationship of that passage to the *Visio S. Pauli*; see *Apocrypha Anecdota*, ed. James, p. 28; see also Wright, *The Irish Tradition*, pp. 127–8.

rivers of hell: 'Et erat flumen igneum et feruens; fluctus autem eius exaltat se super usque ad nubes et ad celum . . . et alia tria que confluunt sicut in eum.'[45] The description of hell in Blickling homily XVI, which refers directly to the *Visio Pauli* as its source, also mentions waters, but clearly represents an alternative redaction in the vernacular, different to any which survives in Latin:

> Swa Sanctus Paulus wæs geseonde on norðanweardne þisne mid-
> dangeard, þær ealle wætero niðergewitað, and he þær geseah ofer
> ðæm wætere sumne harne stan. and wæron norð of ðæm stane
> awexene swiðe hrimige bearwas, and ðær wæron þystrogenipo, and
> under þæm stane wæs niccra eardung and wearga. and he geseah
> þæt on ðæm clife hangodan on ðæm isigean bearwum manige
> swearte saula be heora handum gebundne. and þa fynd þara on
> nicra onlicnesse heora gripende wæron, swa swa grædig wulf. and
> þæt wæter wæs sweart under þæm clife neoðan. and betuh þæm clife
> on ðæm wætre wæron swylce twelf mila. and ðonne ða twigo
> forburston þonne gewitan þa saula niðer þa þe on ðæm twigum
> hangodan, and him onfengon ða nicras. Ðis ðonne wæron ða saula
> þa ðe her on worlde mid unrihte gefyrenode wæron, and ðæs noldan
> geswican ær heora lifes ende.[46]

This passage occurs in a homily on Saint Michael, a character probably involved in the *Solomon and Saturn II* account of the fall of the angels. Immediately preceding the description of this watery hell populated by monster-devils, we are told by the homilist:

> Englas beoð to ðegnunge gæstum fram Gode hider on world sended,
> to ðæm ðe þone ecean eðel mid mode and mid mægene to Gode
> geearniað, ðæt him syn on fultume ða þe wið þæm awergdum
> gastum syngallice feohtan sceolan. Ac uton nu biddan þone
> heahengel Sanctus Michahel and ða nigen endebyrdnessa ðara

---

[45] *Visio Sancti Pauli*, ed. Silverstein, pp. 209–10 ('And there was a fiery and boiling river; its wave-surge mounts up to the clouds and to the heavens . . . and the three rivers there flowed into it'), cited by Wright, *The Irish Tradition*, pp. 128–9; in *Christ and Satan* 101a, hell is described as full of mist, itself a common feature of descriptions of hell, and found in *Moralia* 13.48, CCSL 143A, 697, 'in hoc caliginoso aere'; see Clubb, *Christ and Satan*, p. 68.

[46] *The Blickling Homilies*, ed. R. Morris, EETS os 58, 63, 73 (repr. Oxford, 1967), pp. 208–11 ('So Saint Paul was looking towards the northern region of the earth, where all waters pass down, and he saw there above the water a hoary stone; and north of the stone had grown very rimey woods, and there were dark mists; and under the stone was the dwelling place of monsters and execrable creatures; and he saw hanging on the cliff in the icy woods many black souls with their hands bound; and the enemies in the likeness of monsters were seizing them like greedy wolves; and the water under the cliff was black. And between the cliff and the water there were about twelve miles, and when the twigs broke, then down went the souls who hung on the twigs and the monsters seized them'). The homilies have been renumbered since Morris's edition, so that his XVII is now numbered XVI; see *The Blickling Homilies*, ed. Rudolph Willard, EEMF 10 (Copenhagen, 1960), pp. 38–40. See Wright, *The Irish Tradition*, pp. 133–6, for a discussion of the connections of Blickling XVI and Grendel's mere in *Beowulf* to the *Visio S. Pauli* tradition, and the possibility of a lost vernacular version of the *Visio*; an Old English translation which has survived, but represents an alternative textual tradition is *The Old English Vision of St Paul*, ed. Antonette Di Paulo Healey, Speculum Monographs 2 (Cambridge, MA, 1978).

haligra engla, þæt hie us syn on fultume wið helsceaðum. Hie wæron
þa halgan on onfenge manna saulum.[47]

The *Visio Pauli* also describes guardian spirits who contend against evil
angels every day over the souls of the living, and who report each day back
to God on the merits of their charges.[48] A similar tradition of good and evil
angels contending over souls is also found in Vercelli homily IV (and Napier
XLVI), but significantly is also found in *Solomon and Saturn II*. Solomon's
comment that 'Ðæt sindon ða usic feohtað on' ('it is they who fight against
us', 450) is developed in the dialogue's following question about the
inevitability of death. It can be no coincidence that this following question
is answered by Solomon with an account of guardian spirits contending
with devils.[49] It can be concluded that the formulations of a long version of
the *Visio Pauli*, of the type suggested by Wright, lie somewhere in the
background of this part of *Solomon and Saturn II*. This is suggested not
only by the mention of these contending spirits, but also by the accompanying description of a cold, wet hell.

   Another literary relation for Blickling homily XVI, with its account of
souls falling into their watery hell, which has long been the subject of critical
discussion, is the description of Grendel's mere and its monstrous inhabitants in *Beowulf*:

      No hie fæder cunnon,
      Hwæþer him ænig wæs   ær acenned
      dyrnra gasta.   Hie dygel lond
      warigeað, wulfhleoþu,   windige næssas,
      frecne fengelad,   ðær fyrgenstream
      under næssa genipu   niþer gewiteð,
      flod under foldan.   Nis þæt feor heonon
      milgemearces,   þæt se mere standeð;
      ofer þæm hongiað   hrinde bearwas,
      wudu wyrtum fæst   wæter oferhelmað.
      þær mæg nihta gehwæm   niðwundor seon,
      fyr on flode.   No þæs frod leofað
      gumena bearna,   þæt þone grund wite.   (1355b–68)[50]

[47] Morris, *Blickling Homilies*, pp. 208–9, 'Angels are ministering spirits, sent hither into the world
    by God, to those who with mind and strength merit from God the eternal kingdom; so that they
    should be a help to those who constantly contend against the accursed spirits. But let us now
    entreat the archangel St Michael, and the nine orders of holy angels, that they may be our aid
    against hell-fiends. They were the holy ones ready to receive men's souls.'
[48] *Apocrypha Anecdota*, ed. James, p. 13, lines 19–34.
[49] This link was first noted by Menner, *Solomon and Saturn*, p. 143, and has since been discussed in
    detail by Wright, *The Irish Tradition*, pp. 260–1; both suggest that shared phrasing in the
    passages in *Solomon and Saturn II* 480–501 and Vercelli IV, lines 333–42, may point to a lost
    common source; see *The Vercelli Homilies and Related Texts*, ed. D. G. Scragg, EETS os 300
    (Oxford, 1992), pp. 87–107, at p. 104. Wright notes that a long version of the *Visio Pauli* is the
    likely source, and that the same detail is found in Napier XLVI; see *Wulfstan: Sammlung der ihm
    zugeschriebenen Homilien nebst Untersuchungen über ihre Echtheit*, ed. Arthur Napier (repr.
    Dublin and Zürich, 1967), p. 233, lines 2–12. As the Napier homily identifies Gregory as its
    source, Wright suggests it is possible to surmise that a Latin pseudo-Gregorian homily drawing
    on these traditions lies behind these passages as well.
[50] 'They knew of no father, whether before him any such mysterious spirit had been born. They

The cliff, the frosty groves, and the teaming monsters in waters underneath all point, as Wright has shown in detail, to some literary association between Grendel's mere, the *Visio Pauli* and the Blickling homily. I would suggest that the conception of hell in *Beowulf* and *Solomon and Saturn II*, also a 'wælcealde wic wintre beðeahte', is related to this group of texts, with its lapsed angels falling into a watery pit inhabited by monsters, an association reinforced by the immediate reference of contending guardian spirits and devils. In *Beowulf* the metaphoric association of Grendel's dwelling with hell occasionally comes close to literal identification, and at his death his return home is also his journey to hell (851–2): 'in fenfreoðo feorh alegde,/ hæþene sawle; þær him hel onfeng.'[51] This identification of the mere with the pit of hell is reinforced by the mysterious commingling of fire and water in the nightly sight of 'fyr on flode' ('fire in the stream', line 1367a), an element shared with the depiction of hell in *Solomon and Saturn II*. This is not the only element that the episode of the fall of the angels in *Solomon and Saturn II* shares with *Beowulf*. I have already mentioned that critics have long noted the presence of at least two motifs which may suggest that the *Beowulf* poet has been influenced directly or indirectly by the Book of Enoch. The giant Grendel's descent from Cain clearly echoes the descent of a whole race of monsters produced by unnatural sexual unions between women and fallen angels as described in the Book of Enoch, and the magical sword found by Beowulf in Grendel's underwater lair is the product of giant manufacture (1562, 1679, 1681) and has a hilt decorated with a narrative of the Flood which destroyed this evil race (1687–98).[52]

The fall of the angels in *Solomon and Saturn II* draws together a range of motifs, many of which are found across the Anglo-Saxon literary corpus. Some of the more unusual elements of the poet's description of hell suggest the poem should be seen as part of a group of texts among which associations have previously been noted by a number of scholars, in particular a group of apocryphal homilies which seem to derive from an insular tradition of the *Visio Pauli*. Whether or not the poet of *Solomon and Saturn II* was familiar with the Book of Enoch is difficult to say, but the poem is certainly heir to a number of traditions concerning the fallen angels which may be traced back to this apocryphon. The exact meaning of *insceafte* must remain unclear, but the word clearly refers in some way to demonic procreation, and this is associated here with the use of secret crafts

inhabit a secret land, wolf-cliffs, windy headlands, dangerous fen-paths, there a mountain stream goes down under the darkness of cliffs, the stream under the earth. It is not far from here measured by miles that the mere lies; over that place hang frosty groves, the wood deeply rooted overshadows the earth. There each night a frightening wonder can be seen, fire in the stream. There is none so wise who lives among the children of men that he knows the depth.' See also *Beowulf*, lines 844–52, 1408–32a. All references to the poem cite *Beowulf and the Fight at Finnsburg*, ed. Fr. Klaeber (3rd ed., Boston, 1950).

[51] 'In the fen-refuge he laid down his life, the heathen soul; hell received him there.'

[52] See Kaske, 'Book of Enoch', 421–31. Orchard, *Pride and Prodigies*, pp. 65ff gives an overview of scholarly discussion on the question of the sword and the influence of the Book of Enoch on *Beowulf*.

in the manufacture of weapons, two ideas closely associated with the fallen angels in the Book of Enoch. Whether the presence of the tradition of the monstrous races and weapons forged by them in *Beowulf* suggests a familiarity of that poet with the Book of Enoch, or simply traditions derived from it, is a moot point. But the fact that these traditions are shared by *Beowulf* and *Solomon and Saturn II* is probably no accident. That this is no coincidence is further suggested by associations between the giant lore of *Solomon and Saturn II* and *Beowulf* which have been noted by Andy Orchard,[53] especially in the character of *weallende wulf* ('surging wolf'), 'a famous sea-farer whose dragon-slaying killed him in the end'. This dragon-slaying *wulf*, described as a friend of Nimrod, is finally slain in a wasteland shunned, like Grendel's mere, by ordinary creatures (34–46).[54] Some confirmation of a shared Anglo-Saxon tradition witnessed by the two poems alluded to by Orchard may be offered by the elements of the fall of the angels in *Solomon and Saturn II*. It seems unlikely that the relationship between two poems which share an interest in pagan giants from the early history of the world and the demonic origins of evil can be defined only in terms of the influence on each by a lost (vernacular) version of the *Visio Pauli*.[55] What is more likely is that these connections point not to the widespread character of the traditions which *Solomon and Saturn II* and *Beowulf* share, but to a closer literary association between them than has previously been supposed.

---

[53] Orchard, *Pride and Prodigies*, pp. 82–5.
[54] See also lines 318–22, 198–201; Orchard, *Pride and Prodigies*, pp. 82–5.
[55] See Wright, *The Irish Tradition*, pp. 133–6; Orchard, *Pride and Prodigies*, pp. 40, 47–51.

# 7

# The Book of Enoch and Anglo-Saxon Art

ELIZABETH COATSWORTH

THE influence of The Book of Enoch on Anglo-Saxon poetry, especially but not exclusively on *Beowulf*, has been strongly argued.[1] My initial interest in this topic was aroused because the biblical smith Tubal-Cain (a descendant of Cain) has sometimes been connected with the teaching of smithcraft to men by one of the rebel angels from the story of the Fall of the Angels from The Book of Enoch. In *Beowulf,* the monster Grendel and his mother are described as being of 'the race of Cain', from whom sprang monsters and giants, condemned to the wilderness as a result of Cain's crime, while the sword which slays Grendel's mother is 'the work of giants'.[2] As there are two representations in Anglo-Saxon art that specifically depict Tubal-Cain, and as these have no apparent visual forerunners, it seemed useful to look at The Book of Enoch as a possible source of influence on the two manuscripts in which they appear.

One of these representations is in the Old English Hexateuch (BL, Cotton Claudius B. iv, fol. 10), an eleventh-century translation of the first six books of the bible. In the introduction to the facsimile of this manuscript, the editors note that:

> If we examine the pictures themselves, we find that, after setting out in one direction, they soon change to another, in the sense that *their early interest in extra-biblical material* (my italics) is quickly relinquished for a more straightforward and longer sustained interest in the biblical text itself. At the beginning there is a very promising air of biblical enterprise. The very first picture – that of the Fall of the Angels – is not even related to the biblical text.[3]

This is the first picture, on 2r, immediately following the first five verses in Genesis in which God creates light and separates light from dark (fig. 1). Dodwell and Clemoes do not suggest a source for this illustration, but state

---

[1] See Andy Orchard, *Pride and Prodigies: Studies in the Monsters of the Beowulf-Manuscript* (London, 1995), pp. 64–6. There is a considerable earlier body of research around this subject: see Ruth Mellinkoff, 'Cain's Monstrous Progeny in *Beowulf*: Part I, Noachic Tradition', *ASE* 8 (1980), 143–62; R. E. Kaske, '*Beowulf* and the Book of Enoch', *Speculum* 46 (1971), 421–31. See also Daniel Anlezark, 'The Fall of the Angels in *Solomon and Saturn II*', above.

[2] *Beowulf*, 107ff and 1258ff.

[3] *The Old English Illustrated Hexateuch*, ed. C. R. Dodwell and Peter Clemoes, EEMF 18 (Copenhagen, 1974), p. 65.

Fig. 1. Fall of the angels. The Old English Illustrated Hexateuch, BL, Cotton Claudius B. iv, 2r

that the remainder of the extra-biblical additions, for example the presence of an angel to instruct Adam and Eve (7v), relate to knowledge of the commentaries of St Augustine and to an apocryphal Life of Adam and Eve. It is clear, however, that all this 'extra-biblical material' occurs only in the illustrations to the book of Genesis, and only to its early chapters.

The second manuscript with a depiction of the smith Tubal-Cain – Oxford, Bodleian Library, Junius 11 – also has an extensive surviving programme of biblical illustration, although here it is a poetic paraphrase of the book of Genesis that is illustrated.[4] The poem is that conventionally known as *Genesis A*, together with an interpolation, which has been identified as being from a probable Old Saxon source, known as *Genesis B*, as is customary.[5] This manuscript is probably earlier than the Hexateuch, though not by much: it has been dated to the late tenth or early eleventh century. Both manuscripts have been ascribed to Canterbury, though other centres have been suggested for both.[6] The extra-biblical material in the illustrations in both manuscripts, therefore, relates to Genesis only, and both have some unusual features that are not explained by the sources cited by Dodwell and Clemoes for the Hexateuch.

Junius 11, for example, also has a depiction of the Fall of the Angels very early, on page 3 (fig. 2), although here clearly within an account in the text of *Genesis A* of the rebellion of Lucifer and his angels, and their defeat and fall. The programme of illustrations in this manuscript includes some further extra-biblical additions in relation to the story of Adam and Eve, though not the same ones as in the Hexateuch. On pages 20 and 24, for example, a tempter sent by Satan takes the form of an angel, and on page 36 this tempter is shown on his way back after the successful temptation. These scenes particularly, and some of those sandwiched between them, are a literal rendering of the fall of man as portrayed in *Genesis B*, which includes so much unbiblical material that it can hardly be called a paraphrase. Unfortunately, convincing sources for this material have proved very elusive. In the case of the temptation of Adam and Eve, the artist could be relying on the text of the interpolated material as his source, but this is not the case for all the illustrations to *Genesis A*.

In fact no direct iconographic exemplars for most of the images in either the Hexateuch or Junius 11 have been found. Henderson suggested that the

[4] The illustration of Tubal-Cain is on p. 54. For the illustrations of this manuscript, see Thomas H. Ohlgren, *Anglo-Saxon Textual Illustration: Photographs of Sixteen Manuscripts with Description and Index* (Kalamazoo, 1992). The illustrations are also reproduced in Catherine E. Karkov, *Text and Picture in Anglo-Saxon England: Narrative Strategies in the Junius 11 Manuscript*, CSASE 31 (Cambridge, 2001).

[5] See *Genesis A: A New Edition*, ed. A. N. Doane (Madison, WI, 1978); *The Saxon Genesis: An Edition of the West Saxon Genesis B and the Old Saxon 'Vatican Genesis'*, ed. A. N. Doane (Madison, WI, 1991). See also *The Junius Manuscript*, ed. George Philip Krapp, *ASPR* I (New York and London, 1931).

[6] See Elizbieta Temple, *Anglo-Saxon Manuscripts 900–1066* (London, 1976), cat. no. 58, where it is ascribed to Canterbury, probably Christ Church, and dated *c.* 1000. For a summary of other possible ascriptions, see Paul J. Remley, 'Junius Manuscript', in *The Blackwell Encyclopaedia of Anglo-Saxon England*, ed. Michael Lapidge, John Blair, Simon Keynes and Donald Scragg (Oxford, 1999), pp. 264–66; Karkov, *Text and Picture in Anglo-Saxon England*, p. 35.

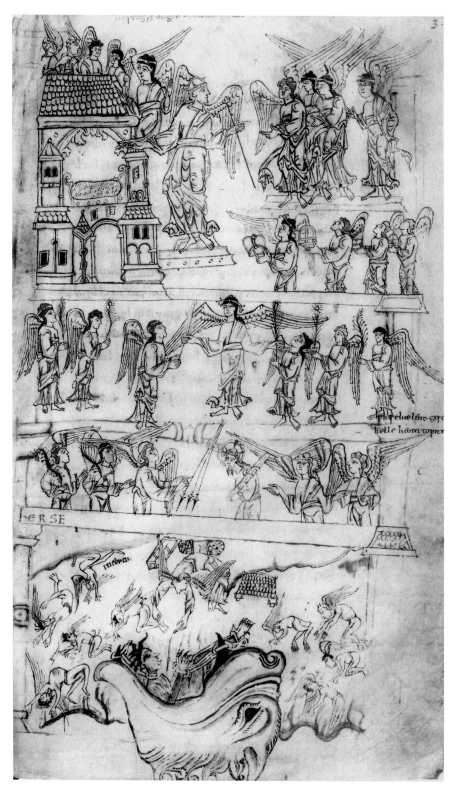

Fig. 2. Fall of the angels. Oxford, Bodleian Library, Junius 11, p. 3

illustrations of both manuscripts imply the existence of a lost Byzantine original, but even on this reading the scenes involving, for example, Tubal-Cain and his family, stand out as having no forerunners.[7] Dodwell and Clemoes, however, strongly argued that the illustrations in the Hexateuch were genuinely innovative.[8] Barbara Raw put forward a case for the derivation of many of the illustrations in Junius 11 from a lost Old Saxon manuscript of *Genesis B*.[9] Broderick pointed out that it was the Utrecht Psalter which had been quarried for motifs which were recombined to produce new images which were independent of direct iconographic sources (and also in many respects of the texts of the poems *Genesis A* and *B*).[10] Karkov in her discussion of Junius 11 emphasises the role of illustration in Anglo-Saxon art as exegesis of the text in its own right, which to my mind makes the case for considering the relationship of illustration to possible sources (which might then be other narratives or other texts rather than illustrations) even more compelling.[11] Both manuscripts also have illustrations of the translation or ascension of Enoch otherwise unique in early medieval art, Junius 11 going so far as to have two, on pages 60 and 61. That in the Hexateuch is on 11v. Could it be that The Book of Enoch was a direct influence on Anglo-Saxon exegesis of Genesis and related themes in poetry and art, as has been argued for *Beowulf*?

The Book of Enoch, also called I Enoch, has never been part of the biblical canon, unlike, for example, Judith or Ecclesiasticus. It is one of a group of pseudepigrapha, essentially a pseudonymous compilation, which cannot be ascribed to a single writer. It has only survived, for the most part, in a very late (fifteenth- or sixteenth-century) Ethiopic version, although substantial portions have also survived in a Greek translation which appear to date from the fifth to sixth centuries, and fragments of an Aramaic version have been found at Qumran. The compilation appears to have been begun in the first two centuries before Christ, but there are additions or revisions, some of them centuries later.[12] It was clearly around and being added to in the very early centuries of the Christian era, and was well enough known for the author of the Epistle of Jude to cite them as scripture. Matthew Black even suggests that a section of the book called the 'parables of Enoch' may owe their presence in the compilation to early Christian interest.

I Enoch is full of detail that makes its appearance in Anglo-Saxon art and thought, although that does not prove it was the source of such detail. It

[7] George Henderson, 'Late Antique Influences on Some English Medieval Illustrations of Genesis', *Journal of the Warburg and Courtauld Institutes* 25 (1962), 172–98, esp. 173 and 194.

[8] *The Old English Illustrated Hexateuch*, Dodwell and Clemoes, pp. 65–73.

[9] Barbara C. Raw, 'The Probable Derivation of most of the Illustrations in Junius 11 from an Illustrated Old Saxon *Genesis*', *ASE* 5 (1976), 133–48.

[10] Herbert R. Broderick, 'Observations on the Methods of Illustration in Manuscript Junius 11 and the Relationship of the Drawings to the Text', *Scriptorium* 37 (1983), 161–77.

[11] Karkov, *Text and Illustration in Anglo-Saxon England*, pp. 7–11.

[12] *The Book of Enoch or I Enoch: A New English Edition*, ed. Matthew Black, SVTP 7 (Leiden, 1985). This is the source of all translations used in this essay.

begins with Enoch's vision, in chapter 1, which closely links the themes of judgment and salvation:

> The words of blessing, according to which Enoch blessed the righteous elect who on the day of tribulation are to destroy all the godless . . .
>   'The great holy one shall come forth from his dwelling . . . and all shall be afraid . . . and the earth shall be rent in sunder . . . and there shall be a universal judgment. But with the righteous he will make peace . . . and he will destroy all the ungodly and convict all flesh of all the works of their ungodliness which they have ungodly committed, and of all the arrogant and hard words which sinners have uttered against him.'

This passage is directly echoed in a passage in the New Testament letter of Jude, verses 5–6, and other epistles and references in the New Testament depend on the same material, for example II Peter VII.4–5, 9–10. In I Enoch it is immediately followed by the legend of the watchers. The watchers are angels, and their fall is described in considerable detail:

> And it came to pass, when the children of men had multiplied, in those days there were born to them beautiful and comely daughters. And watchers, children of heaven, saw them and desired them, and lusted after them; and they said to one another: Come let us choose for ourselves wives from the daughters of the earth, and let us beget children . . . (I Enoch VI. 1–2)
> These [leaders] and all the rest [of the two hundred watchers] took for themselves wives . . . and they began to cohabit with them and to defile themselves with them . . . And they became pregnant by them and bore giants of three thousand cubits . . . These devoured the entire fruits of man's labour . . . Then the giants treated them violently and began to slay mankind . . . Thereupon the earth made accusation against the lawless ones. (I Enoch VII.1–6)
> Asael [one of the Watchers] taught men to make swords of iron and breast-plates of bronze and every weapon for war; and he showed them the metals of the earth, how to work gold, to fashion adornments and about silver, to make bracelets for women; and he instructed them to make antimony, and eye-shadow, and all manner of precious stones and about dyes and varieties of adornments; and the children of men fashioned them for themselves and for their daughters and transgressed. (I Enoch VIII.1–2)

This passage has been held by some to refer to the inherent evil of metalworking, and therefore of smiths, which has coloured some interpretations of the figure of Tubal-Cain.

Enoch's role in his vision is an active one: he appears at some points almost to be a kind of go-between between the fallen angels and God. He is 'taken up', and sent to tell the errant watchers of their doom: 'It has been ordered to bind you in bonds in the earth for all the days of eternity', as he tells them in XIV.5. Enoch has a powerful vision of the throne of God and of the topography of Sheol, which allows for an area in which the souls of the righteous are preserved, separate from those of the forever damned. Redemption of the righteous is therefore associated with the theme of judgement. He is borne aloft in a vision (I Enoch XIV.8), raised aloft, in a chariot of the spirit (LXX.1–2; LXXI.1, 5, 6), returned to earth after one year (LXXXI.5) and ascends for a second time (LXXXI.6).

In the bible, however, Enoch is mentioned only once, though we should note in passing that there are two Enochs in the book of Genesis. The first is a son of Adam's son Cain, and an ancestor of Tubal-Cain: in the Hexateuch at folio 9r, he is depicted in the city built by his father Cain, which was named after Enoch (Genesis IV.17).

The Enoch of I Enoch is the descendant of a later son of Adam, Seth. In Genesis V.18, 21–24 we are told:

> When Jared had lived a hundred and sixty-two years he became the father of Enoch . . . When Enoch had lived sixty-five years, he became the father of Methuselah. Enoch walked with God after the birth of Methuselah three hundred years, and had other sons and daughters. Thus all the days of Enoch were three hundred and sixty-five years. Enoch walked with God; and he was not, for God took him.

This Enoch is the seventh generation from Adam, the sixth from his son Seth; of each of the others in the genealogy, before and after Enoch, it is simply stated that he died. The mysteriousness of the statements that Enoch walked with God, and that God took him, explains the importance of Enoch in later tradition. In Junius 11, the Anglo-Saxon *Genesis A* makes explicit the idea that he did not die an earthly death but was taken up, while living, by the 'king of the angels'.[13]

However, a short passage in Genesis VI.1–4 also has an important connection to the development of the story of Enoch (and incidentally to the interest in depictions of smiths):

> When man began to multiply on the face of the ground, and daughters were born to them, the sons of God saw that the daughters of men were fair; and they took to wife such of them as they chose. The Lord said, 'My spirit shall not abide in man for ever, for he is flesh, but his days shall be a hundred and twenty years.' The Nephilim [giants] were on the earth in those days, and also afterward, when the sons of God came in to the daughters of men, and they bore children to them. These were the mighty men that were of old, the men of renown.

This section is illustrated in the Old English Hexateuch, 13r, by a portrayal of the giants, but this is a straightforward rendering of the biblical text. In the bible, this passage is immediately followed by the story of Noah and the Flood. The Book of Enoch VI to XVI is traditionally held to be an

---

[13] *Genesis A*, 1203–1213.

elaboration of Genesis VI.1–4, although there is also a view that I Enoch represents the earlier material, summarized in Genesis. In this view, the Noah material incorporated in The Book of Enoch is important to it and not merely interpolated.

It is certainly clear in I Enoch that the sons of God who come down and are defiled by the daughters of men are angels. St Augustine's interpretation of Genesis VI, that the children of God refer to the sons of Seth, and the daughters of men to daughters of Cain, and his explicit rejection of Enoch as the author of the Book of Enoch,[14] became the orthodox view, and this is reflected in *Genesis A* and *Beowulf*. The book therefore fell out of favour, but this does not mean that it fell out of use. There is, for example, a fragment of what appears to be a compressed Latin version of one chapter of I Enoch in a ninth-century manuscript once thought to be Anglo-Saxon, but now regarded as Breton, although it was apparently in England by the tenth century.[15] Various writers have seen echoes of I Enoch in a variety of Anglo-Saxon texts apart from *Beowulf*. Patrizia Lendinara, for example, suggested an emendation to a gnomic poem on Cain and Abel, which links the consequences of the slaying of Abel to 'impious beings' who brought weapons to earth, inventing and tempering weapons.[16] Kaske in his study of the influence of The Book of Enoch on *Beowulf* also thought it possible that Bede had direct knowledge of the book, even though his commentary of Jude verses 14–15 is based on St Augustine's views.[17]

The theme of I Enoch is judgment – the first judgment resulting in the Deluge, which is specifically related to the Fall of the Angels, the second the final judgment, to which the book looks forward, and in which the righteous will be released from Sheol into a share of the life to come. It is in effect a vision of the apocalypse. It has been called a star witness to the study of this theme in the emerging Christian church and its literature.[18] Judgment and the salvation of a righteous remnant is also a theme of Genesis itself in the position it accords to the similar theme of the sons of God and the daughters of men in VI.1–4, immediately preceding the story of the Deluge. This relationship is also emphasized in the position of the depictions of the Fall of the Angels, in both the Old English Hexateuch and Junius 11, and in the latter *Genesis A* also begins with an account of the Fall of the Angels. It has been argued that all the texts in Junius 11 taken

---

[14] Augustine, *De civitate Dei*, Libri XI–XXII, CCSL 48 (Turnhout, 1955), Book XV, ch. 23, pp. 488–92, esp. p. 491.

[15] In BL, Royal 5. E. xiii, 79v–80r. See Kaske, '*Beowulf* and the Book of Enoch', p. 423 and Orchard, *Pride and Prodigies*, p. 65 and n. 32 for brief discussion and further references.

[16] Patrizia Lendinara, 'Un'allusione ai Giganti: Versi Gnomici Exoniensi 192–200', *Annali, Sezione Germanica* 16, 2 (1973), 85–98. I am grateful to Patrizia Lendinara for alerting me to this reference. The text of *Maxims I* is in *The Exeter Book*, ed. George Philip Krapp and Elliott Van Kirk Dobbie, *ASPR* 3 (New York and London, 1936), pp. 156–63, with the significant text at p. 163, lines 192–200. See also Bernard J. Muir, *The Exeter Anthology of Old English Poetry* (Exeter, 1994), II.539 for a summary of other discussions of this passage.

[17] Kaske also cites angelic names in the the Book of Cerne and the Enoch references in *Solomon and Saturn* (see below) as evidence of Anglo-Saxon use of I Enoch: Kaske, '*Beowulf* and the Book of Enoch', pp. 422–3. See also Bede, *Super Epistolas Catholicas expositio*, PL 93, cols. 128–29.

[18] Black, *The Book of Enoch*, p. 1.

together should be read as a 'salvation history'.[19] The illustrations would seem to develop this theme further than the words of the text. The comparable position of the Fall of the Angels depiction in the Hexateuch would indicate that there was a similar intention there. The event referred to, however, is certainly in I Enoch and not in Genesis itself. The difficulty is, however, that there could have been other sources for the linked themes of judgement and salvation with or without the fall of Lucifer by the late tenth to early eleventh centuries – for example, the exegesis of Genesis itself, all the many places in the New Testament in which these ideas were taken up and their exegesis, and homiletic material drawing on both the stories and their exegesis.

*The Gospel of Nicodemus*, which does seem to have been well known to the Anglo-Saxons,[20] also mentions Enoch as one of the three who died before Christ and were in heaven already when Christ returned there in triumph with the ancient just after the Harrowing of Hell.[21] This is one interpretation of the phrase that Enoch did not die, but was taken up and 'walked with God'. The iconography of the Fall of the Angels, in both the Old English Hexateuch and in Junius 11, moreover, relates the first judgement visually to the Harrowing of Hell. The mouth of hell represented as the mouth of a lion or dragon-like great beast seems to have been an Anglo-Saxon contribution to iconography, developing the idea of the pit into which Christ bends to rescue the ancient just. It became an established feature of the Harrowing of Hell image in Anglo-Saxon art, most famously in the Tiberius Psalter (BL, Cotton Tiberius C. vi, fol. 15), a mid eleventh-century Winchester manuscript. In the New Minster *Liber Vitae*, 7r, this iconography is used explicitly to combine the themes of the rescue of the just with the Fall of the Angels (fig. 9), and it seems to me likely that this reference would be understood both in the rendering and positioning of the image in the Hexateuch, 2r (fig. 1), and even more particularly in Junius 11 (fig. 2) where the organization of the page layout (p. 3) bears a strong resemblance to that in the New Minster *Liber Vitae*, and is clearly related to it.

I am confident that the placing of the images of the fall of Satan, combined in Junius 11 very clearly with the theme of his binding (an

[19] J. R. Hall, 'The Old English Epic of Redemption: The Theological Unity of MS Junius 11', *Traditio* 32 (1976), 185–208.

[20] For example, Ælfric in *The Old English Version of the Heptateuch, Ælfric's Treatise on the Old and New Testament and his Preface to Genesis*, ed. S. J. Crawford, EETS os 160 (Oxford, 1922, repr. 1969 with additional texts transcribed by N. R. Ker), p. 23; *The Prose Solomon and Saturn and Adrian and Ritheus*, ed. James E. Cross and Thomas D. Hill (Toronto, 1982). In *Solomon and Saturn* (pp. 27 and 73–4), Enoch is described as having been taken up to heaven 'body and soul'. In *Adrian and Ritheus* (pp. 37 and 142), Enoch and Elias (Elijah) weep because they must come back into the world, having long delayed death. In the *Gospel of Nicodemus*, Enoch and Elias expect to return to fight the Antichrist on the Last Day, and to die but to be resurrected in three days; see 'The Gospel of Nicodemus, or Acts of Pilate', in *The Apocryphal New Testament*, ed. M. R. James (Oxford, 1924), pp. 94–146, at p. 140.

[21] See J. Campbell, 'To Hell and Back: Use of the "Descensus ad Inferos" in Old English', *Viator* 13 (1982), 107–58. For Old English translations of the Gospel, see esp. pp. 112–13. The other two figures are Elias (Elijah), who was taken up in a chariot of fire, and the 'good thief' who was crucified with Christ.

important element in the treatment of the Fallen Angels in I Enoch), at the
beginning of Genesis, is neither accidental nor casually experimental: its
placing makes explicit the theme of judgement and redemption. The Fall of
the Angels used in this context might imply I Enoch as a source, but even
though I Enoch describes an area of hell reserved for the righteous who are
to be unbound at the Great Judgement, it is difficult to be certain of a direct
connection to I Enoch because, as already noted, elements of this story are
found also in the New Testament and would also be familiar from many
exegetical sources.

Could this connection be shown, however, by the depictions either of
Enoch himself or of Tubal-Cain, none of which has so far been convincingly
related to any exemplar? In the Hexateuch, 11v shows Enoch not so much
being taken up, as ascending a ladder to converse with a figure with a
cruciferous halo (fig. 3). There are two alternative but not necessarily
exclusive, interpretations of the detail of this scene. The first is that it is a
literal rendering of Enoch ascending to 'walk with God', but it is not
impossible that it also shows Enoch's intercessory role, which comes not
from the bible but from I Enoch. If only the former is meant, it may be
significant that the iconography of the ascension of Christ was *not* used
here. The iconography of the ladder on this interpretation possibly relates
to the dream of Jacob, in which he saw angels ascending and descending.
This is how Karkov sees the ladder that appears in Junius 11, p. 9, in an
image of God's angels moving between heaven and paradise at the creation
of Eve.[22] However, the ladder in Hexateuch 11v may have been intended as
a reference to the cross: in Riddle 55 the cross is explicitly compared to a
ladder leading to the skies.[23] In her study of Junius 11, Karkov strongly
promotes Enoch as a type of Christ,[24] and it may be that this was the
exegetical function of the ladder in Hexateuch 11v. Even so, the intercessory
role of Enoch ultimately depends on I Enoch.

The two scenes depicting Enoch in Junius 11 sandwich the related text
and could be taken to be a mechanical way of covering the repetition of the
phrase that Enoch 'walked with God', although this repetition is not in fact
found in *Genesis A*. In his first appearance, on page 60 (fig. 4), he is nimbed,
carries a book, and he treads on a dragon. This too can be seen as a
reference to the familiar image of Christ treading the beasts, if Enoch is
taken to be an Old Testament forerunner of Christ, but if the dragon is the
dragon of Revelation XII.7–9, 17 and XX.1–3, as has been accepted by
Ohlgren and others, then it is also an indication of knowledge of the active
role of Enoch in the book which bears his name, as an intercessor between
God and the fallen angels.

The second image in Junius 11, on page 61 (fig. 5), *is* dependent on a
model of the ascension of Christ, not the type in which Christ is shown
borne aloft in a mandorla, as in *The Benedictional of St Æthelwold* (BL,
Add. 49598, 64v), but very clearly that of the 'disappearing Christ' like that

[22] Karkov, *Text and Illustration in Anglo-Saxon England*, p. 33.
[23] Riddle 55, lines 4–7, in Krapp and Dobbie, *The Exeter Book*, p. 208.
[24] Karkov, *Text and Illustration in Anglo-Saxon England*, pp. 9–11, 86–8.

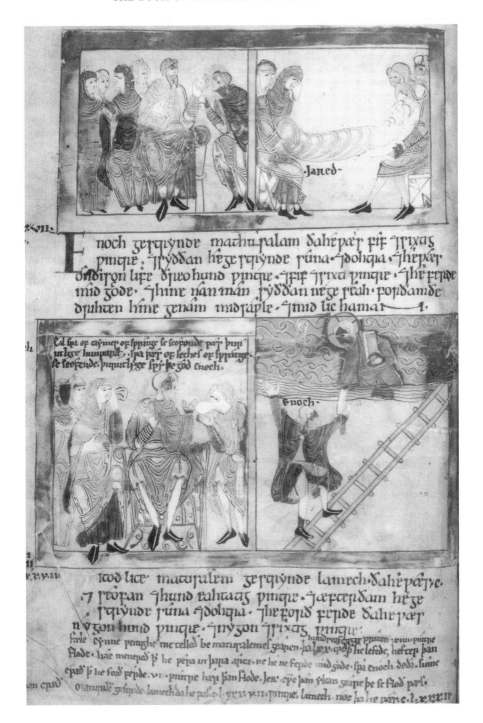

Fig. 3. Ascension of Enoch. The Old English Illustrated Hexateuch, BL, Cotton Claudius B. iv, 11v

ꝺlꝼð pꝼꞇrᵹnꝺ· lꝼðꝼum ꞃunce꞉

ꞇhoch ꞃꝺðan· ꝼꞇlꝺon ꝺom ahoꝼ· ꝼꞃꞇꝺðð ꞃpꝺð ꝼolꝺ꞉ꝼ
pꞃ꞉ꞇa· nallꞇꝼ· ꝼꞇallan lꞇꞇ·ꝺom ꞃoꝛꞇhꞇ ꞃꞇꞇpꝺ· þꞇnoꞇn he
hynꝺꝺ pꝺꞇ· hꝼꞇꝼoꝺ maᵹꞇ· bꞃꝼꞇc blꝺꝺ ꝺaᵹꞇ· bꝼꞇꞇnna
ꞃꞇꞇhynꝺꝺ· þꞇꝺ hunꝺ pꞇnꞇꞇꞇꞇ· hꞇm pꝺꞇ þꞇðꞇn holꝺ·
ꞃoðꞇꞇa palꝺꝺnꝺ· ꞃꝺꞃꞇꞇꞇ hꝼꝺnon· onlꞇc homan· lꞇꞇꞇꝺ·
ꞃohꞇꞇ· ꝺꞃuhꞇꞇnꞇꞇ ꝺuᵹuꝺꝺ· nallꞇꝼ ꝺꞇꞇꝺꝺ ꞃꞇꞇꞇulꞇ· mꞇꝺꝺan
ᵹꞇꞇnꝺꞇꝼ· ꞃꞃa hꞇꞇ mꞇn ꝺoþ· ᵹꞇꞇnᵹꝺ ꞇꞇꞇulꝺꝺ· þonnꝺ· hꞇm
ᵹoꝺ hꞇꞇhꞇnꞇ· ꝼꞇhꞇꞇa ꞇꞇꞇꞇ pꞇꞇꞇ· ꞇꞇꞇnꝺꞇꞇn ᵹꝺꞃꞇnꞇꞇnꞇ· onᵹꞇꞇn
mꝺꝺ· ꞇhꞇꞇna alꝺoꞃ ꞃomꝺꝺ· ꝺꞇc he ꝺpꞇc ᵹꝺꞃꞇꞇꞇ· mꞇꝺ
cynꞇꞇᵹ ꝺꞇᵹlꞇꞇ· oꝼþꞇꞇꞇꞇꞇꞇm lꝺꞇꞇan· lꞇꞇꝺ ꞃꞇꞇꝺn· onþꝺꞇn
ᵹꞇꞇꞇꞇꞇꞇ· ꝼꝺhꞇꞇ ᵹꞇꞇꞇꞇ onꞃꝼꞇꞇꞇ· ꝺꞇn hꞇnꝺ ꞇꞇꞇnonnum
moꝺoꞃ bꞃꞇohꞇꞇꞇ· heþꝺꞇn ylꝺꞃꞇꞇꞇn· ꝼꞇꞃꝺꞃꞇꞇn lꝺꞃꝺꝺ꞉

Fig. 4. First ascension of Enoch; or intercession of Enoch. Oxford, Bodleian Library, Junius 11, p. 60

Fig. 5. Ascension of Enoch. Oxford, Bodleian Library, Junius 11, p. 61

from the Tiberius Psalter, fol. 15 (fig. 6), in which Christ is shown above the apostles in the act of ascending into clouds so that only his lower half remains visible.[25] This scene is adapted in Junius 11, however, to show Enoch *twice*: at the top he is shown ascending; and at the foot of the scene he is shown supported by angels, identified by his Phrygian cap and surrounded by twelve witnesses, possibly meant to be his family. In I Enoch, Enoch is brought back after his first translation bodily by seven angels and placed before the door of his house, and is told he will be removed from the midst of his family, presumably in the same way, a second time. It may be significant therefore that he is shown twice in the same image. These seem quite strong hints that these images are not only exegetical in intent, but also reflect knowledge of the story of Enoch as it is told in I Enoch, and not just from biblical references, *The Gospel of Nicodemus*, or their exegesis.

In a recent study of the Anglo-Saxon goldsmith in art and literature, I found that attitudes towards smiths appeared to vary in relation to con-text.[26] The smith at his forge in art, for example, could represent the purity of God's promises, likened in Psalm 11 to the refining of silver seven times in the furnace, as in the ninth-century Utrecht Psalter illustration of this psalm and in its eleventh-century Anglo-Saxon copy in the Harley Psalter.[27] There are also, perhaps unsurprisingly, considerable differences between the representations of smiths in poetic literature from those in homilies. It is not immediately obvious, therefore, that the depictions of Tubal-Cain in the Hexateuch and Junius 11 imply more than illustration of the immediate biblical text. Both illustrate Genesis IV.22, in which it is recorded that Lamech, a descendent of Cain, took two wives, of whom the second, Zillah, bore Tubal-Cain 'the forger of instruments of bronze and iron', but there is no clear indication in the depiction of either that they are regarded as inherently evil. There are details in both which indicate that they are recording aspects of contemporary practice: for example, the scene in the Hexateuch 10 quite plausibly illustrates the earliest stages of forming a blade or a spearhead.[28] In fact, what realistic detail there is could suggest both to be weaponsmiths, which is interesting in the light of I Enoch VIII.1–2.

However, there was an alternative tradition, which saw the smith as a blessing, rather than a problem. Bede, who is sometimes cited as an example of the influence of the Old Testament Apocrypha, including I Enoch, in fact takes a balanced view. He agreed in his commentary on Genesis in connection with the verse on Tubal-Cain that, if mankind had behaved in accordance with natural law after the expulsion from Eden, it would have had no need for crafts such as metallurgy. He added that nevertheless:

[25] M. Schapiro, 'The Image of the Disappearing Christ: The Ascension in English Art around the Year 1000', *Gazette des Beaux-Arts* 6 ser. (March, 1943), 135–52; repr. in M. Schapiro, *Late Antique, Early Christian and Medieval Art: Selected Papers* (New York, 1979), pp. 267–87.

[26] Elizabeth Coatsworth and Michael Pinder, *The Art of the Anglo-Saxon Goldsmith* (Woodbridge, 2002), esp. ch. 7.

[27] Utrecht Psalter (Utrecht University Library, 32), 6v; Harley Psalter (BL, Harley 603), 6v.

[28] Coatsworth and Pinder, *The Art of the Anglo-Saxon Goldsmith*, ch. 7.

Fig. 6. Ascension of Christ. The Tiberius Psalter, BL, Cotton Tiberius C. vi, fol. 15

there were among God's people men 'learned in all the works of bronze and iron' and of silver and gold as well, but [God] Himself instructed them to apply this art to the construction of His tabernacle. The prophet (Isaiah II, 4) as he was preaching the joys of the Lord's incarnation, also foretold that hurtful works of iron must be taken away and altered for the better.[29]

At the very least, even in biblical exegesis there was a distinction between the smith as an exemplar of fallen humanity, and smiths required for necessity and for the adornment of the church. This distinction is probably also present within the pages of *Beowulf*, since it is hard not to take 'Weland's work' and other references to objects and hangings adorned with gold as other than admiring descriptions.

More to the point in the present context, in the poem *Genesis A* in Junius 11, Tubal-Cain is described in terms which suggest the writer saw him as a benefactor:

Also in that tribe [of Cain] there was at that time a young man called Tubal-Cain. He, a son of Lamech, through the innate power of wisdom was skilled in smithcraft, and through intelligence of mind, the first of men the originator on earth of the forging of ploughs, when the people, town-dwellers, widely knew how to employ bronze and iron.[30]

Many details of the illustrations in the Hexateuch and Junius 11 accord with details from The Book of Enoch, from the importance of the Fall of the Angels as a precursor to the fall of man and to his eventual salvation, to very specific details such as the chained Satan. It is true that much of this detail could have been transmitted through biblical exegesis and homiletic literature rather than from direct knowledge of I Enoch itself. Nevertheless, the representations of Enoch, particularly in Junius 11, do seem to go beyond both the biblical account and that in *Genesis A* and, to my knowledge, beyond any reference to Enoch in Anglo-Saxon literature, even those that hint that the book was known. There seems every indication that the artists of the Hexateuch and Junius 11 took into account a variety of textual as well as visual sources, but while the 'promising air of biblical enterprise' detected by Dodwell and Clemoes in the Hexateuch can also be identified in Junius 11, the aim seems to have been to enrich and emphasise pictorial exegesis of the theology of Judgment and Redemption, rather than to reassert I Enoch as a canonical work.

[29] 'Erant in populo Dei uiri docti in cuncta opera aeris et ferri, necnon et argenti et auri; sed hos ipse hanc artem ad constructionem sui tabernaculi transferre praecepit. Propheta quoque gaudia dominicae incarnationis euangelizans, opera ferri noxia tollenda atque in melius commutanda praedixit': Bede *In Genesim* II, iv, 20–22, in *Bedae Venerabilis Opera (Opera Exegetica)* II, 1, *Libri Quattuor in Principium Genesis*, ed. C. W. Jones, CCSL 118A (1967), 87–8.
[30] *Genesis A*, 1082–9.

# 8

## Judgement and Salvation in the New Minster Liber Vitae

### CATHERINE E. KARKOV

THE New Minster Liber Vitae (BL, Stowe 944), illuminated at the New Minster, Winchester, in 1031, opens with a series of three illuminated pages depicting (1) Ælfgifu and Cnut donating a golden altar cross to the abbey,[1] and (2) an opening depicting the Last Judgement with the saved being ushered into heaven, a struggle for the souls of the saved and the damned, and the archangel Michael locking the door to hell (figs. 7–9). While the donor portrait can be read separately from the Last Judgement as a commemoration of one historical event, the act of donation and the recording of the names of the queen and king were both integral parts of the book as a whole, and significant aids in the couple's eventual salvation, their inclusion amongst the saved at the Last Judgement. The portrait must therefore also be understood as a part of the Last Judgement sequence. The purpose of the Liber Vitae was to provide a record on earth of the names of those to be inscribed in the heavenly Book of Life. It was the earthly parallel to the heavenly Book of Judgement, something the artist has made clear in the repetition of the motif of the open book across the three pages: the book held by the monk at the bottom of folio 6r is mirrored by the book held by Christ at the top of the same page, and by the open books held by the archangel Michael and the demon in the middle register of folio 7r. The contemporary figures of the queen, king and monks on folio 6r stand in readiness to form part of the future procession of the saved into heaven depicted on the verso of the page, and this is emphasized by the fact that the group in the upper left of folio 6v is led by an abbot and an aristocratic lay figure dressed very like Cnut.

Both the iconography of the individual pages and the sequence of illustrations as a whole are unique in Anglo-Saxon art. This set of images was clearly designed specifically for this particular book and the concerns of this particular monastery (and/or abbot). I have considered the meaning and sources of the donor portrait in detail elsewhere,[2] and in this essay I

---

[1] The cross was donated in the 1020s.
[2] Catherine E. Karkov, 'The Image of Emma, Virgin Mother', in *Harald and Harthacnut*, ed. David Hill (Oxford, forthcoming); Catherine E. Karkov, *Authority and the Book: The Ruler Portraits of Anglo-Saxon England* (Woodbridge, forthcoming).

intend to focus on the Last Judgement sequence and the way in which the donor page forms a part of it. This is in fact the only surviving narrative representation of the Last Judgement in all of Anglo-Saxon art; other images commonly identified as Last Judgements, such as the portrait of John the Evangelist on folio 114v of the Grimbald Gospels (BL, Add. 34890, c. 1020), or the tenth- or eleventh-century ivory panel now in the Museum of Archaeology and Ethnology in Cambridge, are more correctly interpreted as scenes of the blessed ascending into heaven or adoring Christ, as they include neither hell and the devil nor the actual moment of judgement.[3] A possible exception is provided by the ninth-century Rothbury cross, on which figures at the top and bottom of the shaft are likely to represent the inhabitants of the kingdoms of heaven and hell.[4] Unfortunately only fragments of the cross survive and we cannot be sure of its iconographic programme. In the Liber Vitae drawings Abbot Ælfwine and his artist were clearly doing something new, as seems to have been the case in all the drawings associated with the abbot, but where might the sources of the illustrations be found, and why might these images have been created for this manuscript at this time? It will be argued here that the pictorial representation of the Last Judgement was developed at Winchester in the eleventh century from a combination of generally popular textual sources (including apocrypha) and specifically Winchester iconographic and historical traditions, and that in addition to its spiritual significance it represented a potent coming together of the concerns of both the contemporary church and court. The New Minster was, after all, founded by the court to minister to its spiritual concerns, and to say daily prayers for the souls of Alfred, Edward the Elder and their descendents.[5]

One of the most unusual elements of the Liber Vitae Last Judgement sequence is the presence of the combination of Mary, Michael and Peter. It is particularly striking that Michael appears no less than three times in the Last Judgement opening: leading the procession of the saved at the left of folio 6v, in the central register of folio 7r, and locking the door to hell in the lowest register of that same page. Mary and Peter are common in Anglo-Saxon manuscript illumination, occurring forty-one times and twenty-five times respectively according to Ohlgren's iconographic catalogue,[6] but Michael is not, appearing only seven times with three of those seven identifications being questionable.[7] The combination of Mary, Michael

---

[3] See Jennifer O'Reilly, 'Early Medieval Text and Image: The Wounded and Exalted Christ', *Peritia* 6–7 (1987–88), 72–118.

[4] See Jane Hawkes, 'The Rothbury Cross: An Iconographic Bricolage', *Gesta* 35.1 (1996), 77–94.

[5] See *Charters of the New Minster, Winchester*, ed. Sean Miller, ASC 9 (Oxford, 2001), xxvi; *The Liber Vitae of the New Minster and Hyde Abbey, Winchester, British Library Stowe 944*, ed. Simon Keynes, EEMF 26 (Copenhagen, 1996), no. 32.

[6] *Insular and Anglo-Saxon Illuminated Manuscripts: An Iconographic Catalogue c. A.D. 625–1100*, ed. Thomas H. Ohlgren (New York and London, 1986).

[7] Salisbury, Cathedral Library, MS 150, fol. 11 (the figure of Libra on the calendar page for September has wings, a helmet and a sceptre, and might possibly be intended as a representation of Michael – feast day 29 September); New York, Pierpont Morgan Library, M. 869, fol. 10 (Arenberg Gospels: Canon Table – figure possibly Michael); Oxford, Bodleian Library, Junius 11, p. 2 (God enthroned with angels), p. 9 (the Creation of Eve with Michael standing in the door to

[See p. 156 for n. 7 cont.]

Figs. 7, 8 and 9 (8 and 9 on following pages).  The New Minster Liber Vitae,
BL, Stowe 944, 6r, 6v and 7r

2.

ALGABYS

and Peter is rarer still, occurring to the best of my knowledge only three times in the corpus of Anglo-Saxon illuminated manuscripts: in the New Minster Liber Vitae, in the Tiberius Psalter (BL, Cotton Tiberius C. vi an Old Minster manuscript), and in a gospel book now in Pembroke College, Cambridge (MS 301), illuminated at either Peterborough or Canterbury c. 1020. If it was indeed illuminated at Peterborough we should note that the abbey had particularly close ties with Winchester, having been obtained and its endowment consolidated by Æthelwold.[8] Robert Deshman has shown that the Benedictional of Æthelwold (BL, Add. 49598), an Old Minster manuscript of c. 973 in which Mary and Peter figure prominently, originally also contained a miniature of St Michael. A possible fifth allusion to the trio can be found in the Junius 11 manuscript in which Michael and a key-bearing angel probably intended as a reference to Peter appear in Genesis, while figures of Mary, and Eve as a type of Mary, appear in both the text and illustrations of Genesis and the text of Christ and Satan.[9] However, only in the New Minster Liber Vitae are the three saints clearly part of the same visual narrative. In the Pembroke College Gospels, as in the Liber Vitae, the three appear at the beginning of the manuscript. They form part of an opening apocalyptic sequence of canon tables consisting of the Lamb with the four symbols of the evangelists facing Christ, Mary facing Michael who holds a sceptre and scales, a trumpeting angel facing Peter, and then Paul leading us into the remaining eight tables containing the rest of the apostles, angels, lions and dragons. In the Liber Vitae Mary, Michael and Peter are again placed at the beginning of the book as intercessors for the queen, king, Winchester community, and those in confraternity with that community. But the two books are very different, and while the gospel book sequence is apocalyptic, it is not a Last Judgement.

One likely iconographic source for the Liber Vitae sequence would have been the famous six-storey decorated tower added to the New Minster under the patronage of King Æthelred II in the 980s. As a point of entrance, the location of the tower in relation to the church would have paralleled the location of the illustrations in relation to the text of the manuscript. According to the description of the tower included in the preamble to the Liber Vitae, the six storeys were dedicated in ascending order to Mary and her virgins, the Holy Trinity, the Holy Cross, All Saints, the archangel Michael and the heavenly powers, and the four evangelists.[10] A direct

heaven), p. 12 (later drawing of Michael fighting dragon) (Ohlgren omits p. 46, the Expulsion); Cambridge, Pembroke College 301, fol. 3 (Canon Table); Oxford, Bodleian Library, Douce 296, 40v (Psalter, etc.: figure in initial Q might be Michael but he has no wings and could be meant to represent Guthlac as the manuscript is attributed to Crowland); BL, Tiberius C. vi, 16v (Tiberius Psalter: Michael fights dragon). Ohlgren also cites Trier, Domschatz Codex 61 (Bibliotheksnummer 134), fol. 9, but this is an eighth-century Insular rather than an Anglo-Saxon manuscript.

[8] Charters of Abingdon Abbey, part 1, ed. Susan E. Kelly, ASC 7 (Oxford, 2000), cxciii, clxxi.

[9] See Catherine E. Karkov, Text and Picture in Anglo-Saxon England: Narrative Strategies in the Junius 11 Manuscript, CSASE 31 (Cambridge, 2001). The connection of the rest of these manuscripts with Winchester may have interesting implications for the suggestion that Junius 11 is a Winchester manuscript.

[10] R. N. Quirk, 'Winchester New Minster and its Tenth-Century Tower', Journal of the British

historical connection between the tower and the drawing is suggested by the identification of the bishop on folio 6v as +*Ælgarus*, presumably Æthelgar, Æthelwold's pupil and the first abbot of the New Minster, the abbot (964–88) under whom the tower was built, who was subsequently bishop of Selsey (980–88) and archbishop of Canterbury (988–90). A formal connection is suggested by the division of the pages into registers which echo, but do not copy exactly, the division of the tower into storeys. However, the parallel is far from exact, and both the meaning and imagery (or lack thereof) of the tower have been called into question.[11] Birthe Kjølbye-Biddle has published a hypothetical reconstruction of the tower,[12] while Barbara Raw has discussed its iconography at some length. According to Raw:

> The ground floor was appropriately dedicated to Mary because she was the source of Christ's human nature . . . The carving of the Trinity, placed above that of Mary, showed Christ's divine origin; the carving of the cross recalled the redemption which came through his incarnation, made possible by the assent of the human mother. The carving of all saints portrayed those people redeemed by Christ who had already reached their home in heaven; that of St Michael and all angels reminded the viewer of the powerful forces who protected him. Finally the figures of the four evangelists symbolized the spreading of the message of redemption throughout the world.[13]

Richard Gem has questioned whether or not the different levels of the tower were indeed decorated with sculpture, but it is clear that the dedications of the various floors alone would have carried the same overall meaning outlined by Raw, even if they lacked sculptural embellishment. Raw focuses on the Christological symbolism and redemptive message of the tower's iconographic program, and stresses its iconic rather than narrative nature, but read together the storeys also suggest a heavenly court and a chronological narrative that runs from the incarnation to the Last Judgement, the latter event signified by the presence of Michael and the symbols of the four evangelists – the four beasts that surround the throne at the opening of Revelation. One also assumes that, as the New Minster was dedicated jointly to the Trinity, Mary and Peter, Peter would have been prominent amongst the saints of the fourth storey – though of course we cannot be certain of this. Admittedly, the tower does not provide an exact match for the Liber Vitae drawings, but it is unlikely that anyone in the Winchester community would have been unaware of the way in which the pages with the procession led by Æthelgar would have referenced their own entrance into the church, past the tower that he had built and towards the altar on

---

*Archaeological Association* 3rd ser. 24 (1966), 16–54; Birthe Kjølbye-Biddle, 'Old Minster, St Swithun's Day 1093', in *Winchester Cathedral: Nine Hundred Years 1093–1993*, ed. John Crook (Chichester, 1993), pp. 13–20.

[11] Richard Gem, 'Towards an Iconography of Anglo-Saxon Architecture', *Journal of the Warburg and Courtauld Institutes* 46 (1983), 1–18.

[12] Kjølbye-Biddle, 'Old Minster', p. 15.

[13] Barbara C. Raw, *Anglo-Saxon Crucifixion Iconography and the Art of the Monastic Revival*, CSASE 1 (1990), pp. 20–1.

which the book would have been displayed. The idea of the Last Judgement implied on the tower of the church, God's kingdom on earth, would have been fulfilled in the imagery of the book showing the final entrance of the community into heaven. The tower does not, however, provide a source for the combination of Mary, Michael and Peter as *intercessors*, but contemporary textual sources do.

Mary, Michael and Peter appear together in prayers, homilies and even charters from a wide range of Anglo-Saxon manuscripts, many associated with the reform centres of Winchester, Worcester, and to a lesser extent, Canterbury. As Mary Clayton has shown, their ultimate source is likely to be the apocryphal *Apocalypse of Mary* in which Mary, the apostles and Michael plead for a respite for the souls of the damned.[14] In the *Apocalypse of Mary* this takes place immediately after Mary's assumption, while in both the prayers and homilies the three plead for, or are intercessors for, the souls of those led before Christ at the final judgement. In Vercelli homily XV, Mary, Michael and Peter plead for, and are each granted one-third of the souls, based on their status as mother of God, leader of the archangels, and possessor of the keys of heaven and hell.[15] Versions of this intercession motif also occur in the 'Sunday Letter' homily in Cambridge, Corpus Christi College 140, Last Judgement homilies in Oxford, Bodleian Library, Junius 121, Oxford, Bodleian Library, Hatton 113, and Cambridge, Corpus Christi College 41, and in prayers in the Bury Psalter, the Portiforium of Wulstan and Ælfwine's Prayerbook – the latter manuscript produced for Ælfwine while he was dean of New Minster in the 1020s. Ælfwine's book contains three prayers that ask for the intercession of Mary, Michael and Peter (along with other saints),[16] a fourth asking for the intercession of Mary and Michael, and a fifth requesting that Peter, doorkeeper and pastor, should intercede for the reader at his death.[17] (We should also note here that it is to Peter the heavenly judge that Ælfwine depicts himself presenting the book.[18]) The table of correspondence of private prayers in Günzel's edition of the manuscript shows that of the prayers to Mary, Michael and Peter, one of the short prayers has a parallel in the later (1060s) Portiforium of Wulstan (Cambridge, Corpus Christi College 391), the second has a parallel in the eleventh-century prayer book BL, Cotton Galba A. xiv (although the prayers are really quite different), and there is no corresponding prayer listed for the third and longest of the three, which requests Mary's intercession, Michael's protection of the petitioner's soul

[14] Mary Clayton, 'Delivering the Damned: A Motif in Old English Homiletic Prose', *MÆ* 55 (1986), 92–102; Mary Clayton, *The Cult of the Virgin Mary in Anglo-Saxon England*, CSASE 2 (Cambridge, 1990), p. 255.

[15] Clayton, *Cult of Mary*, p. 254; *The Vercelli Homilies and Related Texts*, ed. D. G. Scragg, EETS os 300 (Oxford, 1992), pp. 259–60.

[16] *Ælfwine's Prayerbook (London, British Library, Cotton Titus D. xxvi + xxvii)*, ed. Beate Günzel, HBS 108 (London, 1993), items 76.7, 76.9, 76.60, 52.8.

[17] Günzel, 76.51. Yet another prayer to a guardian angel has been added by a twelfth-century hand on folio 74r, the first page of the leaf with the drawing of the 'Quinity'. Günzel notes that the same prayer has been identified in manuscripts from the eighth and twelfth centuries and that in the twelfth-century text the angel is named as Michael (p. 201).

[18] Raw, *Trinity and Incarnation*, pp. 182–6.

on judgement day, and entry into heaven and the locking of the gates of hell from Peter. Moreover, the Devotions to the Cross in the Prayerbook, one of the earliest and largest sets of such devotions to survive from Anglo-Saxon England, show a marked concern for protection at the moment of death and judgement. It is reasonable to conclude that whatever their general popularity in later Anglo-Saxon England, the motif of the intercession of these three saints was particularly popular with Ælfwine, and that it was developed either by him, or under his direction, for the Liber Vitae, a book that is primarily by, for and about the Winchester community and its sense of its own identity under its new abbot.[19] But this was also an identity linked inextricably to the history of the West Saxon kingdom and court, and particularly to the history of royal patronage – the manuscript does, after all, open with an image of royal donation. It is interesting in this regard that the Last Judgement was as much a part of juridical, particularly royal juridical, discourse in the tenth and eleventh centuries as it was of liturgical texts. Mary, Michael and Peter are also invoked in the sanction clauses of a series of sixteen charters issued by Bishop Oswald of Worcester from 966 to the 980s, their issue roughly contemporary with the building of the New Minster tower. The formula is always the same: 'Sca Maria and scs Michahel cum sco Petro and eallum Godes halgum gemiltsien is healden-dum'.[20] The charters then go on to threaten anyone attempting to change or break them with a variety of punishments including damnation: 'gief hwa buton gewyrhtum hit awendan wille God adilgie his noman of lifes bocum and habbe him gemæne wið hine on þam ytemester dæge þysses lifes'.[21] It is unclear why Mary, Michael and Peter suddenly pop up in the charters, appearing in about one-quarter of those issued by Oswald during this period.[22] Worcester had churches dedicated to Mary and Peter, and Julia Barrow has hypothesized the construction of a church or chapel dedicated to Michael at Worcester during Oswald's abbacy, but there is no evidence for the existence of such a structure in the abbey complex until the late thirteenth century.[23] Oswald was also Archbishop of York from 971 to 992, and York too had churches dedicated to Mary and Peter, as well as evidence by the eleventh century for a church dedicated to St Michael in the Belfry. Unfortunately there is no evidence for the existence of the latter

---

[19] Simon Keynes (*Liber Vitae*, p. 69) has suggested that Ælfwine might have been the artist of the drawings in both the Liber Vitae and the Prayerbook.

[20] 'May St Mary and St Michael with St Peter and all the saints of God, be merciful towards those who uphold this [charter]', S 1309, 1312, 1313, 1317, 1320, 1326, 1332, 1337, 1338, 1339, 1342, 1355, 1369, 1372, 1373, 1374. See also *Anglo-Saxon Charters*, ed. A. J. Robertson, 2nd ed. (Cambridge, 1956), pp. 96–7. See also the texts of the charters available on Sean Miller's searchable *Regesta Regum Anglorum*, developed under the auspices of the Anglo-Saxon Charters Committee: http://www.trin.cam.ac.uk/chartwww

[21] 'If anyone, without due cause, attempts to change it, God shall blot out his name from the books of life, and he shall have to account for it to him on the last day of this life', Robertson, *Charters*, pp. 96–7.

[22] Julia Barrow, 'The Community of Worcester, 961–c.1100', in *St Oswald of Worcester: Life and Influence*, ed. Nicholas Brooks and Catherine Cubitt (London and New York, 1996), pp. 84–99, at pp. 89–90.

[23] Barrow, 'Worcester', p. 90.

church prior to the Norman Conquest, and the three saints appear in Oswald's charters prior to his move to York. All things considered, it is far more likely that Oswald's charters were borrowing from the language of judgement and damnation that had become popular in prayers, such as those cited above, as well as in homiletic texts, and the increasingly homiletic tone of the proems of royal charters.[24] Simon Keynes has recently noted the similarities between the imagery of heaven, hell and the Last Judgement (complete with the trumpets of the archangel) in the charters of the scribe 'Æthelstan A' (930s) and the language of Vercelli homily XV and Blickling homily VII.[25] While there may well have been no direct connection between Oswald or Æthelstan's charters and the drawings in the Liber Vitae, the language of the charters is important more generally in a consideration of the imagery of the latter manuscript for two reasons: (1) because of the Liber Vitae's oft-noted resemblance to the New Minster Charter of 966, and (2) because the Liber Vitae is as much a written record of exchange as the charters.

The Liber Vitae and the New Minster Charter are extremely unusual in terms of their contents and their illustration. The two manuscripts are also combinations of religious and secular texts, which seem to have served both a liturgical and an archival function, and the two may have been displayed together on the altar, at least on certain occasions.[26] The frontispiece to the charter (fig. 10) shows Edgar flanked by the patron saints of the New Minster, Mary and Peter, who intercede for him with Christ both here in the charter and at the Last Judgement, as implied by the image of Christ judge to whom Edgar presents the book. There is also of course a typological relationship between Edgar, Peter and Christ, the judges and guardians of their respective kingdoms. The expanded proem of the Charter moves from Creation and the Fall of the Rebel angels, through the Fall of man and the incarnation and ascension of Christ, to close with an anathema granting glory to believers and eternal damnation to unbelievers. Similar threats are repeated against anyone violating the rights of the monks and, in chapters 9 and 10, blessings are requested for those who respect the monks and make donations to the monastery. The latter will have their names recorded in the book of life ('Scriptis decenter eorum in libro uite').[27] Chapters 19 and 20 repeat the blessing on those who give to the monastery, and the curse on those who take from it, wishing for the former a peaceful life and an eternity in paradise, and for the latter divine persecution for their offences and an eternity of suffering in hell.[28] At the end of the proem, that is immediately

---

[24] Simon Keynes, 'The Charters of King Æthelstan and the Kingship of the English', The Toller Memorial Lecture 2001, Bulletin of the John Rylands University Library of Manchester (forthcoming).

[25] E.g. S 416 (931) and S 425 (934). See Keynes, 'Charters of King Æthelstan'.

[26] Keynes, Liber Vitae, p. 27. Ælfwine certainly seems to have been conscious of developments in Winchester under Æthelwold, and it is thought that the office of the Virgin Mary in his Prayerbook, the earliest text of a Marian office to survive, was instituted by Æthelwold (Günzel, Ælfwine's Prayerbook, p. 53).

[27] Keynes, Liber Vitae, p. 27; Miller, Charters of the New Minster, p. 100.

[28] XVIIII. Augenti tribuat rerum cunctarum opifex tranquillum uite presentis excursum . longeuam instantis temporis uitam . futuram eternae beatitudinis talionem . Sufficientem uictualium

[See p. 162 for n. 28 cont.]

Fig. 10.  Frontispiece to the New Minster Charter, BL, Cotton Vespasian A. viii, 2v

after the first request for blessing on believers and damnation for unbelievers, Edgar ponders his own fate, and the way in which he might
achieve salvation through charitable acts (chapter 6). Royal donation to the
abbey is here explicitly linked to salvation, and set within the larger context
of divine and eternal judgement. In addition, divine creation and the
creation of the New Minster are paralleled in the text, and the cleansing
of heaven is famously mirrored in the reform and refoundation of the
abbey.

The iconography of the Charter frontispiece is reflected in that of the
Liber Vitae donor page where the representation of Christ in Majesty
flanked by Mary and Peter alludes to the dedication of the abbey, but also
represents Christ as judge flanked by Mary and Peter as intercessors. While
they were intercessors for all of humanity, the specific implication of the
page is that they intercede here on behalf of the queen and king who are
receiving a veil and crown symbolic of those they will receive in heaven, and
on behalf of the New Minster community who stand in adoration at the
bottom of the page – just as Mary and Peter interceded for Edgar in the
Charter. When we turn to folios 6v and 7r of the Liber Vitae, it is Peter and
Michael who intercede on behalf of both the individual soul at the centre of
folio 7r, and the procession of the saved on folio 6v. We move again from a
specific royal donation and the promise of salvation it brings, to its place
within eternity and the final judgement. As noted above, the New Minster
Liber Vitae, like the Charter also combines religious and secular texts, and
served both a liturgical and an archival function. It contained a record of
donations to the abbey, documentation of royal patronage, an account of
the foundation and history of the abbey (culminating in the dedication
of the tower), and legal documents (including one of the charters [S 1443]
documenting the abbey's foundation in order to serve the spiritual interests
of the West Saxon dynasty), and it might itself be viewed as a form of
written agreement between the monks who were to pray for the souls of the
dead, and the dead who had entrusted them to do so, some in exchange for
land. Eclectic combinations of texts are not unusual in the corpus of *libri
vitae*, as the books could take on so many different forms, but this one
seems to have been written or compiled to a specific agenda. Indeed, the
manuscript is structured such that the history of the New Minster (fols. 8r–
12v, and 57r) is located within the context of the foundation of the English
and West Saxon church, the kingdom of the West Saxons, the English
nation, and of course the 964 reform. There are things missing from the
manuscript, but as it has come down to us it contains the earliest surviving
copy of the will of Alfred (fols. 29v–33r), a tract on the Six Ages of the

---

ubertatem interminabile prosperitatis augmentum . copiosum uirtutum omnium iuuamen. . . .
XX. Minuentem perpetua possideat miseria . In Domini manens persecutione . eius genitricis
sanctorumque omnium incurrat offensam . Presentis uite aduersitas illi semper eueniat . Nulla ei
bonitatis accidat prosperitas . Omnia eius peculia inimici uastantes diripiant . In futuro autem
eterni miserrimum cum edis in sinistra positum damnent cruciatus . si non satisfactione
emendauerit congrua . quod in Domini usurpans detraxit censura. (Miller, *Charters of the
New Minster*, p. 102.)

World with the sixth left open-ended, suggesting that both author and reader are still awaiting the end of it along with Ælfwine, Ælfgifu and Cnut (fols. 33r–34r), two tracts on Anglo-Saxon saints beginning with the conversion and the royal saints of Kent (fols. 34r–39r), a West Saxon regnal list running from King Ine to King Cnut (39rv), and a list of the Winchester community beginning in 964. The purpose of the book seems clearly intended to elevate 'the lesser mortals commemorated into the company of the saints',[29] a point made clear visually by the Last Judgement sequence and its place within the manuscript.

No single one of the works I have cited provides an exact parallel or unequivocal source for the Liber Vitae's Last Judgement sequence: the prayers and homilies give us Mary, Michael and Peter, but in the Liber Vitae we have Mary and Peter, then Peter and Michael; the tower includes a whole heavenly court; and the charters go into great detail about the Last Judgement, salvation and damnation, but rarely provide the names of individual intercessors – the Oswald charters being an obvious exception. It seems likely then, that Ælfwine was borrowing from a number of different sources: the New Minster Charter, and the language of Last Judgement invoked by West Saxon charters in general, the iconography of the New Minster tower that would visually have connected the communities' entry into their church with their entry into heaven, events from the abbey's past, and his own obvious awareness of, if not devotion to, the apocryphal trio of Mary, Michael and Peter as evidenced in his private prayerbook. We should note here that the images in his prayerbook also borrow from a similar variety of sources to create equally innovative compositions.[30] In the prefatory drawings of the Liber Vitae, images and motifs associated with the New Minster and its foundation were combined with motifs from popular liturgical texts to produce the only surviving, possibly the very first, narrative Last Judgement in the history of English art, one that set both the history of the monastery and that of the kingdom before God and in anticipation of the final judgement. The apocryphal trio of Mary, Michael and Peter provided visual assurance that the prayers of the community had been heard, and that help would be on hand in the journey towards salvation.

---

[29] Keynes, *Liber Vitae*, p. 58.

[30] Raw, *Crucifixion Iconography*, pp. 131–3. It may not be entirely coincidental that the motif of the book appears repeatedly in Ælfwine's manuscripts. As already noted, books are one of the devices used to link the donor portrait to the Last Judgement in the Liber Vitae, but they may also be intended as a reference back to the books held by two persons of the Quinity, John, and Ælfwine himself in the Prayerbook, and perhaps beyond that to the book offered by Edgar in the New Minster Charter, the book that was a both a record and a symbol of rule, order and judgement within the monastery. But the book is also a sign of Christ Logos, Christ the Word and his eternal law.

# 9

# The Apocrypha in Anglo-Saxon England:
# The Challenge of Changing Distinctions

JOYCE HILL

A S Fred Biggs notes in the opening sentence to the introduction of this collection, 'the very idea of apocrypha involves making distinctions'. But for the early Middle Ages these are not distinctions that are easy for us to capture, removed as we are from the practicalities of textual transmission, traditions of validation, the niceties of polemical positions, and variations of attitude over time, or even at a given time, as ecclesiastical groups or individuals who have a voice define themselves in terms of what is and is not textually acceptable. These are considerations that have to be taken into account, since the definition of what is 'apocryphal' in Christian terms, though largely stabilized in the modern era within the traditionally structured church, was by no means as stable or as self-evident before the Reformation. True, by the fourth century there were catalogues of acceptable and unacceptable works: the *Decretum Gelasianum* in the West, associated with Damasus I, and the *Stichometry* of Nicephorus of Constantinople in the East, but these often functioned more as reference points for those who wished to support a particular position at a given moment than as definitive lists which determined universal practice. One needs to look no further than the essays in this volume for proof of that point in relation to the *Decretum*.

The essays collected here – and the conference from which they derive – thus put before us two fundamental questions. What were the determining factors in Anglo-Saxon England in establishing what was apocryphal? And how much did it matter? The second of these questions may seem rather radical. But the answer to them both is the same: it all depends on tradition, authority, perception, and polemic. It mattered to different people or different groups at different times and in different ways, depending on how they understood and defined themselves and the available texts in relation to these four dimensions. And to some it did not matter at all. We are back to distinctions again, but distinctions which are fundamentally fluid.

Formally, the distinctions vis-à-vis the Old and New Testaments had already been made. Jerome excluded from the Vulgate Old Testament not only books of esoteric doctrine or dubious provenance, but also those in the

Septuagint for which he had no corresponding Hebrew text. Yet this latter group, which seem to reflect the wider range of books in use among the Jewish community in Alexandria in the second century, when the canon was not finally determined, had a considerable measure of authority and a long-established tradition so that, in terms of distinctions, these have a status which sets them apart from other apocrypha, a distinction that we need to bear in mind as we steer our way through the various apocryphal texts discussed in the foregoing essays. Coatsworth's discussion of the Book of Enoch in art is a discussion of the influence of one of these books, and Enoch also figures prominently in Anlezark's discussion of the Fall of the Angels, for which it was an important medieval source-text, compensating for the paucity of information in the canonical Old Testament. Yet alongside this text Anlezark also refers to the *Vita Adae et Evae*, a text of an altogether different order, in the category of the esoteric or dubious. An issue to be borne in mind here is firstly the simple matter of what texts were available at a particular place and point in time – something that we usually cannot determine directly – and what status a given text would appear to have. As Biggs reminds us, whole bibles were rare, and excluded texts would have been difficult to recognize as such, given the modes and circumstances of textual circulation. Furthermore, the authority of the written word in and of itself should not be discounted in an age of restricted literacy and restricted textual access.

Similar considerations of availability, provision of longed-for 'information', and seemingly indistinguishable status apply when we look at the excluded New Testament material. The spurious or secondary texts that we bring together under the umbrella title of 'The Apocryphal New Testament' is, of course, an artificial collection, unlike the Septuagint exclusions, which were already collected and used within a particular scholarly tradition; in reality, the New Testament Apocrypha is highly diverse in origin, geographically and intellectually, and it is given a collective identification only for modern scholarly convenience. Yet, as we make distinctions in studying the ecclesiastical traditions of Anglo-Saxon England, it is worth bearing in mind the judicious assessment recently made by Elliott in *The Oxford Companion to Christian Thought*:

> Some of the texts are clearly unorthodox, some are tinged with 'heretical' ideas. But in general, this so-called apocryphal literature may be judged as theologically orthodox: it testifies to a vigorous literary activity and to the popular, albeit uncritically received, reading matter of the faithful.[1]

As students of Anglo-Saxon England, we will have reservations, of course, about Elliott's cavalier reference to the 'reading matter of the faithful'. But the essential point is well made: we must not jump to the conclusion that the New Testament exclusions are necessarily wrong, or

---

[1] *The Oxford Companion to Christian Thought*, ed. Adrian Hastings, Alistair Mason and Hugh Pyper, with Ingrid Lawrie and Cecily Bennett (Oxford, 2000), p. 30.

heretical, or inappropriate as stimulants for effective preaching or the inculcation of ways of being or ways of thinking that are good for the souls of the faithful. If we exercise a more severe or more technical set of distinctions, we are in danger of imposing terms of reference which may not be uniformly applicable to the early Middle Ages generally, or to the Anglo-Saxons in particular. It is within this medieval context, rather than in ours, that we must judge the extensive use by the vernacular authors in Anglo-Saxon England of what we might broadly call the New Testament apocrypha: the pseudo-Pauline Epistle to the Laodiceans, discussed by Hall, the Apocalypse of Thomas, discussed by Wright, Anlezark's references to the *Visio Pauli* and the Questions of Bartholomew, Karkov's discussion of the use in art of the Apocrypha of Mary, and O'Leary's discussion of the Apostolic *Passiones*. Lendinara's Sybilline Oracles are not apocryphal in quite the same way, since they purport to be classical rather than Christian, but in the broader spectrum created by the New Testament apocrypha, they stand within a continuum, alerting us yet again to the challenge of making distinctions which were valid for *then* as opposed to *now*. Where, on a continuum, should distinctions be made? And on what grounds? As Lendinara points out, this material is given validating authority by Paul the Deacon and Rabanus Maurus in the context of the Carolingian Reform, which defined its orthodox *renovatio* by making determined distinctions of inclusion and exclusion. In addition, as Lendinara also notes, it was a tradition accepted in England, as evidenced by Bede's *De Die Judicii* and, in the Benedictine Reform period, by the version copied at Canterbury *c.* 1000.

But reservations – distinctions – have to be made; and were made, even at the time. Lendinara points out that Ælfric, in his *Catholic Homilies*, remarked that the Sibyl, although she spoke about Christ's birth, passion, resurrection and Second Coming, was a heathen. This did not, in Ælfric's eyes, invalidate the prophecies; on the contrary, that fact that Christ allowed heathens as well as the prophets to announce his advent confirmed the universal significance of the event. But it points to Ælfric's careful concern for distinctions, which are pertinent to the discussions in these essays. It is well recognized that he was quick to condemn error, *gedwyld*, which is often defined in terms of the avoidance of what we now recognise as apocryphal material. His avoidance of the apocryphal narratives of the Virgin's Nativity and Assumption are cases in point, as Hall notes, even though these were acceptable to contemporary Benedictine reformers in England, including his devoted teacher Æthelwold[2] and those who produced the Winchester miniatures discussed here by Karkov. In this instance, Ælfric takes a rigorous individual stance, which we tend to interpret as evidence of a more severe application of distinctions than prevailing tradition might have prompted – a particularly polemical stance, perhaps,

---

[2] Mary Clayton, *The Cult of the Virgin Mary in Anglo-Saxon England*, CSASE 2 (Cambridge, 1990), pp. 158–67, and Robert Deshman, *The Benedictional of Æthelwold*, Studies in Manuscript Illumination 9 (Princeton, 1995).

as he strives to set standards in the secular church, where understanding was not made subtle by monastic learning.[3] Yet, even within his own work, complications abound, which for us must sound warning notes. On the one hand, he accepts the apocryphal Epistle to the Laodiceans as a canonical text, as Hall points out, perhaps influenced by the context of textual transmission and by patristic acceptance in the person of Gregory the Great, one of Ælfric's key authorities. On the other, he asserts the truthfulness of his narrative about St George (making a firm contrast with those who have peddled unreliable stories) but then, in the telling, feels himself not bound by the details in his key-source legendary, significantly toning down the gory details that are in this Latin source, perhaps out of personal fastidiousness. Nonetheless, in retaining the essential narrative and in asserting its truthfulness, he presents something that is, from a modern perspective, wholly apocryphal.[4] Distinctions are carefully drawn, but although they are presented as being within the framework of an acceptance of orthodoxy and authority as defined by the Carolingian Reform, on which Ælfric extensively drew, they are distinctions that can be varied to suit the immediate purpose, and perhaps even personal taste. It is a salutary reminder that the situation may be complex, even at a given period, and even for a given individual.

It is a truism that the winners are the writers of history. In the present context, that tends to give priority, as we look back to earlier periods, to those who seem to be framing their distinctions in ways analogous to our own; those who favour the canonical over the apocryphal; those whose definitions of orthodoxy are textually based in ways that have defined subsequent ecclesiastical traditions. The value of this book is to challenge those terms of reference, to open up for careful study texts that are too often devalued or dismissed, and to reveal for us the depth and complexity of these traditions. By providing us with a set of essays that put the apocryphal at the centre instead of at the dismissive outer edges, this book begins to shift the focus onto what were, for the Anglo-Saxons, traditions that were far more important and influential than we often allow ourselves to admit. Modern distinctions have necessarily prevailed in bringing together a book on 'apocrypha'. But perhaps its lasting value will be in opening up the question of what such distinctions might actually have meant in Anglo-Saxon England.

---

[3] There are times when one suspects that some of Ælfric's avoidance tactics in the *Catholic Homilies* are adopted because he mistrusts the capabilities of his non-monastic audience. Thus the rigour of his distinctions might to some degree be determined by the immediate context, rather than being an absolute definition of his own position within the intellectually more sophisticated monastic context. In his *Preface to Genesis*, for example, produced in response to a request from a secular patron, he agonizes at length about the inability of the unlearned or poorly trained to appreciate the spiritual sense of somewhat titillating details such as, in this case, Jacob's four wives; what can be coped with in more learned circles might well be a problem elsewhere.

[4] *Ælfric's Lives of Saints*, ed. Walter W. Skeat, EETS os 76, 82, 94, 114 (1881–1900; repr. as 2 vols. 1966), I.306–18. See Joyce Hill, 'Ælfric, Gelasius and St. George', *Mediaevalia* 11 (1989 for 1985), 1–17.

# Index